HR Analytics

HR Analytics
Understanding Theories and Applications

Dipak Kumar Bhattacharyya

Professor, School of Human Resource Management,
Xavier Institute of Management, Bhubaneswar

Los Angeles | London | New Delhi
Singapore | Washington DC | Melbourne

First published in 2017 by

⊛SAGE TEXTS

SAGE Publications India Pvt Ltd
B1/I-1 Mohan Cooperative Industrial Area
Mathura Road, New Delhi 110 044, India
www.sagepub.in

SAGE Publications Inc
2455 Teller Road
Thousand Oaks, California 91320, USA

SAGE Publications Ltd
1 Oliver's Yard, 55 City Road
London EC1Y 1SP, United Kingdom

SAGE Publications Asia-Pacific Pte Ltd
3 Church Street
#10-04 Samsung Hub
Singapore 049483

Published by Vivek Mehra for SAGE Publications India Pvt. Ltd, typeset in 10/12 pts Stone Serif by Fidus Design Pvt. Ltd., Chandigarh 31-D.

Library of Congress Cataloging-in-Publication Data Available

ISBN: 978-93-860-6271-0 (PB)

SAGE Team: Amit Kumar, Indrani Dutta, Apoorva Mathur, Apeksha Sharma and Rajinder Kaur

To
My wife and children

Thank you for choosing a SAGE product!
If you have any comment, observation or feedback,
I would like to personally hear from you.

Please write to me at contactceo@sagepub.in

Vivek Mehra, Managing Director and CEO, SAGE India.

Bulk Sales

SAGE India offers special discounts
for bulk institutional purchases.

For queries/orders/inspection copy requests,
write to **textbooksales@sagepub.in**

Publishing

Would you like to publish a textbook with SAGE?
Please send your proposal to **publishtextbook@sagepub.in**

Subscribe to our mailing list

Write to marketing@sagepub.in

CONTENTS

PREFACE

HR analytics or predictive decision-making processes in human resources can be facilitated by big data when we are able to capture, cure, store, share, transfer and analyse big data to study the trends of human resource management (HRM) systems of an organization. Apart from HR analytics, big data also help in other business decisions, with predictability. HR analytics is the science of HRM, based on big data. We can say big data are the superset and HR analytics is the subset. With the increased spate of competition, and complexities of business, organizations globally are depending on their human resources for sustainability. All decisions on human resources—be it on recruitment, performance management, succession planning, training, compensation design and talent management—now require a more scientific approach. With big data, such a scientific approach to an HR decision-making process is possible, developing various predictive models. With less risk of decisional errors, therefore, HR analytics is becoming a more effective tool for HR decision-making processes.

HR analytics being predictive can help an organization to look forward on their human resources with appropriate decisions. Decision-making processes being more scientific, HR analytics not only reduce decisional errors but also help in cost optimization. For example, a decision on the launch of a training programme, when leveraged on the past trend from big data, can help in predicting the return on investment (ROI) with less chances of error. Again extrapolating the trend, we can understand the long-term effects of such training in terms of building competencies of the participants, incremental changes in performances and supporting of business goals of organizations. Also with HR analytics, it is possible to assess the implications of HR decisions on organizational business. With all these, HR analytics can make decision-making process more effective and cost-efficient.

HR analytics tools consider both statistical analysis and predictive modelling for HR decisions. When required, the implications of HR decisions on other functions of an organization can also be assessed; this helps in optimization. Also with HR analytics, we can automate our operational HR decisions, thus reducing the decisional delay, responding on real-time basis. Often we dilute HR intelligence with HR analytics. HR intelligence making use of HR metrics, dashboards and scorecards helps us to understand the actual happening. HR analytics, on the other hand, making use of predictive modelling, multivariate testing and statistical analysis helps us to understand the reasons for the actual happening and, in the process, helps to initiate the appropriate actions to stop the recurrence of such happenings. Therefore, HR analytics is an effective tool for fact-based HR decision-making with a forward-looking approach.

In organizations, HR analytics can help in assessing the true value of people, understanding their present and future needs, identifying the potentials among them, ensuring the right-fit between the people and the job, and ensuring their retention. With optimum resource allocation, organizations can balance HR costs with appropriate investment in human capital development and other such areas. Both sustainable and strategic HRM (SHRM) practices are possible through HR analytics. With cause–effect relationships between human resources and business, HR analytics can provide meaningful insights into the organization to sustain and grow in a competitive environment.

Keeping in view all the above issues, this book has been designed for HR students and professionals to acquaint them with the theories, applications and practices. This book has been written keeping pace with the syllabi of business schools, professional bodies and universities in India and abroad. Professionals also can learn the basics of HR analytics for its non-technical way of presentation. This book is divided into eight self-paced chapters, covering all the core areas of HR analytics.

CHAPTER OUTLINE

Chapter 1 discusses the basics of HRM functions, their process of development, strategic focus; helps thinking of HRM as a process, as a system, as human capital management (HCM) functions, as control functions; and then introduces HRM and HR analytics.

Chapter 2 focuses on HR decision-making and HR analytics. This chapter introduces HR decision-making, changing pattern of HR decision-making, analytics-based HR decision-making, predictive modelling of HR decisions and HR decision-making with cross-functional inputs.

Chapter 3 introduces HR analytics, discussing on its concepts, processes, history, predictive modelling, importance and benefits, and framework and models.

Chapter 4 elaborates on HR business processes and HR analytics, focusing on concepts of HR business processes, statistics and statistical modelling of HR research and HR decision-making, HR research tools and techniques, data analysis for human resources, HRIS for HR decision-making, HR metrics, HR scorecard and HR analytics as a tool for HR decision-making.

Chapter 5 covers forecasting and measuring HR value propositions with HR analytics, elaborating on concepts of value propositions and HR decisions, sustainability in HR decisions, HR analytics and HR value propositions, HR optimization through HR analytics, HR forecasting, HR plan and HR analytics and predictive HR analytics.

Chapter 6 discusses HR analytics and data, introducing the concepts of HR data, HR data and data quality, HR data collection, big data for human resources, transforming HR data into HR information, process of data collection for HR analytics, data collection for effective HR measurement, HR reporting, data visualization, root cause analysis and datafication of human resources.

Chapter 7 introduces HR analytics and predictive modelling, elaborating on the basics of HR analytics and predictive modelling, different phases of HR analytics and predictive modelling, examples of predictive analytics, data and information for HR predictive analysis, predictive analytics tools and techniques, and practical processes of using predictive analytics for HR decisions.

Chapter 8 wraps up the discussions of this book, elaborating on HR analytics for future, introducing the basics of HR analytics in future, details of HR future, generic future HR skill-sets and knowledge, ethical issues in HR analytics and empowerment of human resources with HR analytics.

SPECIAL PEDAGOGIC FEATURES

The pedagogic features of this book include the following:

- It has been written in simple language for both academia and practitioners.
- It has balanced discussions on theories and practices.
- It has chapter-specific case studies, both at the beginning and at the end.
- The section 'Practitioners Speak' has been provided with a topical issue in each chapter.
- General and critical review questions have been provided at the end of each chapter. The answer key to the MCQs has been provided on the companion website.
- Key words have been incorporated.
- Special notes on corporate practices have also been provided.

ACKNOWLEDGEMENT

At the outset, I must acknowledge my wife Sutapa, who is my constant source of inspiration. I also acknowledge my faculty colleagues, namely Professor Arun Kumar Paul, Professor Sandipan Karmakar and Professor Bhaskar Basu, who had been consistently supporting my endeavour with technical support. Special thanks to the reviewers of SAGE, who helped me develop this manuscript. Also, I acknowledge with gratitude the constant support of the editorial team of SAGE.

I would be grateful to receive critical comments from the readers of this book. I can be reached at dkbhattacharyya@yahoo.co.in or dkb@ximb.ac.in.

Dipak Kumar Bhattacharyya

ABOUT THE AUTHOR

Dipak Kumar Bhattacharyya has a PhD in management from the University of Calcutta. He has served in industry in a training and organizational development role for about 15 years. Thereafter, for the last two and half decades, he has worked with several management institutes in India in various capacities such as a director, a dean, the head of the department, a professor and so on. Presently, he is working as a professor at the Xavier Institute of Management, Bhubaneswar, India. He is also a visiting faculty of XLRI, Jamshedpur. Professor Bhattacharyya has extensive consultancy experience in human resources, quality management, human resource planning, compensation design, organizational development and restructuring areas. He has published 30 books on various HR management topics and has contributed more than 100 papers in various journals of national and international repute.

1

HUMAN RESOURCE MANAGEMENT FUNCTION OVER THE YEARS

LEARNING OBJECTIVES:

After reading this chapter, you will be able to understand:

- Introduction to HRM functions
- Process of development of HRM functions
- Strategic focus in HRM practices
- HRM as a process
- HRM as systems
- HRM and HCM functions
- HRM and control
- HRM and HR analytics

INTRODUCTORY CASE

Wipro's Innovative Cost Cutting Without Pinching Employees' Pocket and Job

Unlike other companies, India's third largest software exporter, Wipro, is innovative in managing HR costs. Wipro does not cut salaries, never says no to promotion and never stops giving increments, even though an economic downturn at times puts the company in a difficult patch. And the company does all this by giving its employees the option to work for less number of days in a week or avail sabbatical. Project Enrich and Project Rejuvenate are the two components of such a programme, which Wipro feels could give them a new lifeline without employees' resentment.

Project Enrich is for the bench employees who are given the option to work just for 10 days in a month with 50 percent cut in their total compensation package. Project Rejuvenate is earmarked for senior employees. Under this scheme, employees are given the opportunity for sabbatical to pursue their hobby. They are also allowed to join a non-governmental organization (NGO). During this period of sabbatical, such employees receive only 25 percent of their total compensation package.

In both the programmes, the company could get good responses. Such voluntary participation of employees could enable Wipro to address the concern of rising HR costs, particularly during the economic downturn.

INTRODUCTION

Human Resource Management (HRM) as a concept is of recent origin. Its gradual acceptance in organizations, across the globe, could make it the most important function in any organization, in terms of competitive advantages, strategic relevance and sustainability. With its beginning as a personnel management function for productivity enhancement during the end phase of World War I (1918), HRM as a function has developed primarily to promote the concept of humanization of work (Bhattacharyya, 2015). Organizations, across the globe, are now facing the challenges of technological change, rising competition, rise of consumerism, structural change in employment relationships and various other macro-economic and social changes. Such changes redefined the process of managing human resources, making employees as partners of the organizations and their management as a business-aligned function.

HRM is defined as the management of organizational human resources. This definition of HRM considers HRM from normative perspectives. Pioneering researchers who had viewed HRM from normative perspectives are Boselie (2002) and Schemerhorn (2001). Boselie (2002) defined HRM as a 'process of shaping employment relationships to achieve individual, organizational and societal goals'. This obviously requires managers to relate their decisions with the prevalent policies and practices. Schemerhorn (2001) defined HRM as a 'process of attracting, developing and maintaining a talented and energetic workforce to support organizational mission, objectives, and strategies'. Both the definitions are normative. Only contextually these two definitions are different. For Boselie, achieving stakeholders' goals, which even include society, is also important, while Schemerhorn focuses on achieving organizational goals. Broadly, the normative approach to HRM concepts covers all HRM functions such as Human Resource Planning (HRP), recruitment, employee relations, compensation management, training and development, performance management, motivation, organizational change and development, team development, work-life balancing, employee engagement talent management.

Descriptive and conceptual perspectives of human resource: Descriptive perspective of HRM emphasizes on fact-based HRM practices, and the conceptual perspective helps us to relate facts to each other.

Over the years, complexities of business have added two more perspectives of HRM, i.e., **descriptive** and **conceptual**. The descriptive perspective of HRM emphasizes fact-based HRM practices, and the conceptual perspective helps us to relate facts to each other. Unlike normative perspectives, descriptive and conceptual perspectives of HRM do not have theoretical base, but these two perspectives are the trend-setters to set the premise for the development of HR analytics and predictive HR decision-making process.

In this chapter, we will first examine the stage-wise process of the development of HRM concepts from historical perspectives. Further, HRM concepts will be examined from different perspectives such as strategy, process, systems, human capital (HC) and human control. In every stage, we find the need for HR analytics for an improved HR decision-making process. This chapter sets the ground for subsequent chapters in this book.

HISTORY OF DIFFERENT HRM PERSPECTIVES

At the outset, it is important to clarify our ideas on HRM models, theories and perspectives. HRM models pertain to detailed descriptions of objectives, capabilities, processes and standards of human resources, following which we can achieve strategic intents of HRM in organizations. Therefore, HRM models help us to integrate an HRM strategy with HRM processes and structure. Also, HRM models provide clear principles for designing roles and responsibilities of human resources, help organizations to achieve results through competitive positioning in the market and also detail HR responsibilities for managing the administrative processes.

HRM theories are certain principles on which HR practices are based. Theories generate ideas or propositions to explain facts and events in HRM, namely reasons for typical behaviour of employees. For example, various employee motivation theories explain reasons for employees' behaviour to satisfy their unmet needs.

Perspectives in HRM denote our outlook to consider something. For example, we view organizational change always from a negative perspective.

Although we value such finer distinctions between these three terms, operationally we hardly find any differences. Here also these terms have been used interchangeably, meaning they are one and the same.

Theoretically, we need to examine different HRM perspectives, particularly in the context of different school of thoughts, i.e., **Michigan** and **Harvard**. Fombrun et al. (1984) pioneered the Michigan approach to HRM. This perspective of HRM emphasized the need for adopting organizational policies, which can have effect on the individual performance of the employees. In a sense, this perspective acknowledged the need for the strategic orientation of an HRM function. Harvard approach, pioneered by Beer et al. (1984), emphasized the need for the alignment of employees with the organization and management. This emphasized the need for developing the strategic vision of HRM functions, primarily to assess the extent of integration of HRM practices with the organizational policies. Both the approaches, in a sense, acknowledged the important role of HRM, elevating it to the level of a strategic function.

Michigan School: This school of HRM emphasizes on the need for adopting organizational policies, which can have effect on the individual performance of the employees.

Harvard School: This school emphasizes on the need for the alignment of employees with the organization and management, developing the strategic vision of HRM functions.

However, in the following paragraphs, a detailed discussion on various HRM models has been made, primarily to facilitate the understanding of the readers on how HRM functions are differently viewed by different organizations.

The Harvard model is also termed by the authors as the map of HR territory. Acknowledging the existence of multiple stakeholders, the model recognizes a neo-pluralist approach and emphasizes the soft side of HRM. Neo-pluralist approach here indicates valuing of diversity, valuing equal power of the groups and so on. This model of HRM is influenced by the human relations school of thoughts. As a natural corollary, the model believes in developing organizational culture based on mutual trust and team work. The model primarily recommends the need for considering employees as assets rather than cost to the organizations.

In contrast to the Harvard model, the Michigan model or the matching model recommends the need for 'tight-fit' between the HR strategy and the business strategy. The model focuses towards the harder side of HRM and, therefore, suggests the need for matching human resources with the jobs. As the model puts the business strategy as the prime concern for the organizations, consider human resources like any other resource to facilitate achieving organizational objectives.

The guest model of HRM integrates both hard and soft approaches of HRM. As per this model, such integration can be achieved with congruent business and HR strategies for achieving organizational goals. Here also the model considers human resources like any other resource of the organizations. However, the model is flexible, as it recommends the need for the organization and human resources to be more adaptable to the changing dynamics of business and the work environment. Other two focus areas of this model are: high commitment and quality. While high commitment can be achieved when employees are able to identify themselves with the organizations, quality is achieved through the process of effective management or the human resources.

In addition to the aforementioned points, based on the researches of Legge (1989) and Bratton and Gould (1999), and many others, we could classify HRM models into: normative, descriptive-functional, descriptive-behavioural and critical-evaluative types.

The normative model or perspective of HRM divides HRM into hard and soft types. Hard types of HRM are more focused on the Harvard model linking HR management to organizational strategy. Hard types emphasize linkage of all HRM functional areas such as HRP, job analysis, recruitment and selection, compensation and benefits, performance management and employee relations with the corporate strategy. Soft HRM, on the other hand, emphasizes considering people as assets rather than resources, thereby laying more stress on organizational culture, development, leadership, con-flict management and so on to increase trust and collaborative performance. Primarily this approach makes the assumption that anything good for the organization is also good for the employees.

The descriptive-functional model or perspective of HRM emphasizes the need for adopting the pluralistic approach in managing employment relations. The descriptive-behavioural approach considers that employees' behaviour mediates strategies and performance of organizations. Hence, it recommends the need for controlling attitudes and behaviours of human resources, matching with the strategic requirements of the organizations, to achieve organizational goals. The critical-evaluative model of HRM focuses on balancing the asymmetries of power between the organization and the employees, enforcing strategic control.

Relatively from a different perspective, Storey (1989) developed the HRM model (named after him) encapsulating the total preventive maintenance (TPM) approach. The model suggests HRM has synonymity with TPM, as like TPM, HRM also believes in holistic approach with certain set of inter-related policies. This model rests on certain beliefs and assumptions, strategic focus on qualities, acknowledging the role of line managers, and also on certain key levers. The primary belief and assumption of this model is that human resources, although an important factor of production, is different. Hence, the model suggests the need for careful nurturing of human resources, considering it as valuable assets, and so also believing employment relationship based on commitment and not compliance. As human resources is of strategic quality, the model suggests the need for managing it with the full knowledge and support from the top management of the organizations. The model acknowledges the important role of line managers in managing human resources; it recommends the need for delegating the management of human resources to the line or operational people. Finally, the model also emphasizes the need for focusing on the culture of the organization, i.e., the values, beliefs and assumptions.

Again we can analyse HRM also from **resource-based** and **behavioural** perspectives. The resource-based perspective differentiates one organization from another in terms of the available resource-mix, i.e., physical, organizational and human resources. Available resource-mix or heterogeneity of resources of organizations contributes to their productive potentiality. Out of various resource-mixes, resources which are sustainable and difficult to imitate can give distinct competitive advantages to the organizations (Prahalad & Hamel, 1990; Rangone, 1999). Researchers on HRM across the world are equivocal that human resources of an organization can only ensure sustainable competitive advantages to any organization. With human resources, therefore, every organization tries to stay competitive and become sustainable. This requires organizations to focus on talent management practices, embracing suitable HRM strategies and aligning HRM functions with organizational goals and objectives.

Resource-based perspective: Resource-based perspective differentiates one organization from another in terms of available resource-mix, i.e., physical, organizational and human resources.

Behavioural perspective of HRM: It focuses on embracing those HRM practices which can churn desired employees' behaviour for achieving organizational goals and objectives.

The behavioural perspective on HRM focuses on embracing those HRM practices which can churn desired employees' behaviour for achieving organizational goals and objectives (Naylor et al., 1980). Organizations vary their goals and objectives, based on their business mission and plans. Such variations in goals and objectives are accomplished through different strategies and behaviours; this obviously requires different HRM practices (Snell, 1992) and focuses on external fit, i.e., contingency variables such as size, technology, ownership, location and so on (Delery & Doty, 1996; Huselid, 1995; Legge, 1995). Using the behavioural perspective, Schuler and Jackson (1987) tested Porter's three generic strategies (Porter, 1985) aligning with different HRM practices. This study's results indicated that when organizations select an HR policy and practices appropriate to particular generic strategies, they can achieve higher work performance. This obviously legitimizes our understanding that organizations need to achieve strategic-fit with their HRM practices to achieve the best results.

Examining HRM from the aforementioned context, today we find the compelling need to take HR decisions in alignment with the goals, objectives and strategies of the organizations. HR decisions are no longer taken in silos; rather such decisions are taken with a holistic approach, duly understanding probable decisional effects and initiating the appropriate actions to balance the decisional adversities, if any. HR decisions with such a futuristic look require us to make use of HR analytics and predictive models.

HRM AND STRATEGY

Again when we examine HRM from the strategic perspective, we find that an HR strategy is the pattern of decisions concerning policies and practices associated with the HR system. Organizational HR system encompasses all functional areas and, hence, helps in framing organization-wide strategies. Today, embracing the competency-based SHRM approach, HR managers focus on developing human resources for sustainable competitive advantage. In managing human resources strategically, HR managers can make use of HR analytics. However, for deeper understanding, we need to have more clarity on SHRM. Miles and Snow (1995) defined SHRM as an HR system tailored to the demands of the business strategy. Wright and McMahan (1992) could see it as HR activities that enable organization to achieve its goals. Obviously these definitions see human resources more as a proactive function to create and shape the business strategy (Sanz-Valle et al., 1999). In terms of the range of activities, according to Mabey et al. (1998), SHRM encompasses the social and economic contexts, establishes relationships between SHRM and business performances, develops the managerial style for new forms of organization and, finally, facilitates in building organizational capability through knowledge management practices. All these SHRM activities can become more effective when these are powered by HR analytics.

Universalistic approach: This approach scouts for those policies or practices that contribute to organizational gains in general.

Contingency approach: This approach aligns organization-level strategic positions with specific choices and practices to achieve the intended results.

Configuration approach: This approach focuses on more holistic approaches to examine how a pattern of several independent variables can influence organization-level strategies.

SHRM is also seen from universalistic, contingency and configurational perspectives (Delery & Doty, 1996). The **universalistic** or best practices approach scouts for those policies or practices that contribute to organizational gains in general. Researchers such as Arthur (1994) and Huselid (1995) have contributed to the universalistic theory. **Contingency** and **configurational** perspectives believe that SHRM practices focus on achieving the strategic intents through shaping behaviours and outcomes. The contingency approach aligns organization-level strategic positions with specific choices and practices to achieve the intended results (Schuler & Jackson, 1987). Many empirical studies, namely, aligning organizational compensation systems with the strategies (Begin, 1993; Gomez-Mejia & Balkin, 1992) and so on could reinforce this approach. Configuration theorists, however, focus on more holistic approaches to examine how a pattern of several independent variables can influence organization-level strategies. This approach is based on the principles of equifinality (Doty et al., 1993), i.e., believing that organizational strategic intents can be achieved through different courses of actions. Configuration approaches to HRM strategy have been studied by different researchers such as Wright and McMahan (1992), Becker and Gerhart (1996) and Schuler and Harris (1991). While Wright and McMahan argued the need for the alignment of organizational HRM systems with their strategy, Becker and Gerhart observed that the architecture is more important than specific practices. Schuler and Harris on the other hand observed the relationships between Deming-type quality approaches and organizational strategy with the configuration of HRM practices. Deming's 14 points on quality management are certain recommended set of managerial practices to achieve quality and productivity in organizations. Whatever may be the approaches embraced by the organizations, HR analytics undoubtedly can play a crucial role, with data and information, so that HR managers can make their strategic choices as scientific as possible.

Again while we examine the critical role of HR strategy, we observe researchers such as Katz and Khan (1978) and Jackson and Schuler (1995), who had emphasized the importance of employee behaviours for achieving the strategic intents. Researchers such as Barney (1991) and Prahalad and Hamel (1990) from a resource-based perspective suggest that human resources provides sustainable competitive advantage for an organization. This is because human resources is characteristically rare, inimitable and non-substitutable sources for achieving competitive advantage. Other resources do not have such characteristic feature. Human Capital Theory of Becker (1964) suggests strategic importance to human resources like other economic assets as knowledge, skills and abilities of the people has economic values. This concept later developed the human resources accounting by Flamholtz and Lacey (1981) and others. The transaction cost theory of Williamson (1981) suggests that a strategic HR approach can ensure cost minimization, as this will enhance periodic monitoring and governance. The agency theory of Eisenhardt (1989) suggests that a strategic approach to human resources aligns agents' (employees) and principals' (employers) interests and thereby ensures streamlining of employment relations and systems within the organization.

All the earlier discussed theories justify the alignment of human resources with an organization-wide strategy, and these can be grouped under rational choice theories of human resources. As opposed to this, we have **institutional** (DiMaggio & Powell, 1991; Meyer & Rowan, 1977) and **dependency** (Pfeffer & Salancik, 1978) theories on HR strategy. These theories focus on constituency-based interest. This is because the strategic approach to human resources is not empirically proved as a contributor to organizational performance. More specifically, the institutional theory argues the need for strategic acceptance from stakeholders; the dependency theory, on the other hand, argues this will unduly enhance the level of influence over the organizations (from human resources) and thereby will defeat the purpose. Hence, there exists a need for balancing.

Institutional theory: This theory argues the need for strategic acceptance from stakeholders.

Dependency theory: This theory argues that strategic acceptance from stakeholders can unduly enhance the level of influence over organizations from human resources; hence, there exists the need for balancing.

Prima facie, environmental, organizational, institutional and technological factors are potential influencers in a strategy. The relative importance of each such factor will depend on organizational characteristics. SHRM, therefore, requires formulation of HR objectives, strategies and policies. SHRM can be strengthened by HR analytics, as with the availability of data and information, organizations can make their best strategic choices to achieve the goals and objectives.

REINFORCEMENT OF HR STRATEGY FACTORS WITH HR ANALYTICS

Here, we are discussing how HR strategy factors can play a pivotal role in achieving organizational success. All HR strategy factors can be substantially influenced by HR analytics. These have been classified in Table 1.1.

■ **Table 1.1:** HR Strategy Factors

Recruitment and Selection	Strategically, an organization needs to determine whether it should outsource or recruit employees on direct pay-roll. If it is on direct pay-roll, whether it should be contractual or permanent. While recruiting, potential employees should be selected based on multi-skill attributes or specialization? There are other issues such as can the recruited employees be groomed for future leadership positions? Can they be developed, retained and considered in organizational talent pool, etc. All these strategic recruitment and selection decisions can be facilitated by HR analytics. HR managers can take strategic recruitment and selection decisions, leveraging data and information from the HR analytics solutions. In fact, HR analytics are largely used by the organizations across the globe for strategic recruitment and selection-related decision-making. Also, a large number of software vendors provide dedicated solutions for strategic recruitment and selection decision through their workforce analytics suites.
Career Development	Career development, *per se*, is one of the critical strategic HRM functions. Integrating career development with talent management functions, organizations can enhance their strategic competence and can sustain and grow. Career mapping, succession planning, management development and organizational development (OD) initiatives are the important areas of activities covered under this area. Most of the HR analytics solutions are known as talent analytics applications.
Performance Management	Performance management is essentially an employee development function. Hence, this can supplement talent management activities of the organization also. With systematic performance feedback, employees can self-assess their strengths and weaknesses, and accordingly can pace their self-development with organizational support. Organizations also can design effective employee development programmes, balancing employees' and organizational needs. Designing effective performance management systems for measuring the performance of employees is also a strategically relevant HR decision. Performance-management-related decision-making processes can be reinforced by HR analytics. Like workforce analytics, here also we have some available HR analytics solutions.
Training and Development	Training and development functions are again another strategically relevant HR activity. HR analytics can facilitate training and development functions with relevant data and information developing in-house training, return on investment (ROI) models for evaluating training, training budgets, training transferability and so on.

| Compensation Designing | With suitable compensation and benefits programme, organizations can not only optimize the cost of compensation but also attract and retain talent. Strategic compensation designing requires organizations to benchmark with the peer group companies, and even with the best paying companies, so that organizations can remain competitive in the market. Issues such as compa-ratio (comparative ratio) to measure equity/inequity, compensable factor for decisions on pay design and so on require data and information, which can be made available through HR analytics solutions. |
| Human Resource Planning (HRP) | HRP-related activities are also strategically relevant, as these can provide vital information on future manpower requirement with different set of competencies, assess the in-house availability of manpower and match the same with the future manpower requirements to understand the gap, predict the availability of a talent pool and so on. Some workforce analytics solutions can reinforce such decision-making processes, making data and information available. |

Source: Author.

Apart from the earlier listed strategically relevant HR functions, other HR functions such as managing discipline and industrial relations, grievance handling, managing trade union activities and so on can also be facilitated by HR analytics. Today's HR managers require data-driven decision-making, as with the complexities of business, intuitive decision-making processes have become more risk-prone. Hence, without HR analytics, a strategic HR decision-making process may become futile.

PRACTICE ASSIGNMENT

Visit any organization and list its HR functions, suitably identifying the degree of their strategic focus in such functions. Indicate your perceived degree of strategic focus assigning weight.

The HRM function today is, therefore, much more integrated and strategically aligned. The increased strategic importance of HRM means that HR managers must demonstrate how they can contribute to the goals and missions of an organization. Obviously for this reason, HRM functions today need to be measured and evaluated. All these once again legitimize the importance of HR analytics.

HUMAN RESOURCE MANAGEMENT AS A PROCESS

Tracing the process of development and growth of the world economy, we find that in 1990s, people or people-centric approaches in managing organizations have received the importance. For example, total quality management (TQM) practices to achieve organizational excellence throughout the 1990s focused on people-related issues as key drivers for organizational change and transformation. Subsequently, the six-sigma approach to achieve zero defects also laid emphasis on the people-centric approach. Looking at some of the excellence models, such as

European Foundation of Quality Management (EFQM), Shingo Prize Model and Malcolm Baldrige Model, it is evident that people-centred issues have received the highest attention over technology and process. Obviously, such renewed focus on HRM made it necessary for us to focus on effective HRM practices with support of data and information. The six-sigma approach suggests recreating an existing process to make it error free. At the six-sigma level, we need to perform at 99.999666 percent accuracy, i.e., natural occurrence of defects can only be 3.4 in one million jobs. The EFQM, Shingo Prize, Malcolm Baldrige and so also the Investors in People Models consider HRM as critical input to enhance business success. Some of the common HRM criteria considered by these models are

- Planning, managing and improving the human resources.
- Identifying, developing and sustaining people's knowledge and competencies.
- Involving and empowering people.

Thus, HRM inputs have a significant impact on the performance of an organization. Hence, to ensure HRM process is more effective, HR managers need to improve their decision-making process more and more, using HR analytics.

HUMAN RESOURCE MANAGEMENT AS A SYSTEM

A system is an entity that maintains, exists and functions as a whole, interacting with its parts. Therefore, the behaviour of any system depends on how its parts are interrelated. Parts are the elements or components but they have inter-connectivity. For example, Hay's performance evaluation system has several components. Sear's three C (compelling place to work, compelling place to shop and compelling place to invest) has 74 elements or parts to evaluate a particular employee on how far he/she is meeting the three C requirements. The ISO 9000 quality system has several elements or parts which together make one quality assurance system. An individual element of ISO 9000 quality system hardly has any significance, unless it integrates with the total system. Therefore, the properties of a system are the properties of the whole.

Hard system approach: This approach to human resource uses well-defined systems to formulate goals, resolve identity problems, ascertain and evaluate options, and finally select and implement rational plan to achieve the desired outcome.

Soft systems approach: This approach focuses on understanding what the purported HR system should do and how it should behave. More logically it can be considered as an approach to refer to a problem situation with the intention of developing a conceptual model that defines how the system should operate.

When we consider HRM has a system, different elements or components of HRM such as procurement (HRP, recruitment and selection function), maintenance (compensation, discipline and industrial relations) and development (performance appraisal and training and development) act as parts. Checkland (1984) used systems engineering principles while categorizing an HRM system into hard and soft categories. The **hard system approach** deliberates on organizational requirements and identifies ways to meet such requirements. Thus, this approach using well-defined systems formulates goals, identifies problems, ascertains and evaluates options, and finally selects and implements a rational plan to achieve the desired outcome. For these reasons, hard systems are considered as a task-focused approach. The **soft systems approach**, on the other hand, focuses on understanding what the purported HR system should do and how it should behave. More logically, it can be considered as an approach to refer to a problem situation with the intention of developing a conceptual model that defines how a system should operate.

PRACTICE ASSIGNMENT

Indicate your understanding of HRM as a process and as a system.

For both hard and soft system approaches of HRM, HR analytics can support the effective decision-making process.

Likewise, we also consider HRM as a technique and a business process. A technique is a process, style and method of doing something. It might be the only way to do it or it might be a version of the possible methods. HRM as a business process provides critical support to value addition to organizational process. For example, for operating processes, employees' skills and competencies are instrumental for value addition. Both for considering HRM as a technique and as a business process, we need to make use of HR analytics.

Reviewing various theories and approaches to HRM functions, we can assess the changing roles, duties and responsibilities of HR managers. Traditionally, HR managers were responsible to systematically monitor and comply with the people management issues in the organizations. However, today HR managers need to pace with the changing needs of the organizations, making their HR practices more strategic and sustainable with more capable human resources, which require continuous development and retention. For such changing roles, HR managers need to dissuade from an intuitive decision-making process, as a standalone approach. To make their decision-making process more and more aligned with the business goals of the organizations, HR managers require data and information support for which obviously HR analytics can play a crucial role.

When HR functions are powered by HR analytics, HR managers can play the role of a **strategic partner**, employee advocate and so also of a change champion. Ulrich (1997) mentioned about such modern roles of HR managers. HR managers as strategic partners contribute to the development and also in accomplishment of the organization-wide business plans and objectives. The HR business objectives are to support the attainment of the overall strategic business plan and objectives. At the tactical level, HR managers design suitable work systems to support organizational strategies. People achieve success and develop their capability in line with the strategic intent of the organizations, with the facilitation support of human resources. Therefore, strategic partnership of human resources exerts impact on HR services such as design of work systems, recruitment, compensation management, performance management, career development and so on.

Strategic partner role: HR managers as a strategic partner contribute to the development and also the accomplishment of organization-wide business plans and objectives.

Employee advocate role: HR managers make use of their expertise in nurturing a work environment that motivates people to spontaneously contribute to organizational needs.

As **employee advocate**, HR managers make use of their expertise in nurturing a work environment that motivates people to spontaneously contribute to organizational needs. People by developing their problem-solving skills would feel responsible to set their own goals, achieve the same through self-empowerment and develop a sense of ownership of the organization. The scope of the employee advocacy role for HR managers, therefore, encompasses wide range of issues concerning organizational culture and climate. Competency development, commitment to customers, employee development opportunities, employee assistance programmes, strategic compensation designing, OD and so on are some of the initiatives taken by HR managers in this direction.

Change champion: As change champions, HR managers constantly evaluate the effectiveness of an organization, understand the need for change, assess the need for knowledge and skill to execute the change process and also manage the employees' resistance to change.

As **change champion**, HR managers constantly evaluate the effectiveness of the organization, understand the need for change, assess the need for knowledge and skill to execute a change process and manage the employees' resistance to change.

The extended roles of HR managers are policy formulators, internal consultants, service providers and monitors.

Such extended roles of HR managers radically transform the HR functions, requiring HR managers to power their decision-making process more and more with data and information support. More predictive approach to HR decision-making is now considered necessary, so as to pre-judge the decisional impact. Such understanding can help HR managers to design suitable HR decisions that can help in achieving the strategic intents with minimum risk of failure. For all these reasons, today's HR functions are increasingly driven by HR analytics.

We can better appreciate the HR manager's role if we go through the advertisement for an HR manager of a large organization, as presented in Table 1.2.

■ **Table 1.2:** Sample of Job Description of an HR Manager

Job Title	HR Manager
Responsible to (line)	General manager
Responsible to (function)	HR head
Responsible for (line)	Steel manufacturing human resources
Purpose/Role	Provide a professional, integrated HR service aligned to the business strategy of an organization.
Key aims and objectives	– Capable to use creative and innovative methods to harmonize diverse HR and business concepts and policies. – Develop and implement integrated and coherent HR strategies to suit the local environment, aligning with organizational objectives. – Optimize the deployment of human resources – Frame suitable HR policies, procedures and systems in accordance with organizational HR values. – Work within budget.

Prime responsibilities and duties	– To contribute and assist in the development and achievement of corporate objectives through support and advice to management on the optimum deployment of human resources including the development of supporting strategies, policies and procedures.
	– Develop, introduce and maintain appropriate HR policies, procedures and systems, which are aligned with the organization.
	– Assist in the expansion and enhancement of sustainable business.
	– To manage the implementation of the company's HR strategy.
	– Ensure business compliance with policies, procedures and legislations.
	– Develop and implement recruitment programmes which comply with all legal requirements, code of practice and organizational policy.
	– Develop suitable remuneration packages for employees based upon sound market information.
	– Re-source vacancies in a prompt, professional and cost-effective manner.
	– Develop and manage budgets within HR function.
	– Contribute to the development of HR strategy for the organization.
	– Develop and progress appropriate resource strategies and plans with relevant line management.
	– Development and administration of policies for assigning staff away from their normal workplace.
	– Ensure effective implementation of health & safety policy.
Allied occasional duties	– Implementation of the company's disciplinary and grievance procedures.
	– Advising management on maintaining good employee relations.
	– Contribute to the development of manpower and succession plans.
	– Produce timely and accurate management information and reports on human resources.
	– Advise line management on appropriate labour law issues.
	– Work closely with other aspects of the operation to facilitate the development and harmonization of common areas.
Core competencies	– Openness.
	– Safety, health and environment.
	– Drive for excellence.
	– Self-motivation.
	– Flexibility.
	– Adaptability.
	– Perceptiveness.
	– Interpersonal awareness.
	– Communication.
	– Cross-cultural awareness.
	– Business and commercial awareness.
	– Influencing leadership.
	– Knowledge of working with HR analytics.
	– Exposure to predictive decision modelling.

Source: Author.

MORE CLARITY ON ROLES OF HR MANAGERS

Using the example in Table 1.3, we can understand how an organization can assign weight to different functional/competency areas of an HR manager. However, this varies from organization to organization. While in one organization, strategic perspective may get less weight, in another it may receive the highest.

■ **Table 1.3:** Assigning Weight to Functional/Competency Areas of Human Resources

Behaviour	Category	Definition
Strategic perspective	B	Focus on issues to support the broad organizational strategy. Maintain a broad view and understand and consider the interests and aims of different stakeholders both inside and outside the organizations.
Maximizing potential	A	Develop systems and strategies befitting for the development of human resources at all levels of the organization. Create and nurture an environment that motivates people to achieve results.
Negotiation and influencing	A	Practice negotiation and influencing skills to persuade and exert influences over people using logic and reason. Successfully sell the benefits of the ideas that provide acceptable solutions for all both inside and outside the organization.
Respect and value diversity	A	Understand the cross-cultural differences and be sensitive to social and racial differences. Ensure equal employment opportunity to all irrespective of their social, cultural and racial differences.
Effective communication	B	Ensure transparency in communication (without compromising with the organizational confidentiality). Help people to understand clearly organizational needs, instructions and decisions. Make the communication style more adaptive to organizational needs and check the understanding of employees.
Planning and organizing	B	Effectively plan activities for self and others. Build milestones into plans, monitor progress and adjust plan to respond to changes. Make sure plans provide clear direction to people. They understand what is expected of them.
Personal responsibility	A	Be responsible for self and others' actions. Manage the situations and problems, leading by example, which demonstrates a commitment and determination to succeed. Focus on continuous learning and development.
Problem-solving	A	Develop problem-solving skills for self and others, applying different analytical techniques and understanding complex information issues.

Source: Adapted from Bhattacharyya (2012).

Complexities of HR functions today made it impossible for HR managers to work without data. It is said that without data HR managers cannot be strategic. Also, HR managers today need to be business partners and, hence, be able to use metrics to relate HR strategies with the organizational performance. However, HR metrics have its limitations, as these are not dynamic and capable to take descriptive and correlational decisions. For modelling predictive HR decisions, HR analytics is now increasingly becoming more important.

Visit any organization and illustrate the change champion role of their HR manager. Give your answer, duly listing the nature and degree of changes which the sample organization faced over the years.

TRANSITION OF HUMAN RESOURCE MANAGEMENT TO HUMAN CAPITAL MANAGEMENT

The present trend in organizations is to consider people as HC because they are the important assets for the growth and sustenance of an organization. Economist Adam Smith (1977[1776]) for the first time used the term HC primarily to legitimize the payment of higher wages to those who invest time and put effort to acquire skill. It is expected that these workers will contribute more to the organizations in terms of their performance and productivity. In management, HCM concept was formalized by Becker (1962) and subsequently by Schultz (1982). Schultz research was focused on individual household's decisions on investment in HC, more in the form of financing the education for the children. Becker could relate such households' decisions with the firms' investment decisions in knowledge creation to develop the people as capital to the organization. Since then, we find many scholarly pieces of work on HC, emphasizing the need for its continuous development for sustainable competitive advantages of the organization. HC is differentiated from other assets which we use for the accomplishment of business goals of the organizations. Organizations gain competitive strength leveraging aggregate knowledge, skill, positive attitude and abilities of its people. Hence, investment in people in the form of training and development, improvement of the quality of work-life, support of work-life balance, general health improvement among others, improve the asset value of people. The renewed focus on human resources, naming it as HC, is a major transition from control to commitment approach (Bhattacharyya, 2012), as asset precepts legitimize investment on people for incremental benefits in terms of performance and productivity, which can strengthen the organizations. Commitment orientation to HRM requires HR managers to be the facilitators to develop employees to establish link between individual and organizational goals. In achieving the business results, in organizations, issues related to people often supersede technologies, strategies and other operational excellence. Issues related to people receive attention only when organizations fail in achieving the positive results of their efforts. HCM is also interchangeably used as the talent management approach, as HCM process focuses on building the talent of people. We carefully craft the word people replacing our previous thought process, i.e., human resources, as the resource concept is constrained by our mindset of exploiting human resources like any other resources for one-way gain of the organizations, and we also feel constrained to consider people as an expense item. Considering people as assets, we buy the idea of investment on people to build their capabilities, which maximizes their contribution to organizations.

However, we have also some criticism on the HCM concept, as it equalizes with other resources and can be owned, bought, sold or traded. The approach is more like considering people as an inventory which is not expandable, rather renewable for improved use in future, when investments are made. Our criticism on HCM further extends to the dilution of the social enterprise model of an organization, which focuses on achieving a common goal. Considering people as capital at the disposal of the organization subjugates them as inert disposable assets, when they fail to perform. HCM reduces performance management systems to a more stocktaking process for HC to estimate whose asset values appreciate or depreciate, and accordingly take decisions on investment or divestment. In this process, performance management as a tool for feedback and collaboration loses its importance. Also, the criticism on HCM centres on the commercialization of HR function, as it is metrics driven, and like other operating and financial reviews makes review of capital value of people in financial terms.

Despite such criticism, the concept of HCM is gradually replacing HRM, as evident from various organizational practices. Organizations today are using strategic HCM approach, aligning people with the business and strategies for consolidating their gain (Bhattacharyya, 2013).

SUSTAINABLE COMPETITIVE ADVANTAGE THROUGH HUMAN CAPITAL

The term sustainable competitive advantage is well defined by Hofer and Schendel (1978) as the unique positioning of the organization that enables them to outperform in relation to their competitors. It is the value-creating capabilities of the organization that cannot be replicated by others. Lowson (2002) argued that it can be created leveraging knowledge, know-how, experience, innovation and unique use of information. Similar studies by Barney (1991) earlier focused on its essence of inimitability. Barney further contended that sustainable competitive advantage can only be built on strategies leveraging the internal strengths of the organizations. Internal strengths of the organizations can only be built on the possession of distinctly valuable resources over its competitors.

Reviewing the publications of scholarly researches, it is evident that till the 1990s, organizations worldwide predominantly viewed the external environmental forces as their basis for strategy framing for their competitive positioning in the market (Barney, 1991, 1995; Grant, 1991, 1998), leveraging their financial and technological resources. Human resources was considered as a tool to supplement such strategies (Boxall, 1999; Schuler & Jackson, 1999) to extend support in the process of value creation (Porter, 1998). However, we observe the departure from this thereafter because of imitable properties of this approach. The resource-based view (Becker & Gerhart, 1996; Pfeffer, 1994) shifted our focus from external to the internal context for building sustainable competitive advantages (Barney, 1991; Grant, 1991, 1998). Proponents of this view argued that organizations should focus on acquiring, deploying, developing and retaining their resources, rather than the competitive positioning in the market (Colbert, 2004). Organizational resources are assets, such as human resources, intellectual capital, capital equipment, that, however, do not have the potential of establishing a competitive advantage in isolation (Grant, 1998). Accordingly, resources have to be utilized in bundles, or combinations, which then lead to the development of organizational capabilities that can be viewed as a source of competitive advantage. Similarly, Prahalad and Hamel (1990) maintain that the establishment and sustainability of a competitive advantage rests on the organization's ability to determine, develop and nurture core competences, which they define as collective learning in an organization, while Lado and Wilson (1994) proposed that the creation of competitive advantage necessitates organizational competencies, i.e., their resources and capabilities, which strengthen their strategies to enhance values.

Barney (1991) differentiated between the competitive advantage and sustained competitive advantage, arguing that firm's strategy on competitive advantage does not consider present and future competitors, while sustained competitive advantage considers this, thereby restricting the competitors' present or future to imitate. While considering people as the core driver of sustainable competitive advantage for any organization, scholars such as Barney (1995), de Wit and Meyer (2004) and Grant (1998) also considered the importance of organizational resources. Grant's (1998) classification of organizational resources into tangible (financial and physical), intangible (culture, reputation and technology) and human recognized the importance of all these resource constructs for organizational success. However, human resources have been considered more crucial of attaining the success in organizations (Becker & Gerhart, 1996; Doorewaard & Benschop, 2003; Kamoche, 1999; Pfeffer, 1994; Wright et al. 1994; Wright et al., 2001; Ulrich & Lake, 1991). Burke (2005) recognized the importance of human resources to bring changes in organizations to survive in competition. The distinctive qualities of human resources, e.g., people's competency (aggregation of knowledge, abilities, skills, attitudes and experience), help in gaining sustainable competitive advantages for the organization. These distinctive qualities being the differentiators for firm's sustainable competitive advantage legitimize the concept of HC in place of human resources. This extension of thoughts to HC later prompted many scholars to rename HRM to HCM. Dessler's (2005) definition of HC as knowledge, education, training, skills and expertise corroborates with this distinctive approach to human resources. The difference in these two approaches, i.e., human resources and HC, rests on the difference in the approaches of cost minimization (in the case of HRM) and investment in HC (Kane et al., 1999).

Huselid et al. (1997) maintain that to achieve competitive advantage through HC, organizations need to be in possession of HC that is value adding, unique, inimitable and non-substitutable, while to meet these conditions a set of HRM practices is required. Batt (2002) distinguishes three dimensions of HRM systems that lead to the acquisition and retention of the relevant HC: First, the recruitment of people with respective skills and investment in their initial training; second, work design that fosters discretionary and continuous learning through cooperation with co-workers and, third, performance-based incentives. Thus, mere possession of human resources does not lead to the establishment and sustainability of competitive advantage; it requires building and developing human resources into core competence or organizational capability. Hence, high-quality HC needs to be supported by effective HRM to add to the competitive value of an organization. Mueller (1996) emphasized the relevant role of tacit knowledge, thus proposing that explicitly defined and formalized HRM practices do not form basis for the development and sustainability of competitive advantage. Boxall (1999) proposed that a distinction should be made between HC advantage and human or organizational process advantage, where the first embraces hiring and retaining high-quality people with tacit knowledge and the latter refers to processes. Each of these two advantages may lead to value creation; however, according to Boxall and Purcell (2008), they work best in combination with each other. Besides, the authors maintain that though human resources may be viewed as a source of competitive value, they have to be managed to lead to the establishment of a sustained competitive advantage, which in turn necessitates an HRM system for it, in contrast to single HR policies and practices, to make it inimitable (Boxall & Purcell, 2003). Ulrich and Brockbank (2005) build their HR value proposition on the following five elements: knowledge of external environment, meeting needs of external and internal stakeholders, development of HR practices, organizing human resources and effective HR function. These criteria point to the significance of both human resources and their effective management, and support the idea that to create value for the organization the two have to work in close combination.

Lawler (2005) maintains that though the value of HR function is undoubted, it could be further enhanced by assuming a business partner's role in the organization and offering the following three lines of products: administrative services (e.g., hiring, training and so on.), business partner services (e.g., HR system development) and strategic partner services (e.g., strategic differentiation of HR practices). Wright et al. (2001) proposed that in order to acquire a sustainable competitive advantage, an organization has to be superior in all areas of strategic HRM: HC pool (knowledge, skill and ability), employee relationships and behaviour (psychological contract and organizational citizenship) and people management practices (staffing, training, rewards, appraisal, work design, participation, recognition and communication).

Development of sustained competitive advantage is supported by other theories, such as, the knowledge-based view (Price, 2007) that emphasizes the critical role of unique knowledge ownership; the role behaviour theory that maintains the necessity of different role behaviours for different means of strategy implementation and views HRM as a primary means of behaviour management and the HC theory that assumes that the value of human resources, just as any other type of capital, lies in their ability to contribute to organizational productivity (Schuler & Jackson, 2005). Stavrou and Brewster (2005) pointed out to the following four perspectives that acknowledge the significance of HRM in the establishment of sustained competitive advantage: (a) organizational learning, i.e., creation of competitive advantage through innovation, change and rapid renewal; (b) external and internal fit of organizational practices, resources and capabilities; (c) engagement in change processes, identification of threats and opportunities, and acting as an intermediary between stakeholders and the business and (d) core competency development and deployment.

The extensive literature review suggests organizations with a strategic HCM approach can successfully compete, survive and grow in the long run. Theoretical framework of strategic HCM is embedded in the core concepts of HCM, per se, and how it gradually replaces the established concepts on HRM, especially in the context of organizational practices. Table 1.4 documents this.

By now we have observed that strategic HCM practices enhance organizational capabilities to sustain and grow in competition. However,

■ **Table 1.4:** Theoretical Framework of Strategic HCM

Core Concepts	Theoretical Contributions	Relationship with HCM
The economics route	Adam Smith (1977[1776])—Recommended payment of higher wages to workers who invest time and effort to acquire skill.	Laid the foundation of HCM.
The management relation	Becker (1962), Schultz (1982), Vroom (1964), Coff and Kryscynski (2011), Ployhart and Moliterno (2011)—Schultz viewed investment on human capital in terms of households' decisions on financing education for the children, while Becker relates such households' decisions with firms' investment in knowledge creation to develop people as capital to the organization.	Institutionalized HCM in organizations.
The debate on its legitimacy	Porter (1998) and Prahalad and Hamel (1994)—Discarded that people are core part of the organizational value chain and core competencies. People are critical and support the organization.	Acknowledged the criticality of the people but not accepted people as capital to the organization.
The strategic need	Bartlett and Ghoshal (2002), Ulrich & Brockbank (2005) and Ingham (2006), Sturman et al. (2008), Lawler and Boudreau (2012)—Agreed that managing people as capital we make HCM a strategic function of the organization.	Acknowledged the strategic role of HCM.
The knowledge-based view	Price (2007)—Emphasized the critical role of unique knowledge ownership for human capital for sustainable competitive advantage.	Agreed that firms by investing in human capital can own it and leverage it for sustainable competitive advantages.

Source: Bhattacharyya (2013).

we are still not very clear about the concept from organizational point of view, and we do not observe any commonality or even some degree of agreement on its major drivers. HC is embodied in the knowledge of people (Coff, 2002). Traditionally, HC is acquired by the organizations while they hire people with new knowledge and skills (Coff & Kryscynski, 2011). However, from here we have shifted our focus on the need for developing HC at the organization level (Ployhart & Moliterno, 2011). Many organizations prefer to invest in specific HC development (Barney, 1991; Nonaka, 1994; Sturman et al., 2008). Although organizations benefit from this approach, but to what extent it benefits the individual employees in terms of their future career progression both within and outside the organization, is yet to be empirically tested. Many critics to the HCM approach, for such propensity of firms to restrict investment in firm-specific areas, are already vocal about the dilution of the social enterprise model. The social enterprise model of organizations makes people work together happily to achieve a common goal. In contrast, HCM, as observed by some critics, dilutes the social enterprise model and reduces people to livestock (Wookey, 2012). However, there is nothing wrong in such approaches of the organizations, as long as HCM is truly practised. Wookey (2012) again suggested a people-centric approach to HCM to maintain the sanctity of social enterprise, integrating it with the essence of 'connection, communication and collaboration'. This literally requires a participative approach in designing HCM programmes. Some of the core drivers of HCM, evident from the literature review and organizational practices are: leadership, employee engagement, knowledge sharing, developing capabilities of people and manpower optimization (both in terms of its utilization and management). Effective leadership for HCM requires transparent top-down communication, inclusiveness of people through introduction of suggestions and feedback, reduced hierarchical barrier and facilitation. For HCM, employee engagement, among others, requires organizational commitment to acknowledge good performance of people through rewards. Employees' feel more engaged with the organization when they participate in setting their performance targets, and they can enjoy work-life balancing. Knowledge sharing requires constant training support, team work culture and mutual information sharing. This succeeds building capabilities of people as they become more innovative. Capability building, therefore, requires promoting a culture of innovation and continuous training, creating career development opportunities for the employees and scaling up to the quality of a learning organization. Manpower optimization requires clarity in work processes, congenial working conditions, accountability and a robust performance management system.

In organizational practices, we observe the evidence of HCM drivers that can be construed as core constructs (Lawler, 2009). Hence, the effective-ness of any organizational HCM practice can be understood when the organization recruits, manages, trains, retains talent and manages perfor-mance, considering people as capital to the organization. As HC value has to be assessed time to time, many organizations develop their own

HCM analytics and, with computer support, track the movement for appropriate intervention to sustain and increase the HC value. Many software vendors also provide standard HCM analytics, which organizations adapt to their requirements. When organizations align their HCM practices with their mission, goals and objectives, it becomes strategic. With a strategic HCM approach, an organization can enhance its performance. This linkage stems from the resource-based view discussed earlier. Evidently, it also has its roots to Vroom's (1964) expectancy theory. The generic model of strategic HCM, based on Fitz-enz (2000), therefore, centres on acquisition, maintenance, development and retention. Contributing factors to strategic HCM have been identified based on the degree of universality in its approach, especially in the context of organizational practices and the relevant literature support on the same.

Organizational sustainability, according to Dyllick and Hockerts (2002), is achieved through meeting the needs of the present and future stakeholders. HRM balances such needs through productive internal work relationships, meeting the expectations of employees and the society (Arnold, 2005). Ehnert (2009) advocated the practice of sustainable human resources for this purpose, defining it as a process of balancing an organizational goal with human resources with a long-term focus. Sustainable OD through motivation and job satisfaction was identified as an important prerequisite (Deal & Jurkins, 1994; Erez & Earley, 1993). From HR perspectives, organizational sustainability is achieved when the organization is able to make itself an 'employer of choice'. Sustainable HR practices encompass training, engagement, employee communications and talent acquisition. Practices, however, vary from organization to organization, depending on their specific needs.

> **Organizational sustainability:** This is achieved through meeting the needs of the present and future stakeholders.

Innovation or sustainable OD essentially requires organizations to be policy driven. This among others requires organizations to bring changes in processes, develop and empower human resources, balance the present and the future needs and also meet expectations of different stakeholders. With HR analytics it is possible for organizations to manage their HRM functions as HCM functions with long-term focus on sustainability and growth.

EMERGENCE OF HUMAN RESOURCE CONTROL SYSTEMS

Along with the theories and researches on the changing pattern of HR functions, simultaneously we also observe the trend in measuring HR activities over the years. First such observation was the emergence of the concept of **HR control systems**.

Snell (1992) defines HR control as the alignment of actions of employees with an organization. In HRM, the concept of control is embedded with the 'agency theory'. In terms of this theory, managers acquire and allocate resources and are empowered to act as control agents. As control agents, HR managers focus on controlling the variation in the behaviour of

> **HR control systems:** It is primarily the adoption of certain HR practices that can enforce behavioural changes in employees, when the results are not meeting the expected standards.

employees and the outcome. While behavioural control is enforced through structuring of activities (Child, 1973), outcome and output control is possible when it is measurable (say key performance indicators or key performance areas and so on). Japanese researcher Ouchi (1977) suggested the need for behavioural control when outcome or output deviates from the expected standards. Organizations try to enforce behavioural and output control with appropriate HR practices.

Thus, HR control systems are primarily adoption of certain HR practices that can enforce behavioural changes in the employees when the results are not meeting the expected standards. HR managers enforce HR control through the execution of the monitoring, directing, evaluating and rewarding activities of the employees (Anderson & Oliver, 1987). In addition, HR managers have another important responsibility to enforce HR control through input control. Input control in human resources is primarily enforced through the adoption of effective recruitment and selection process. Here again, HR managers make use of quantitative information to measure the knowledge, values, attitudes and behaviours of the prospective employees to assume the degree of fit with the organizational culture and value systems. With input control, HR managers can address the future performance problems, check attrition and drive the culture of teamwork. Even with HR control systems, HR managers can ensure functional autonomy to employees and make them good performers and the right-fit with the culture of the organizations. In such cases, HR managers need to consider an HR function as a process of commitment maximizers, rather than cost reducers (Arthur, 1992). HR control and HR commitment represent two distinct approaches to shape employee behaviours and attitudes at work. The goal of control of HR systems is to reduce direct labour costs, or improve efficiency, by enforcing employee compliance with specified rules and procedures and basing employee rewards on some measurable output criteria (Eisenhardt, 1985; Walton, 1985). In contrast, commitment HR systems shape desired employee behaviours and attitudes by forging psychological links between organizational and employee goals. In other words, the focus is on developing committed employees who can be trusted to use their discretion to carry out job tasks in ways that are consistent with organizational goals (e.g., Organ, 1988). In general, the commitment of HR systems was characterized by higher levels of employee involvement in managerial decisions, formal participation programmes, training in group problem-solving and socializing activities and by higher percentages of maintenance, or skilled, employees and average wage rates. The existence of the control and commitment variations in organizations is generally thought to be associated with certain organizational conditions. Most HR strategy researchers have taken a behavioural perspective (Snell, 1992). Research using this perspective rests on the often implicit assumption that the successful implementation of a business strategy requires a unique set of employee behaviours and attitudes and that a unique set of HR policies and practices will elicit those behaviours and attitudes (Cappelli & Singh, 1992). Alternatively, control theory researchers (e.g., Eisenhardt, 1985;

Ouchi, 1979; Snell, 1992) have noted that the use of a control system depends on managers.

MEASUREMENT TOOLS USED IN HUMAN RESOURCE CONTROLLING

To enforce control in HR functions, organizations still use relatively less analytical tools. However, scholars such as Sullivan (2004) and others have enriched this area, providing new insights into HR metrics. These apart, HR control is possible through generating data based on employee satisfaction surveys and periodic HR audits, and through various statistical analyses of employee responses and data. The real problem starts after such data collection, as HR managers need to collate these with their vital HR decisions to enforce control in the organizations. Sullivan's HR metrics provide some quick fix solutions to such problems of interpretation, but in true sense, we cannot draw a borderline on HR metrics, as organizations' approaches to the management of resources widely varies. For example, strategically, an organization may like to recruit people with mono-skill (i.e., narrow or single skill set) and make these people redundant once the job process changes. But in other cases, organizations may be interested in recruiting multi-skilled people, to ensure time-to-time skill renewability, thereby keeping pace with the changing business process.

Some of the core HR metrics such as cost of turnover, cost of recruitment process, training costs, productivity costs, percentage improvement in workforce productivity, degree of employee engagement data, average performance appraisal score, percentage of diversity hires, employee retention data, compensation and benefits data and so on are vital to enforce HR control.

Using such metrics, HR managers enforce control. HR tools such as HR scorecard and so on can also supplement the HR control process in the organizations. In fact, when employees are taken through the HR scorecard and are facilitated to understand its application and interpretation, they themselves can enforce self-control to keep them aligned with the organizations.

Again a distinction is made between the HRM practices that focus upon enhancing employee commitment and the ones that increase control of the owner-manager over employees and the production process. These two aspects of HRM practices are considered as the two extremes on a continuum, where HRM practices tend to be either more committed or more control oriented. This debate, however, is not new, as it is evident from McGregor's (1960) Theory X and Theory Y, which suggests the need to achieve both control and consent of employees to maintain or improve performance (Legge, 1995). Also, the debate on control–commitment dichotomy extends to various other dimensions of organizations such as organization structure versus management style, autocratic versus democratic decision-making, mechanistic versus organic organizations, tasks versus interpersonal-oriented styles, transactional versus transformational leadership, direct control versus responsible autonomy (Friedman, 1977) and Tannenbaum and Schmidt's (1958) continuum (tell–sell–consult–join). These management styles and practices either emphasize the maintenance of tasks through direct forms of control or the nurturing of interpersonal relationships through indirect or self-control of employees (Van Engen, 2001).

HR control systems, therefore, are composed of various HR practices that lead an organization to the accomplishment of its established objectives. Based on the dimensions of the traditional versus high-commitment work system as proposed by Beer et al. (1984), Walton (1985) explicitly proposed the distinction between commitment and control strategies within an organization. Given the assumption that HRM consists of a series of internally consistent HRM practices, which combine into a specific HRM system, it can be argued that HRM systems are either control or commitment oriented. HR control systems are characterized by a division of work into small, fixed jobs for which individuals can be held accountable, and direct control with managers supervising rather than facilitating employees (Walton, 1985). This type of HRM system aims at reducing direct labour costs, or improves efficiency, by enforcing employee compliance with specified rules and procedures (Arthur, 1994; Eisenhardt, 1985; Walton, 1985). In contrast, commitment-oriented HRM systems are characterized by managers who facilitate rather than supervise. This type of HRM system emphasizes employee development and trust, establishing (psychological) links between organizational and personal goals. Commitment here is seen as an individual's bond with an organization, referred to as attitudinal (affective) commitment (see Allen and Meyer, 1990).

HR control systems have two dimensions: (a) organization-wide control and (b) self-regulating autonomous control by the employees. Box 1.1 explains how HR control systems is enforced in organizations, in the context of HR practices of De La Rue.

Box 1.1   Self-regulating Control at De La Rue

De La Rue is the world's largest commercial security printer and papermaker, producing over 150 national currencies and a wide range of security documents such as passports, fiscal stamps, travellers' cheques and authentication labels. In business since 1813, De La Rue is a member of the FTSE 250 and employs over 4,000 people across 31 countries.

Lead by CEO, Martin Sutherland, De La Rue is currently driving forward a programme of operational improvement, aimed at increasing efficiency and improving shareholder value. As part of the drive to improve productivity, De La Rue introduced 'My Contribution', to empower all individuals to drive improvements. 'My Contribution' programme enables employees from any De La Rue Unit to implement HR.net, a powerful web-enabled HR system, developed by Vizual Business Tools plc. Through the installation of HR.net, the company intended to automate a range of HR processes as well as to consolidate information held in disparate, preexisting HR systems, on to one central database, housed at the company's head office. Using the latest '.net' technology, HR.net allows any manual HR process to be replicated in electronic form and enables a wide variety of tasks to be carried out by employees on a self-service basis. In addition, HR.net has a highly flexible, customizable workflow engine, to make suggestions aimed at increasing efficiency. All ideas are evaluated, and those likely to generate greater operational efficiency or cost saving are translated into projects. The project has already led to some 1,500 ideas being put forward by employees, with 250 being resourced as projects. Following the inception of 'My Contribution', and in order to achieve the full benefits from the programme, it became clear that a reporting system was required that would allow suggestions to be received from employees around the globe and then tracked through to review investment, implementation and recording of benefit which enables organizations not only to automate standard HR procedures but digitize a range of other (non-HR specific) business processes. As any business process can be defined and recreated within HR.net, organizations have the opportunity to not only streamline the HR function but refine processes and create cost-efficiencies in other areas. De La Rue managers soon realized that HR.net could be used to facilitate 'My Contribution': HR.net's powerful workflow and project tracking technology could be exploited to support the programme and, as the company had already invested in the HR.net system, no further capital expenditure was required.

HR control systems, both for HR cost optimization and enhancing employees' commitment, were so far managed with HR metrics. But complexities of business today require us to manage it with HR analytics to ensure decisions are predictive to evaluate the possible outcome well in advance for bringing changes in decisions.

Examining HR functions from different perspectives, it is now clear to us that modern HR functions need to be powered by HR analytics; else, HR functions will fail to align with the business and strategies of the organizations. We can understand this reviewing the job requirements of human resources/people analysts of some world-class organizations. One such example is illustrated in Box 1.2.

Box 1.2   People Analysts: The New Job Profile for HR Managers

Google always searches for talent in all areas of organizational activities. One thing common for all recruitments at Google is the emphasis on analytic skills. With analytic skills, Google expects its managers can make use of data, and with their research and analytic insights, they would be able to come out with innovative solutions to business problems. The company believes that with analytic skills people become more detail oriented, inquisitive and problem-solvers. A diagnostic mindset makes people successful in their jobs. For example, a people analyst at Google is part of the HR team. Google expects a people analyst to be able to conduct data analyses, regressions, factor analyses, t-tests and ANOVAs, in addition to their capabilities to identify issues, frame hypotheses, conduct surveys, have capability to use metrics and synthesize data for effective decision-making.

For Facebook, a people analyst is a visionary who feels excited to use data to drive HR-related business decisions. They will commit them for employee-related research, develop models for predictive decision-making and help the company to maximize the ROI in people. Facebook calls it the HR business intelligence function. HR managers in Facebook are expected to have knowledge in statistical analysis, applied research design and multivariate statistical analysis.

(Box 1.2 continued)

Amazon expects its human resources or people analyst to be able to identify actionable insights and to drive its HR investments and talent management decisions. It requires statistical analysis of large data sets and provides solutions, designs HR scorecard and dashboards, develops benchmarks with peer group and other world-class organizations and so on. They are expected to possess deep business insights and strategic orientation with the ability to frame hypotheses, interpret results, curiosity and attention to minute details.

For Shell global, human resources or people analysts are expected to take evidence-based decisions, making use of data. They provide valuable and strategic inputs to top management team of an organization, so that their business decisions can reflect on these. Combining human resources and business data they assess the opportunities and risks. Apart from deep human resources insights, Shell expects them to be able to carry out advanced and predictive analytics, regression analysis, multi-level analysis, factor analysis, decision tree and longitudinal analysis.

For Schlumberger, HR analysts capture, analyse and report HR trends. Based on their analysis, they focus on the continuous improvement of HR policies and standards. DuPont India expects its HR analysts to be able to align its human resources with their South Asia human resources, understand business priorities and translate the understanding in terms of HR plans and programmes and so on.

In many world-class organizations, an HR analyst's role even extends to the identification of business challenges, so that organizations can bring desired changes and make them future ready.

Summary

Over the years, HRM has become the most important function in organizations, as it ensures competitive advantages, strategic relevance and sustainability. In this chapter, we have examined HRM from the perspectives of strategy, process, systems, HC and human control.

We could analyse that irrespective of different approaches and thoughts of HRM, HR decisions in organizations cannot be taken in silos. HR decision-making needs to align with the goals, objectives and strategies. Obviously for such futuristic look, HR decision-making requires the use of HR analytics.

Reviewing the strategic perspective of human resources, it is clear that like any other economic assets, knowledge, skills and abilities of the people have also economic values. Hence, aligning human resources with the organization, it is possible to optimize cost and at the same achieve business goals of the organization. HR managers can address HR strategy factors more professionally when they make use of HR analytics.

When we manage human resources as a process, we observe the importance of people-centric approaches. For example, in adopting TQM practices or six-sigma practices, or in complying with excellence models such as EFQM, Shingo Prize Model, Malcolm Baldrige Model or Capability Maturity Model, we emphasize people-centric approaches along with processes. With HR analytics, we can better manage human resources as a process.

Likewise, when we see human resources as a system, as HCM, as cost or even as a sustainability issue, we find that an HR decision-making process can be made more and more effective with HR analytics.

This chapter concludes reviewing the changing role of HR managers as human resources/people analyst in several world-class organizations, and finally with a chapter-end case study on Toyota, whose recent case of failure is attributable to the failure of HR functions of the organization.

General Review Questions

1. Briefly explain the process of development of HRM functions.

2. Discuss the differences between resource based and behaviour perspectives of HRM. Can HR analytics support HR functions when an organization manages it from a behavioural perspective?

3. Explain why HR functions require to be managed strategically.

4. Discuss how HR functions can be managed as a process. Can we manage HRM function as a system also? Answer with some examples.

5. Explain the changing roles, duties and responsibilities of HR managers.

6. Explain the process of transition of HRM to HCM.

7. Discuss how HR can give sustainable competitive advantage to an organization.

8. Explain the concept of HR control systems. How does the concept of commitment differ from HR control?

9. Reviewing HR functions from different perspectives, explain how HR analytics can ensure value addition to HR department.

10. Write short notes on the following:

    - HR cost
    - Resource-based view of human resources
    - Configuration approach to human resources
    - Contingency approach to human resources
    - HR analytics
    - Predictive modelling of HR decisions
    - Normative human resources
    - Descriptive model of human resources
    - HCM

Multiple Choice Questions

1. Indicate which of the following is not categorized as a macro-economic change for HR function:

    a. Rising competition
    b. Rising consumerism
    c. Structural change in employment
    d. Technology-enabled human resources
    e. None of the above

2. Select the correct statement: 'HRM is normative because…'

    a. It shapes employment relationships
    b. It shapes employment relationships to achieve individual goals
    c. It shapes employment relationships to achieve organizational goals
    d. It shapes employment relationships to achieve societal goals
    e. It relates decisions with the prevalent policies and practices

3. Descriptive perspective of HRM denotes

   a. Describing HR functions in details
   b. Relating facts to each other
   c. Laying emphasis on fact-based HRM practices
   d. Focusing on predictive HR decision-making process
   e. None of the above

4. Identify which of the following is not the correct statement for the Harvard approach to HRM:

   a. It was pioneered by Beer et al.
   b. It emphasized the need for aligning employees with the organization
   c. It emphasized the need for developing strategic vision of HRM
   d. It was pioneered by Fombrun et al.
   e. It emphasized the need for the integration of HRM practices with the organizational policies

5. Identify which of the following is an incorrect statement:

   a. Heterogeneity of resources of organizations contribute to their productive potentiality
   b. Sustainable resources can give distinct competitive advantages to the organizations
   c. Sustainable resources of one organization can be imitated by another organization
   d. Human resources of an organization can ensure sustainable competitive advantages
   e. None of the above

6. Which one of the following is relevant for today's HRM:

   a. HR decisions are not taken in silos
   b. HR decisions are holistic
   c. HR decisions need to be futuristic
   d. HR decisions need to be powered by HR analytics and predictive models
   e. All of the above

7. Indicate which of the following is an incorrect statement about SHRM:

   a. It is pattern of decisions concerning policies and practices
   b. It is an HRM system
   c. It helps in framing organization-wide strategies
   d. It embraces competency-based strategic HRM approach
   e. It recommends use of HRM as reactive function

8. Which of the following approach of SHRM is based on the principles of equifinality:

   a. Heuristic
   b. Universalistic
   c. Contingency
   d. Configurational
   e. None of the above

9. Configurational perspective of strategic HRM denotes

   a. Best practices approach
   b. Policies and practices that contribute to organizational gains in general
   c. Holistic approach to examine how a pattern of several independent variables can influence organization-level strategies
   d. Alignment of organization-level strategic positions with specific choices and practices to achieve intended results
   e. None of the above

10. HR analytics cannot play a desired role when SHRM embraces

    a. Universalistic approach
    b. Configurational approach
    c. Heuristic approach
    d. Contingency approach
    e. None of the above

11. Agency theory of HRM lays emphasis on which of the following:

    a. Managing human resources like HC
    b. Managing human resources like cost
    c. Strategic alignment of employees' and employers' interest
    d. Institutional approach in managing human resources
    e. Dependency approach in managing human resources

12. Indicate which of the following is not a common HRM criterion as per different models of excellence:

    a. Planning, managing and improving the human resources
    b. Identifying, developing and sustaining people's knowledge and competencies
    c. Involving and empowering people
    d. Managing human resources as a cost function
    e. None of the above

13. Procurement function of HRM does not include

    a. HRP
    b. Attracting talent
    c. Performance evaluation
    d. Recruitment and selection
    e. None of above

14. Development function of HRM does include

    a. HRP
    b. Attracting talent
    c. Performance evaluation
    d. Recruitment and selection
    e. None of above

15. Hard systems approach to HRM is

    a. Task-focused approach
    b. Identifies problems
    c. Ascertains and evaluates options
    d. Selects and implements rational plan
    e. All of the above

16. HRM is a technique because

    a. It is a process
    b. It is a style
    c. It is a method of doing something
    d. All of the above
    e. None of the above

17. When HR functions are powered by HR analytics, HR managers can play the role of

    a. Strategic partner
    b. Employee advocate
    c. Change champion
    d. All of the above
    e. None of the above

18. Strategic partnership of human resources exerts impact on HR services like

    a. Design of work systems
    b. Recruitment
    c. Compensation management
    d. Performance management and career development
    e. All of the above

19. Employee advocacy role of human resources encompasses issues concerning:

    a. Organizational culture and climate
    b. Competency development
    c. Employee development opportunities
    d. Employee assistance programmes
    e. All of the above

20. Extended roles of HR managers do not include role of

    a. Policy formulations
    b. Internal consultants
    c. Evaluating the effectiveness of the organization
    d. Service providers
    e. Monitors

21. To sustain competitive advantage, HRM focuses on the following, except

    a. Organizational learning
    b. Innovation
    c. External and internal fit of the organization
    d. Core competency development and deployment
    e. Compensation cost minimization

22. Identify the statement which is not relevant to HR control:

    a. It is alignment of actions of employees with the organization
    b. It is embedded with the agency theory
    c. It focuses on controlling the variation in employees' behaviour
    d. It focuses on controlling employees' training and development
    e. It focuses on controlling the variation in outcome

23. HR managers enforce HR control through the execution of

    a. Monitoring
    b. Directing
    c. Evaluating
    d. Rewarding
    e. All the above

24. HR commitment denotes

    a. Reducing direct labour costs
    b. Improving efficiency

    c.   Enforcing employee compliance
    d.   Shaping desired employees' behaviours and attitudes
    e.   All of the above

25. Control–commitment dichotomy extends to various other dimensions of the organizations, except

    a.   Organization structure versus management style
    b.   Transactional versus transformational leadership
    c.   Mechanistic versus organic organizations
    d.   Job versus task
    e.   Autocratic versus democratic decision-making

Critical Review Questions

1. Review some HR decisions of some organizations (collect inputs from web-based information) and critically comment how such HR decisions could have been better with HR analytics. (Hint: Search from the web some recent cases of organizational failure, study those relating with the failure of human resources and then go for answering the question.)

2. Prepare a case for the legitimacy of HR analytics in managing today's HR functions in organizations.

PRACTITIONER SPEAKS

HR head of X & Co. considers his HR functions as standalone and accordingly he takes HR decisions in silos. Explain the types of problems HR head of X & Co. is likely to face, and how he can minimize the problems.

CASE STUDY

Looking Beyond Gas Pedals—How Human Resources Lead to Toyota's Failure

Toyota today is riddled with quality problems. Quality was once the pride USP of this company. The problem reached to such a critical level that the company had to recall almost 9 million cars worldwide. Obviously, this led to significant lowering of the brand value of the company, and drop in sales. John Sullivan (2010) attributes such failure of Toyota to poor HRM function of the company. Sullivan added that while hull design flaw contributed to this catastrophe, the root cause of the problem was human error. Human error at times caused for factors which could be beyond the control of employees. It cascades for the actions of the senior management. People at operations level may have inadequate information and poor job training.

Toyota's poor HR practices, which Sullivan classified under eight categories, attributed to such mechanical failure, causing recalling of their supplies. Such HR practices are: rewards and recognition, training, hiring, performance management process, corporate culture, leadership development and succession, retention and risk assessment. In all these HR practices, the company failed to integrate with the business goals. Moreover, HR decisions were not backed with data, rather it were in accordance with the existing systems and standards. Hence, systemic failure of management contributed to quality problems and subsequent recalling of cars, resulting several-billion-dollar loss to the company. With data-driven HR decisions, HR managers could have been more analytic and predictive in foreseeing such problems and warned the top management well in advance.

Note: Inputs for this case study was from Sullivan (2010).

Question: In the context of this case study, do you think Toyota could make a difference with HR analytics? Elucidate your answer.

REFERENCES

Allen, N. J., & Meyer, J. P. (1990). The measurement and antecedents of affective, continuance and normative commitment to the organization. *Journal of Occupational Psychology, 63*(1), 1–18.

Anderson, E., & Oliver, Richard L. (1987). Perspectives on behavior-based versus outcome-based salesforce control systems. *Journal of Marketing, 51*(October), 76–88.

Arnold, E. (2005). Managing human resources to improve employee retention. *Health Care Management, 24*(2), 132–140.

Arthur, J. B. (1992). The link between business strategy and industrial relations systems in American steel minimills. *Industrial and Labor Relations Review, 45*(3), 488–506.

———. (1994). Effects of human resource systems on manufacturing performance and turnover. *Academy of Management Journal, 37*(3), 670–687.

Barney, J. (1991). Firm resources and sustained competitive advantage. *Journal of Management, 17*(1), 99–120.

———. (1995). Looking inside for competitive advantage. *Academy of Management Executive, 9*(4), 49–61.

Bartlett, C. A., & Ghoshal, S. (2002). Building competitive advantage through people. *MIT Sloan Management Review, 43*(2), 34–41.

Batt, R. (2002). Managing customer services: Human resource practices, quit rates, and sales growth. *Academy of Management Journal, 45*(3), 587–597.

Becker, B. E., & Gerhart, B. (1996). Human resources and organizational performance: Progress and prospects. *Academy of Management Journal* [Special Issue: Human Resources and Organizational Performance], *39*(4): 779–801.

Becker, Gary, S. (1962). Investment in human capital: A theoretical analysis. *Journal of Political Economy, 70*(2), 437–448.

———. (1964). *Human capital.* New York: National Bureau for Economic Research.

Beer, M., Spector, R., Lawrence, P., Quinn Mills, D., & Walton, R. (1984). *Human resource management: A general managers perspective.* Glencoe, IL: Free Press.

Begin, J.P. (1993). Identifying patterns in HRM systems: Lessons learned from organizational theory. In J. Shaw, P. Kirkbride and K. Rowlands (Eds.), *Research in Personnel and Human Resource Management,* 3 (pp. 3–20), Greenwich, CT: JAI Press.

Bhattacharyya, D. K. (2012). *Human resource management* (3rd ed.). New Delhi: Excel Books.

———. (2013). Evidence based strategic human capital management: A study on Durgapur Steel Plant (DSP). In Patricia Ordonez de Pablos and Robert D. Tennyson (Eds.), *Strategic approaches for human capital management and development in a turbulent economy* (pp. 53–72). IGI Global.

———. (2015). *Training and development: Concept and theories.* New Delhi: SAGE Publications.

Boselie, P. (2002). *Human resource management, work systems and performance: A theoretical-empirical approach* (Dissertation thesis). Erasmus University, Rotterdam: Netherlands.

Boxall, P. (1999). The strategic HRM debate and the resource-based view of the firm. In R. S. Schuler and S. E. Jackson (Eds.). *Strategic human resource management*. Oxford: Blackwell Publishers.

Boxall, P, & Purcell, J. (2003). *Strategy and human resource management*. London: Palgrave Macmillan.

———. (2008). *Strategy and human resource management*. Hampshire: Palgrave Macmillan.

Bratton, J., & Gould, J. (1999). *Human resource management: Theory and practice*. London: Macmillan.

Burke, R. J., & Cooper, C. L. (Eds.). (2005). *Reinventing human resource management: Challenges and new directions*. London: Routledge.

Cappelli, P., & Singh, H. (1992). Integrating strategic human resources and strategic management. In D. Lewin, O. S. Mitchell and P. D. Sherer (Eds.), *Research frontiers in industrial relations and human resources* (pp. 165–192). Madison, WI: IRRA.

Checkland, P. (1984). Systems thinking in management: The development of soft systems methodology and its implications for social systems. In H. Ulrich and G. J. B. Probst (Eds.), *Management of Social Systems* (pp. 94–104). Berlin: Springer-Verlag.

Child, J. (1973). Strategies of control and organizational behavior. *Administrative Science Quarterly, 18*(1), 1–17.

Coff, W. R. (2002). Human capital, shared expertise, and the likelihood of impasse in corporate acquisitions. *Journal of Management, 28*(1), 107–128.

Coff, R., & Kryscynski, D. (2011). Drilling for micro foundations of human capital-based competitive advantages. *Journal of Management, 37*(5), 1429–1443.

Colbert, B. (2004). The complex resource-based view: Implications for theory and practice in strategic human resource management. *Academy of Management Review, 29*(3), 341–358.

de Wit, B., & Meyer, R. (2004). *Strategy: Process, content, context* (3rd ed.). London: Thomson Learning.

Deal, T., & Jurkins, W. (1994). *Managing the hidden organization strategies for empowering your employee*. Oxford: Oxford University Press.

Delery, J. E., & Doty, H. D. (1996). Modes of theorizing in strategic human resource management: Tests of universalistic, contingency, and configurational performance predictions. *Academy of Management Journal, 39*(4), 802–835.

Dessler, G. (2005). *Human resource management* (10th ed.). Upper Saddle River, NJ: Pearson Education.

DiMaggio, P. J., & Powell, W. W. (Eds.). (1991). *The new institutionalism in organizational analysis*. Chicago, IL: University of Chicago Press.

Doorewaard, H., & Benschop, Y. (2003). HRM and organizational change: An emotional endeavor. *Journal of Organizational Change Management, 16*(3), 272–286.

Doty, D. H., Glick, W. H., & Huber, G. P. (1993). Fit, equifinality, and organizational effectiveness: A test of two configurational theories. *Academy of Management Journal, 36*(6), 1196–1250.

Dyllick, T., & Hockerts, K. (2002). Beyond the business case for corporate sustainability. *Business Strategy and the Environment, II*(2), 130–141.

Ehnert, I. (2009). *Sustainable human resource management: A conceptual and exploratory analysis from a paradox perspective*. Berlin: Physica-Verlag.

Eisenhardt, K. M. (1985). Control: Organizational and economic approaches. *Management Science, 31*(2), 134–149.

———. (1989). Building theories from case study research. *Academy of Management Review, 14*(4), 532–550.

Fitz-enz, J. (2000). *The ROI of human capital*. New York: AMACOM.

Flamholtz, E. G., & Lacey, J. M. (1981). *Personnel management, human capital theory, and human resource accounting*. Los Angeles, CA: Institute of Industrial Relations, University of California.

Fombrun, C., Tichy, N. M., & Devanna, M. A. (Eds.). (1984). *Strategic human resource management*. New York: John Wiley & Sons.

Friedman, A. L. (1977). *Industry and labour*. London, Macmillan.

Gomez-Mejia, L. R., & Balkin, D. B. (1992). *Compensation, organizational strategy, and firm performance*. Cincinnati, OH: South Western Publishing Company.

Grant, R. M. (1998). *Contemporary strategy analysis: Concepts, techniques, applications*. Malden: Blackwell Publishers.

———. (1991). The resource-based theory of competitive advantage: Implications for strategy formulation. *California Management Review, 33*(3), 114–135.

Hofer, Charles W., & Schendel, D. (1978). *Strategy formulation: Analytic concepts*. St. Paul, MN: West Publishing.

Huselid, M. A. (1995). The impact of human resource management practices on turnover, productivity, and corporate financial performance. *Academy of Management Journal, 38*(3), 635–672.

Huselid, M. A., Jackson, S. E., & Schuler, R. S. (1997). Technical and strategic human resource management effectiveness as determinants of firm performance. *Academy of Management Journal, 40*(1), 171–188.

Ingham J. (2006). Closing the talent management gap. *Strategy HR Review, 5*(3), 20–23.

Jackson, S. E., & Schuler, R. S. (1995). Understanding human resource management in the context of organizations and their environments. In M. R. Rosenzweig & L. W. Porter (Eds.), *Annual review of psychology* (Vol. 46, pp. 237–264). Palo Alto, CA: Annual Reviews.

Kamoche, K. (1999). Strategic human resource management within a resource-capability view of the firm. In R. S. Schuler and S. E. Jackson (Eds.), *Strategic human resource management*. Oxford: Blackwell Publishers.

Kane, B., Crawford, J., & Grant, D. (1999). Barriers to effective HRM. *International Journal of Manpower, 20*(8), 494–515.

Katz, D., & Kahn, R. L. (1978). *Social psychology of organizations* (2nd ed.). New York: John Wiley & Sons.

Lado, A. A., & Wilson, M. C. (1994). Human resource systems and sustained competitive advantage: Competence-based perspective. *Academy of Management Review, 19*(4), 699–727.

Lawler, E. E., III. (2005). From human resource management to organisational effectiveness. *Human Resource Management, 44*(2), 165–169.

———. (2009). *Make human capital a source of competitive advantage. Organizational Dynamics, 38*(1), 1–7.

Lawler, E. E., III, & Boudreau, J. W. (2012). Creating an effective human capital strategy. *H.R. Magazine, 57*(8), 57–59.

Legge, K. (1989). Human resource management: A critical analysis. In J. Storey (Ed.), *New perspectives in human resource management*. London: Routledge.

Legge, K. (1995). *Human resource management: Rhetorics and realities*. London: Macmillan Business.

Lowson, R. (2002). The implementation and impact of operations strategies in fast-moving supply systems. *Supply Chain Management: An International Journal, 7*(3), 146–163.

Mabey, C. Salaman, G. & Storey, J. (1998). *Human resource management: A strategic introduction* (2nd ed.) Oxford: Blackwell Publishers.

McGregor, D. (1960). *The human side of enterprise*. McGraw-Hill (annotated ed., McGraw-Hill, 2006).

Meyer, J. W., & Rowan, B. (1977). Institutional organization: Formal structure as myth and ceremony. *American Journal of Sociology, 83*(2), 340–363.

Miles, R. E., & Snow, C. C. (1995). The network firm: A spherical structure built on a human investment philosophy. *Organizational Dynamics, 23*(4), 5–17.

Mueller, F. (1996). Human resources as strategic assets: An evolutionary resource-based theory. *Journal of Management Studies, 33*(6), 757–785.

Naylor, J. C., Pitchard, R. D., & Ilgen, D. R. (1980). *A theory of behavior in organizations*. New York: Academic Press.

Nonaka, I. (1994). A Dynamic Theory of Organizational Knowledge Creation. *Organization Science, 5*(1), 14–37.

Organ, D. W. (1988). *Organizational citizenship behavior: The good soldier syndrome*. Lexington, MA: Lexington Books.

Ouchi, W. G. (1977). The relationship between organizational structure and organizational control. *Administrative Science Quarterly, 22*(1), 95–113.

———. (1979). A conceptual framework for the design of organizational control mechanisms. *Administrative Science Quarterly, 25*(9), 833–848.

Pfeffer, J. (1994). Competitive advantage through people. *California Management Review, 36*(2), 9–28.

Pfeffer, J., & Salancik, G. R. (1978). *The external control of organizations: A resource dependence perspective.* New York, NY: Harper & Row.

Ployhart, R. E., & Moliterno, T. P. (2011). Emergence of the human capital resource: A multilevel model. *Academy of Management Review, 36*(1), 127–150.

Porter, M. E. (1985). *The competitive advantage: Creating and sustaining superior performance.* New York: Free Press.

———. (1998). *The Competitive advantage: Creating and sustaining superior performance.* New York: The Free Press.

Prahalad, C. K., & Hamel G. (1990). The core competence of the corporation. *Harvard Business Review, 68*(3), 79–91.

———. (1994). Strategy as a field of study: Why search for a new paradigm? *Strategic Management Journal, 15*(S2), 5–16.

Price, A. (2007). *Human resource management in a business context* (3rd ed.). London: Thomson Learning.

Rangone, A. (1999). A resource-based approach to strategy analysis in small-medium sized enterprises. *Small Business Economics, 12*(3), 233–248.

Sanz-Valle R., Sabater-Sanchez, R., & Aragon-Sanchez, A. (1999). Human resource management and business strategy links: An empirical study. *International Journal of Human Resource Management, 10*(9), 655–671.

Schemerhorn, J. R. (2001). *Management.* New York, John Wiley & Sons.

Schuler, R. S., & Harris, D. L. (1991). Deming quality improvement: Implications for human resource management as illustrated in a small company. *Human Resource Planning, 14*(3), 191–207.

Schuler, R. S., & Jackson, S. E. (1987). Linking competitive strategies with human resource management practices. *Academy of Management Executive, 1*(3), 207–219.

———. (Eds.) (1999). *Strategic Human Resource Management.* Oxford: Blackwell Publishers.

———. (2005). A quarter-century review of human resource management in the US: the growth in importance of the international perspective. *Management Review, 16*(1), 11–35.

Schultz, T. W. (1982). Investment in entrepreneurial ability. *Scandinavian Journal of Economics, 82*(4), 437–448.

Smith, A. (1977[1776]). An inquiry into the nature and causes of the wealth of nations. Chicago, IL: University of Chicago Press.

Snell, S. A. (1992). Control theory in strategic human resource management: The mediating effect of administrative information. *Academy of Management Journal, 35*(2), 292–327.

Stavrou, E. T., & Brewster, C. (2005). The configurational approach to linking strategic human resource management bundles with business performance: Myth or reality? *Management Review, 16*(2), 186–201.

Sturman, M. C., Walsh, K., & Cheramie, R. A. (2008). The value of human capital specificity versus transferability. *Journal of Management, 24*(2), 290–316.

Storey, J. (1989). Introduction: From personnel management to human resource management. In J. Storey (Ed.), *New Perspectives on Human Resource Management.* (pp. 1–18). London: Rutledge and Kegan Paul.

Sullivan, J. (2004). End equal treatment today! Focus on top performers. *Human Resources, 58*(1), 10–11.

———. (2010, February 15). A think piece: How HR caused Toyota to crash. Available at: http://www.ere.net/2010/02/15/a-think-piece-how-hr-caused-toyota-to-crash/ (accessed on 28 April 2015).

Tannenbaum, R., & Schmidt, W. (1958). How to choose a leadership pattern. *Harvard Business Review, 36*(2), 95–101.

Ulrich, D. (1997). *Human resource champions: The next agenda for adding value and delivering results.* Boston, MA: Harvard Business School Press.

Ulrich, D., & Brockbank, W. (2005). *The HR value proposition.* Boston, MA: Harvard Business School Press.

Ulrich, D., & Lake, D. (1991). Organizational capability: Creating competitive advantage. *Academy of Management Executive, 5*(1), 77–92.

Van Engen, M. L. (2001). *Gender and leadership: A contextual perspective* (Dissertation thesis). Tilburg University: Netherlands.

Vroom, V. H. (1964). *Work and motivation*. New York: John Wiley & Sons.

Walton, R. E. (1985, March–April). From control to commitment in the workplace. *Harvard Business Review*, *63*(1) 77–84.

Williamson, O. E. (1981, November). The economics of organization: The transaction cost approach. *American Journal of Sociology*, *87*(3), 548–577.

Wookey, J. (2012). Why human capital management really needs a social model? Available at: www.tlnt.com/2012/5/02/why-human-capital-management-really-needs-a-social-model (accessed on 14 February 2014).

Wright, P. M., Dunford, B. N., & Snell, S. A. (2001). Human resources and the resource-based view of the firm. *Journal of Management*, *27*(6), 701–721.

Wright, P. M., & McMahan, G. C. (1992). Theoretical perspectives for strategic human resource management. *Journal of Management*, *18*(2), 295–320.

Wright, P. M., McMahan, G. C., & McWilliams, A. (1994). Human resources and sustained competitive advantage: A resource-based perspective. *International Journal of Human Resource Management*, *5(2)*, 301–326.

FURTHER READINGS

Begin, J. P. (1991). Strategic employment policy: An organizational systems perspective. Englewood Cliffs, NJ: Prentice Hall.

Erez, M. & Earley, P. C. (1993). Culture, self-identity and work. New York: Oxford University Press.

Flamholtz, E. G. (1979). Towards a psychotechnical systems paradigm of organizational measurement. *Decision Sciences*, *10*(1): 71–84.

Nonaka, I. (1991). The knowledge-creating company. *Harvard Business Review*, *69*(6), 96–104.

Pinnington, A., & Edwards, T. (2000). *Introduction to human resource management*. Oxford, London: Oxford University Press.

Torrington, D., & Hall, L. (1998). *Human resource management* (4th ed.). London: Prentice Hall.

Tyson, S. (1995). *Strategic prospects for HRM*. London: Institute of Personnel and Development.

APPENDIX

HR Research Through HR Analytics

HR analytics can also help us in developing relevant approaches for successful management of organizations through HR research. When HR managers manage HR functions and take HR decisions with a research bent, they can get better results. HR research is defined as a rigorous scientific activity, capability for which can be developed through systematic knowledge acquisition. In organizations, HR research can be tailored to solve specific decisional problems. Through HR research, HR managers can understand how organizations are structured and function, what could be the right approaches for decision-making, what may have a potential effect on the operations of organizations, what HR strategies can be the right-fit for achieving business goals and so on.

While using HR analytics, we follow the typical HR research approach, such as finding causal relationships between variables, how we can control the effect or caused variable for achieving organizational goals and so on. In many cases the effect or caused variable needs to be eliminated or strengthened, which can be better done once we adopt an HR research approach. Also, HR research can provide descriptive research outputs that can be useful in many operational and strategic HR decisions. For example, through HR research we can understand various costs of operations and accordingly can focus on reducing costs with appropriate changes in the operations.

With HR analytics, we can carry out pure, objective, evaluative, applied and action researches in human resource. Pure basic research in HR requires more theoretical knowledge in line with the needs of the academic world. In fact, pure research is our source of knowledge, as it helps in developing our core knowledge. Objective research is carried out in framing objectives and hypotheses, and then based on the data analysis and statistical interpretation, testing the validity of our existing knowledge in a specific situation. Evaluative research analyses the effectiveness of a specific issue, namely we can study how effective is performance-related pay (PRP) over fixed pay, when we relate it with the employees' performance. Through this research, HR managers can develop 'scientific neutrality' in managing HR functions. Applied research is specific to solve a problem. For example, HR managers may be required to study an effective leadership style for employees' motivation. Obviously, this research requires HR managers to first apply their relevant knowledge to test how effective is the leadership style of the company in motivating employees. Action research improves our existing stock of knowledge, based on the way a problem is solved.

For all the aforementioned types of HR researches, HR analytics can immensely help in churning data to information, and thereafter, making use of statistical analysis and tests.

Another important aspect of HR research is concept mapping that helps in HR analytics. It is a formative assessment and research tool which visualizes relationships between concepts. It helps in assessing our cognitive map: with the help of a diagram explaining relationships between concepts. Also, it can stimulate and organize the generation of new ideas.

All these HR research issues are relevant for HR analytics, as through HR analytics, today we can successfully do HR researches.

HR DECISION-MAKING AND HR ANALYTICS

INTRODUCTORY CASE

Coping with the Challenge of Talent Retention

Managing talent is increasingly becoming a critical issue for a Pune-based automobile spares manufacturer of India. With successive acquisitions, including acquisitions abroad, the company now emerges as one of the biggest automobile spares manufacturer in the world. The company observes, despite its inclusive talent development approach, a very high talent attrition rate. Talent attrition in general is attributable to factors such as inter-industry mobility of workforce for the effect of cross-skilling, globalization and workforce demography. However, at the organization level, it is difficult to assess which factors are more dominating the mindsets of the talented people to change their job. The company believes this is largely for their lack of insight into HR data. HR data analysis on why employees leave their job, basis of their recruitment and data on the same, how capable they are in delivering the jobs, what is their engagement level with the organizations, what is the compa-ratio of compensation and benefits, what training and development programmes have been conducted for such job leavers and so on can help the company to understand the underlying reasons for talent attrition. Such understanding can help the company to decide on effective talent retention strategies. The company has decided to invest in HR analytics for better insights into such critical HR issues.

INTRODUCTION

Globally, organizations are shifting their focus on evidence-based management practices. Evidence-based management practices facilitate conscientious decision-making, with effective use of available evidences (data support) so that decisional outcome can benefit the organization and the stakeholders. The concept of evidence-based management was pioneered by researchers such as Pfeffer and Sutton (2006) and Briner et al. (2009). In human resources, we make investments in building capabilities of the organizations, and so also of the employees. We attract and retain talent to sustain in competition. With HR analytics such decisions in organizations can be more and more evidence based, leading to a more realistic cross-functional approach. Analytics-based HR decisions, being evidence-based, are more value adding, futuristic and sustainable.

Analytics *per se* is defined as scientific data manipulation. **Business analytics (BA),** therefore, is scientific data manipulation for better business decisions. BA literally indicates the application of mathematical and statistical techniques. Primarily in operations research, economics, marketing and financial functions, BAs are in use for quite some time and also being taught in all management programmes for several decades. Use of BA in HR decision-making process is of recent origin. In fact, its use started getting our attention, once we started looking at the HR function from the point of view of organizational strategy and sustainability. In Chapter 1, we have elaborated on this issue. With big-data-enabled BA, organizational decision-making processes have undergone many changes, and today the organizational decisions (operational, business and strategic) are more predictive, rather than analysing static decisional impact in terms of decisional outcomes. **Predictive decision-making process** being more and more holistic and being capable to assess the decisional outcomes right in the beginning, helps managers in calibrating their decisions, so that adverse effects of decisions, if any, can be minimized and the overall decisional impact can benefit both the organizations and the employees. Today, BA tools are more subject and function specific, of which HR analytics is one of such example. HR analytics is a predictive decision-making tool capable to manipulate the big data and assess the decisional impact before its occurrence, letting the decision-makers to alter, change or intervene to improve the decisional outcomes. However, before we go for a detailed discussion on HR analytics, let us first understand HR decision-making and how over the years, the HR decision-making process was powered by metrics, correlational analysis and now by analytics.

Business analytics (BA): BA is scientific data manipulation for better business decisions. It literally indicates the application of mathematical and statistical techniques.

Predictive decision-making process: It is more holistic and capable to assess the decisional outcomes right in the beginning, helping managers in calibrating their decisions.

HR DECISION-MAKING

HR decisions are characteristically different from non-HR decisions in organizations, both in terms of its scope and complexities. Cases of organizational failure are largely attributable to wrong HR decisions. A good example is decisions on talent recruitment and selection. Despite adoption of multiple approaches for making the selection process in true sense a successive hurdle technique, we observe selected talent become unproductive, unfit for team work, unable to integrate with the culture of the organization and so on. Those who are the right-fit decide to quit the organization unpredictably, causing increased cost of talent replacement.

Prima facie a decision-making process is our judgement for any action. An HR decision-making process, therefore, can be defined as HR managers' judgemental thoughts on an action. As most of the HR decisions are encompassing all stakeholders of the organizations, it is always prudent to reinforce HR decisions with supportive data and information. Obviously for this reason today, we observe increasing acceptance of HR analytics as an important tool for HR decision-making.

An effective HR decision-making process requires the integration of critical thoughts and information. HR managers develop critical thoughts using their professional skill and competence, while business information are made available through big-data analysis. Critical thoughts of HR managers are also moderated by evidence-based HR decision-making (Rousseau & Barends, 2011). In the process of emulating best practices, HR managers get influenced by organizational experiences, more specifically in terms of cognizance to decisional consequences. Data-driven HR decision-making is in practice in organizations for quite some time. In fact, researchers such as Locke (2009) and Charlier et al. (2011) could observe that an HR decision-making process, across organizations, has the richest scientific evidence. This signifies that organizations have already embedded a data-driven HR decision-making process, for their sustenance. Evidence-based HR decision-making, in its current stage of development, signifies factoring of managerial practices and decision-making with couple of factors such as evidence-based indicators and metrics, procedural justice and ethical issues, stakeholders' interests and so on. In all such cases, the use of big-data and HR analytics can help.

HR managers largely feel constrained in their decision-making process for couple of reasons, such as organizational systems, regulatory influences, social influences and stakeholders' responses. Most of the HR decisions in organizations often neglect the stakeholders' interests, resulting gradual decline in their performance and brand value. For example, 'say on pay' is a critical issue for shareholders (Bhattacharyya, 2013). In India, it is yet to gain popularity, but in Europe, America and a couple of other industrially advanced countries, this issue is gaining importance. 'Say on pay' means exertion of shareholders' right to vote against or for the proposed executive compensation packages of organizations, which have been approved by the compensation committee, and put up for vetting before the shareholders' annual general meeting. Shareholders' today are more informed for the information availability from various shareholders' advisory services. Even though shareholders' voting effect is non-binding for the company, but when they vote against, companies dissuade them to implement the increased compensation package, fearing decrease in market capitalization and dilution of their brand value.

Similarly, HR decisions on the redesigning of a performance standards, introducing new key performance indicators (KPIs), without factoring the employees' responses, often create crisis for the organizations. On the positive node, diversity inclusive policy design, or creating new career anchors for the employees for increasing career development opportunities for the employees, may have significant effect in terms of reduced employee attrition. It also helps organizations to enhance their brand value, which can attract new talent to join the organization (Bhattacharyya, 2015).

Data-driven HR decisions, which we call HR analytics, even though considered to be the best and scientific, are not to be considered as sacrosanct. Even in today's dynamic business environment, HR analytics is a means to an end. HR decisions which can be made analytics bound are particularly non-strategic in nature. These are more operational. Walmart's manpower planning model helps it assess how with every additional headcount its sales revenue changes. Hence, before the start of their day, managers here first decide manpower allocation, using the prudence of cross-utilization, balancing the customers' services and queuing problems in sales outlets. Apparently, this is an operational issue, but having high strategic significance, as over and under engagement of manpower can affect the company's sales revenue and so also the profit or the bottom line. Similarly, in workforce planning, analytics can help interpreting the transition probabilities of managerial employees' attrition, to decide on the current recruitment level of executive/managerial employees, pacing with organizational future leadership programme. Here, HR analytics can only lend support in strategic workforce planning, making data available and interpreting the attrition trend in an organization. Therefore, with HR analytics, operational HR decisions can achieve success with high degree of precision, and strategic HR decisions become less risk-prone.

Analytics-based HR decisions can significantly reduce the decisional bias. Often a typical confirmation bias, i.e., propensities of HR managers to support their decisions with available information, which is a typical problem of bounded rationality, lands them into a problem of wrong decision-making with negative consequences. For example, HR managers, often under pressure, hasten their recruitment decisions without adequate verification of the antecedents of employees who later transpire to be problem employees for the organization. Similar decisional bias in HR functions may occur due to a consensus effect (result of groupthink), deadline effect (to achieve the target within the mandated time), ethics effect (issues pertaining to ethical compliance), regulatory effect (pertains to legal compliance issues) and also the branding effect.

Professionally designed HR analytics make use of statistical models to predict the future, or the implications of current HR trends, including decisions on critical future organizational issues, such as sustainability, growth, revenues and bottom-line changes. Many consulting organizations have developed such predictive decision-making suites with their HR analytics packages.

However, despite such enhanced technology-enabled HR analytics and predictive decision-making support, and despite organizational investments in such resources, many HR managers even to date are not able to reinforce their HR decision with strategic insights. They still believe in intuitive decision-making process, with poor strike rate of success. Very few organizations today audit their HR decisions. Some of the very well-known organizations that invest in such annual audit could surprisingly identify wrong HR decisions not only increased the cost of litigation but even affected their sales revenue, and ultimately their profitability.

Powerful HR analytics can predict how employees' satisfaction cascades to customers' satisfaction, which in turn leads to repeat buying. Similarly, employees' satisfaction leads to their increased level of motivation, productivity and performance. Strategically, therefore, organizations need to invest on enhancement of employees' satisfaction. One possible area is investment in building their positive attitude. Through HR analytics, firms can appropriately conclude what could be contributing to employees' positive attitude. Characteristically, HR analytics, therefore, is not just availability of big data but it includes use of statistics and research design for specific HR decisional issues, and then making use of relevant data, both within and outside the organization, for predictive decision-making. Using HR analytics, HR managers can effectively align their HR functions with the business and legitimize the strategic significance of human resources in organizations.

Predictive analytics: It can assess the probability of future occurrence of an event, which may have significant implications on HR decisions.

We have already said that HR decision-making processes over the years have been increasingly becoming data driven. When we analyse the evolution process of HR analytics, we can appreciate also the changing pattern of HR decision-making. With **predictive analytics**, HR decision-making processes have now become more encompassing, integrated, strategic and business aligned. While in the beginning phase of data-driven HR decision-making process, HR managers were contended with the use of metrics, complexities of business gradually increased the scope of HR decision-making, requiring HR managers to understand the correlations between variables. Finally in the current phase of the development of HR analytics, for effective HR decision-making, HR managers focus on both causation and predictions. With predictive analytics, HR managers can envision the future landscape, and factoring such outcome, i.e., implications of their current decisions on future, they can make their decision-making process more and more effective. Figure 2.1 illustrates different phases of development of data-driven HR decision-making. The use of metrics is identified as the phase of descriptive analytics; the use of correlation (to study the relation between different variables) is identified as correlation analytics, while the HR analytics in its current form is known as prescriptive/predictive analytics.

A survey by IBM in 2010 indicated that HR decision-making process is increasingly becoming prediction and causation based. Obviously for this reason, technology vendors (including IBM) are now making available HR analytics packages that are capable to make scientific, predictive and causation-based studies. However, HR managers, across organizations are still not very comfortable to make use of predictive analytics packages, as this requires good understanding of statistics in interpreting data.

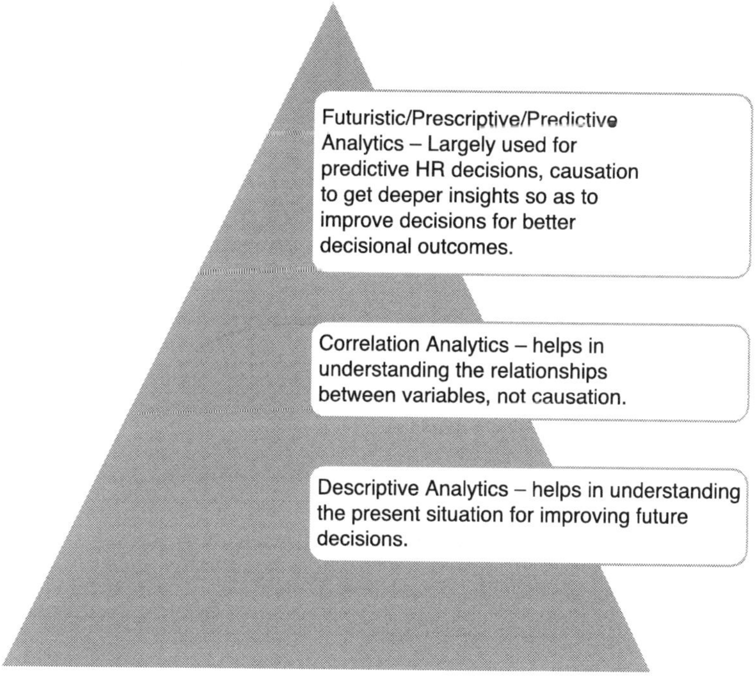

Futuristic/Prescriptive/Predictive Analytics – Largely used for predictive HR decisions, causation to get deeper insights so as to improve decisions for better decisional outcomes.

Correlation Analytics – helps in understanding the relationships between variables, not causation.

Descriptive Analytics – helps in understanding the present situation for improving future decisions.

■ **Figure 2.1:** Phases of Development of HR Analytics
Source: Author.

Broadly, HR decision-making can be categorized in two types: financial decisions and data-driven decisions. **Financial HR decisions** are ROI on training or any other financial impact of HR decisions taken in organizations. **Data-driven HR decisions** are those which are facilitated by HR analytics. Box 2.1 explains the data-driven HR decision-making in Google with the help of HR analytics.

Financial HR decisions: Common types of decisions under this category are: ROI on training, any financial impact analysis relating to HR decisions and so on. Such decisions are most metrics driven.

Data-driven HR decisions: HR decisions based on HR analytics.

Box 2.1   HR Analytics Is not a Panacea for Google

For Google, innovation is the major driving force. As the company expects its people to be innovative, so also they create the right ambience to create an enabling culture of workplace innovation embracing innovative HR practices. Think of perks, those are unique at Google. We cannot get gourmet food in office canteen, except in Google. A barber shop and sleeping pods are yet other unique perks for Googlians. Google does this not just to create headlines in the corporate news but to reflect how serious it is in managing its people. With research inputs from behavioural science, Google continuously upgrades its PiLab (People & Innovation Lab). With Google analytics, the company tries to get deeper insights into HR issues, and manages supports and develops its human resources to remain on the top. Thus, while Google analytics provide the insights, Google's innovative HR practices reinforce the support to achieve the excellence. Thus, standalone use of HR analytics is not a panacea for Google.

Descriptive HR Decision-making

Descriptive HR decision-making process: It makes use of metrics or HRIS to get insights into decisional issues and then take decisions. It can be reinforced by correlational of the decision-making process also.

Descriptive HR decision-making process makes use of metrics or human resources information systems (HRIS) to get insights into decisional issues and then take decisions. For example, high employee attrition rate is an indicator of poor employee engagement programme in an organization, may be for less competitive compensation and benefits, less opportunities for employees' growth and development and so on. HR managers once getting higher rate of attrition, as per the conventional practices of descriptive decision-making, may check the earlier listed areas and correct the situation, wherever required. A descriptive HR decision-making process can be reinforced by a correlational HR decision-making process, discussed in the subsequent paragraph. Many organizations are now strengthening their HRIS with HR analytics, i.e., the process of shifting from descriptive and correlational decisions to an analytics-based decision-making process.

Functionally, HR analytics are more dynamic than HRIS, as these can extend to the collection of micro-management data, factor individual employee-level information, assess their pattern of predictable behaviours and propensities and so on. In contrast, HRIS is capable to factor in macro-level data. A good way to differentiate between descriptive and predictive HR decision-making process is summarized in Table 2.1.

Thus, it is clear how predictive HR analytics can facilitate better HR decision-making process, optimizing the resource constraint of the organizations.

■ **Table 2.1:** Descriptive Versus Predictive HR Decisions

Descriptive/Correlational HR Decisions	Analytic/Predictive HR Decisions
Basic details of the employee: – Number of years Mr X has been working with us – CTC of Mr X – Performance rate of Mr X – Average rate of absenteeism of Mr X – Average man-days of training of Mr X	Basic details of the employee: – Number of years Mr X will continue working with us – Likely CTC of Mr X after 10 years – Likely rate of absenteeism of Mr X after five years – Number of man-days of skill-change training required by Mr X after five years
Specific career-related information : – How many years Mr X has been working at the same job level? – Was Mr X recommended for promotion by his superior? – What merit rating Mr X got over the last 3 years? – What seniority score Mr X has at present?	Specific career-related information: – Number of promotions need to be given to Mr X in his career span of next 10 years in the organization. – Year-wise likely rate of performance of Mr X in next 10 years – Year-wise merit rate of Mr X for next 10 years – Year-wise seniority score of Mr X for next 10 years

Descriptive/Correlational HR Decisions	Analytic/Predictive HR Decisions
Retrospection/Hindsight information such as ratio, metrics, data in absolute numbers and so on.	Futuristic/Foresight information such as probability or likelihood, hidden pattern and so on
Tools are: tracking signal, dashboard, Gantt chart, review reports and so on.	Tools are: mathematical and statistical models, predictive models, forecasting models and so on.

Source: Author.

Correlational HR Decision-making

Correlational HR decisions help us to assess the determinants of key variables. It refers to the study of strong or accurate relationship, to assess the goodness of fit. Based on such assessment, HR managers can understand the possible effect of their decisions and accordingly can calibrate their decision, to minimize the risk of adverse consequences, if any. On a positive note, it also helps in making changes in the decision for eliciting better results. For example, PRP may be correlated with the change in employees' performance. PRP calculation formula may be changed to give more weightage on individual performance or group performance, for getting better individual performance results or group performance results. For effective correlation of HR decisions, it is important for HR managers to first understand which are the variables that interact with each other and how manipulating such variables, the HR decision-making process changes. Once such patterns are understood, HR managers may establish link between variables. However, it is important to understand that correlation is not causation. To prove causation, we require performing a controlled experiment. Correlation occurs when two things are associated with each other but are not bound by cause and effect relationships. Causation is the connection between two events, where one is the cause, while the other one is the effect. For assessing the causation, we need to make use of HR analytics. Correlational HR decision-making is facilitated by HR metrics.

> **Correlational HR decision-making process:** It helps in assessing the relationships between two variables. Measuring such relationships, HR managers can understand the possible effect of their decisions and accordingly calibrate their decision, to minimize the risk of adverse consequences, if any.

Predictive HR Decision-making

Predictive HR decision-making process rests on big-data analysis. Two commonly used predictive HR decision-making tools are causation and regression analysis. Through regression analysis we estimate the trend pattern, and accordingly make our decision more robust. Multiple regression analysis can study the relationship between or among variables, and thus, can influence the HR decision-making process with more precision and level of accuracy. Causation analysis is different from correlation analysis. Through correlation we can understand the relationships between two variables, but that does not speak that one causes the other. For example, less pay may correlate with poor productivity, but we cannot say poor productivity is caused by less pay. In causal analysis, we consider that the independent variables are the causes of the dependent variable.

> **Predictive HR decision-making process:** It rests on big-data analysis. Companies such as Google and Facebook extensively use big data sets to manage their core businesses, and so also HR functions.

For this, we require hypothesis framing and testing to understand the phenomenon.

Companies such as Google and Facebook extensively use big data sets to manage their core businesses and so also HR functions. These companies align their human resources with their organizational strategies and business plans. We call it predictive HR decision-making as manipulating the big data such organizations can develop their mathematical models for estimating the likely outcomes of their HR decisions, and accordingly can go for well-thought interventions to churn better outcomes for both organizations and employees. Since a predictive HR decision-making process can even be extended to individual employee level, it can ensure better HRM and can truly leverage HR potentialities for the benefit of the organizations. Justification for the use of predictive modelling for HR decision-making has been explained in Box 2.2.

Box 2.2   Why Predictive Modelling for HR Decision-making?

Anticipating what might happen in future requires human resources to make use of predictive analytics. Predictive analytics require the knowledge of mathematics and statistics. One important area of human resources where predictive analytics have become almost essential is organizational decisions on talent management. Although we have evidences in the corporate world that talent sourcing decisions are taken more intuitively by the CEOs of companies (namely Apple, Yahoo, Google and so on.), we have more pieces of evidence on mistakes of organizations on this count. Any mistake in talent-related decisions is costly; hence, it requires foresight. Honestly speaking, the number of variables that merit consideration of HR decision-makers on talent is many, and is difficult for manual interpretation. Using mathematics and statistics, with the big data, HR managers can generate algorithms, processing voluminous data, and then can take critical HR decisions, which may be less prone to error. Here lies the importance of predictive analytics. HR managers, with actionable insights, can develop advance-level rubrics for decision-making, and can ensure talent is not only appropriately sourced or recruited but also developed and retained in the organizations. Talent analytics help in predicting whether the recruited talent will continue with the organization or not and whether organizations should invest on such employees to build their future capabilities. Such understanding to a great extent can help in minimizing the risk of managing talent in organizations. Also, predictive models using talent analytics can assess the talent management process with business-related issues. In addition, predictive analytics also help in profiling and segmenting employees' attrition and loyalty analysis, forecasting recruitment, profile matching for recruitment and also analysing the sentiments of the employees. Primarily, predictive modelling helps in understanding potential future trends in all areas of human resources, which can influence the business outcomes.

Often, we believe that HR analytics, or predictive HR decision-making processes, have diminished the importance of HR metrics. But this is not correct. HR metrics continue to support HR decision-making, and with analytics, decisions become more effective. Over the years, the pattern of HR metrics has also changed. At the outset, we started with efficiency metrics, focusing more on cost, productivity, ROI and so on. These metrics are basically intended to assess the efficiency of HR functions. Gradually, a new set of HR metrics started to evaluate the human capital (HC), as HC is now being considered strategic and sustainable resource support for the organizations. Today, organizations make use of strategic HR metrics that focus on assessing the strategic knowledge and skill sets, competencies, quality of cross-functional teams, ratio of pay at risk and so on. Strategic HR metrics assess the impact of human resources on the business outcomes of organizations and at the precision level even extend to the assessment of the impact of HR functions on customers, processes, people and the finance of organizations.

ANALYTICS HIGHLIGHT

Today, HR analytics is not an option, it is a necessity. With the increased complexities of business, the importance of HR analytics will continue to rise. Realizing this, HR managers today volunteer to accept responsibilities even for financial issues, prefer to collaborate with other departments, interpret data with a holistic perspective and involve in framing HR strategy in alignment with the overall strategy of the organization.

CONCEPT AND DEFINITIONS OF ANALYTICS

Often we confuse analytics with metrics. It is wrong. Analytics can give better decisional insights than metrics. Analytics can enhance the power of the data and encompass all managerial functions and decision-making processes. Powered by analytics, HR managers can manipulate their decisions which can benefit both the organizations and the employees. For example, HR decision to enhance performance can benefit both the organizations, in terms of increased performance results, and the employees, in terms of higher earnings (performance incentives).

Analytics can enable us to integrate our knowledge with the data, and thereby, direct us to appropriate actions. It can also help us in making predictions. With metrics we can only assess the trend of past functions and accordingly we can hypothesize what would be our future actions. Analytics can make predictions about the future. Many organizations currently use metrics to report how different business entities are functioning. For example, a recruiting function may examine metrics such as recruiting cycle time or cost to recruit, benchmarking them against past performances as well as other organizations. These metrics help the organization understand *how* its recruiting processes performed. Analytics, on the other hand, can help a recruiting function realize *what* factors make recruiting cycle time and costs higher or lower. For example, having recruiters focus on sourcing fewer positions may lead to shorter cycle times for hiring new candidates. Analytics is used to gain understanding on why something happened or what will happen; while metrics are reactive, analytics are predictive.

Often we confuse big data with analytics. But big data per se is not analytics. Big data indicate high volume, variety and velocity of data. In many organizations, big data remain unutilized, as managers fail to connect these with their business decisions. But when these are used as inputs to analytics, they become meaningful, as these can facilitate more accurate and holistic decision-making, predictive modelling of decisions and so on. In some organizations, unstructured and untapped portion of big data are called as dark data. But, dark data also can facilitate in predictive modelling of the decisions. For example, Procter & Gamble's disparate move to make their products future ready, mapping the changing expectations of the future customers, makes use of dark data also. Dark data are data which organizations collect in course of their regular data collection but fail to make use of the same for any meaningful analysis. Similarly, compensation and benefit expectations of generation Z can be mapped from their present consumption pattern, health index and education level.

Organizational propensities to make their decision-making processes powered by analytics eventually emerges from their urge to align human resources with their business goals and strategies, realizing people can only give sustainable competitive advantages. Globally, organizations which are now using HR analytics believe their performance and productivity have significantly increased, for the enhancement of the quality of their decision-making processes. Some organizations even concede that the use of HR analytics could enhance their competitive advantages. Variation in HR decision-making pattern in organizations has been explained in Box 2.3.

Box 2.3   HR Decision-making Pattern Varies with the Organizations

The pattern of HR decision-making process across organizations widely varies. Many organizations believe that giving employees the right to work flexibly can be a better reward than monetary effects. Royal Bank of Scotland (RBS), e.g., follows this approach. 3M, another globally known company, makes its people to strategically contribute to innovation. Recognizing the fact that risk and innovation complement each other, the company could successfully create a culture of innovation, which it feels is also a reward to its employees to feel more and more engaged with the organization.

Microsoft believes human resources play a strategic role in its business performance. With an analytic approach to talent management and flexible work styles, the company embraced most innovative HR practices for creating a culture of collaboration and cooperation. This is also a perceived reward for the employees of Microsoft. Making workplace innovation 'business as usual', employees at Microsoft feel more engaged.

IMPORTANCE AND SIGNIFICANCE OF HUMAN RESOURCE ANALYTICS

For organizations, HR analytics provide scientific facts to human resources. Reviewing the framework of HR analytics, introduced in several organizations, we find that it starts at the outset with the identification of key business concerns, focus on strategy and long-term sustainability issues. After this, we go forward with assessing the available knowledge and competencies' set in the organizations. Gaps, if any, need to be met through appropriate interventions before we proceed to the next step, i.e., the analysis of organizational data. At the end, results are communicated, examining which, HR managers decide for appropriate interventions, well in advance, to improve the decisional outcomes or to reduce the adverse effect of decisional outcomes. This is a working model of HR analytics.

For operational ease, in many organizations HR managers at the beginning start with descriptive analytics, i.e., the use of metrics, to understand the current syndrome. Gradually, HR managers start the use of statistics and research methodology for better analysis of decisional outcomes, and finally, HR managers use HR analytics to predict how HR decisions influence business results and align with the strategies of organizations. With prediction results, HR managers can alter or improve HR decisions.

Although in the corporate world it is largely believed that HR analytics can significantly alter and improve HR decision-making, and bring holistic change in organizations, some HR managers still believe that such assumptions are more over pitched. With standalone use of HR analytics, HR managers believe they can influence the HR decision-making process, establishing a link between HR decisions and employees. More appropriately, HR analytics help in diagnosing HR issues, which can facilitate in taking prevention actions through appropriate interventions.

We can understand the importance and significance of HR analytics, once we create a business case, and then analyse how it can facilitate in holistic decision-making. Maersk, a Denmark-based large conglomerate, made use of HR analytics to study how its employee engagement programmes can enhance managerial commitment, improve training effectiveness and workplace safety. For Maersk, workplace safety is a business-critical issue.

Why HR analytics is important for organizations? We do not have any simple answer to this question. But reviewing organizational experiences, when we document the typical trends in HR decision-making process, we can truly understand the significance of HR analytics. Review indicates that in most of the organizations HR decisions are made in silos.

When decisions on investments in people are made in silos, and even without any data, organizations may fail to understand the benefits of investments, like the ROI on training.

However, all HR decisions are not measurable in terms of business outcome. A good example of this is employee engagement. Hence, if a company feels that its investment in employee engagement will enhance the sales revenue and expect HR analytics to provide such information, it would perhaps be more aspirational. A better way to look into this, perhaps, is measuring the change in the attitude of the employees. It is like improved employee engagement can contribute to the development of positive employees' attitude, which leads to enhanced sales revenue as sales improve with improved customers' relationships. Hence, the significance or importance of HR analytics needs to be understood in terms of the analysis of its effects on the HR decision-making process.

Again, the influence of HR decisions is very much culture specific. Hence, what could be seen in an organization need not be universalistic. Thus, if we feel what Google could do with HR analytics, we also can, it is certainly not logical and realistic. Therefore, the other significant characteristic of HR analytics is that it is time consuming, as connecting people data with business may not yield quick results.

HR analytics require cross-functional knowledge. Today's HR managers need to understand that interpreting people data in silos take them nowhere. Rather, people data require interpretation in alignment with other functional areas of organizations.

With HR analytics, it is also possible to fix responsibilities and make people accountable for their work.

BENEFITS OF HR ANALYTICS

HR managers earlier limited their information requirements to certain basic areas, analysing what they could understand in terms of measurement of the trend of HRM practices in organizations. The complexities of business and the growing importance of human resources on organizational long-term sustainable nature of human resource information are now changing. Hence, with HR metrics what was earlier possible, i.e., gauging the rate of absenteeism, attrition, cost of compensation and so on, cannot just satisfy the HR decision-making process. Today, we require our HR managers to assess employee engagement, predict the requirement of future talent in organizations and relate employee satisfaction with customer relationships management (CRM) practices and other alike.

With HR analytics, HR managers can predict the trend, which helps them to take wise decisions, evaluating different decisional alternatives, based on the big data set. For example, with a holistic approach to data analysis, HR managers can assess which employees are going to continue with the organization and which not. Hence, while drawing a succession plan, and while investing on building the future leadership skill, organizations can make a strategic choice. HR analytics also benefit in scenario planning, i.e., envisioning the future changes and drawing the future strategic interventions to correct such situations. For example, making effective use of HR analytics, HR managers can assess when they will be facing leadership crisis and who are the possible employees available in the organizations to take up future leadership roles. Similarly, HR managers can also make out how their performance management systems help in identifying the employees' potentiality for their proper development and in what way PRP can benefit the organization to get increased spate of performance from the employees. With interpretive skills, HR managers can even take data-driven information across the functional boundaries. For example with high performance incentives, how the cost of compensation of the organization gets affected. Does it reduces organizational competitiveness or enhances it, can be assessed with interpretive skills.

With increased understanding of the business goals of the organizations, HR managers can align their HR decisions which facilitate achieving the business results. Similarly, mapping organizational strategies, HR managers can adopt their HR plans and programmes which can help in achieving the strategic intents and so on.

We have a number of vendors for HR analytics. Top leaders in HR analytics are: Oracle, SAP, IBM and so on. These apart, we have a number of small vendors also. Depending on the functional requirements, an organization can choose an appropriate vendor to customize HR analytics solutions.

STEPS TO IMPLEMENT HR ANALYTICS

Organizations, across the globe, are now using HR analytics to take effective HR decisions in alignment with the business goals and strategies. In many organizations, however, the use of HR analytics, or analytics-mediated HR decision-making, gets restricted in some function(s) of HRM. For example, most of the organizations use HR analytics in managing their talent. In fact, such use is so extensive that we also see the use of the term 'talent analytics' to indicate HR analytics. The idea behind to sustain and grow organizations need to be talent driven and HR management needs to be more and more development focused. Hence, HRM integrates with talent management.

To implement HR analytics or talent analytics, based on industry practices, the following steps can be recommended:

- Clarity on HR analytics: HR managers are still not very clear about the meaning, concept and scope of HR analytics and how it can help in better HR decision-making processes in organizations. Some HR managers even misconstrue HR metrics and HR analytics as one and the same. For example, HR metrics can help us in measuring the rate of attrition, while HR analytics with big data can help us, even at the precision level, to predict who are going to stay or leave the organization. With reference to analogies and business cases, we have to clarify the differences between HR metrics and HR analytics, and help HR managers to take their informed decisions about choosing HR analytics to facilitate their future decision-making processes.
- Top management acceptance: HR analytics require investment in terms of buying technology support, software solutions, training and so on. Unless the top management of an organization accepts in principle the need for HR analytics, human resources cannot get it for their decision-making support. Therefore, human resources has to first take the top management into confidence, so that resources can be committed for HR analytics. With a detailed mapping on requirement analysis, human resource needs to showcase how quality of HR decisions gets improved, when HR analytics are used. Also, how improved and predictive HR decisions can align with organizational business and strategies for long-term growth and sustainability.

- Incremental approach in implementation of HR analytics: Many organizations invest in HR analytics expecting to bring total change in HR decision-making processes. But this is a wrong approach. Often, experiences may be negative. An incremental approach to implement HR analytics solutions, i.e., to start with choosing its implementation only in one or two HR functions to improve the HR decision-making process, is considered to be more appropriate. Moreover, such an approach helps HR decision-makers to get adjusted with technology-enabled decision-making processes. HR managers slowly transcend to tech-savvy, build their capabilities and make their informed choice about the usage of HR analytics.
- Design common glossaries and definitions on HR analytics: We can call it the need for designing an HR analytics dictionary. This will ensure common understanding of the terms and clarity in the process encompassing HR analytics. The whole idea is to ensure consistency.
- Develop cross-functional team: To implement HR analytics in organizations, it is always desirable to form a cross-functional team. When HR managers operate in silos, they fail to understand the implications of HR decisions on business goals and strategies of organizations. Also, they fail to relate HR decisions to other functional areas, such as operations, marketing and finance. Moreover, HR managers themselves may not always be confident and competent to comprehend statistics and mathematics to design predictive decisional models. With a cross-functional team, all these problems can be addressed.
- Train the people: In addition to the vendor-supported training, ensure reinforced training for all those who will be using HR analytics. More training reinforcement ensures better clarity, and people can feel confident to use HR analytics for their decision-making processes.

CRITICAL HR DECISION-MAKING AND HR ANALYTICS

In critical HR decision-making processes, namely talent acquisition or recruitment and selection, many organizations come out with their detailed decisional guidelines. Such guidelines ensure decisional consistency and so also can immune HR decision-makers from any future liability, including legal hassles. Moreover, recruitment and selection are serious HR functions, first because of choosing the right candidate and then for the need of predicting their retention probabilities. Hence, from organizations' point of view, recruitment is investment.

What could be the appropriate decisional guidelines for the decision-making largely depends on the organizations, the level of recruitment, the prevailing legal norms and restrictions and so on. A tentative decisional guideline for the recruitment of a hypothetical organization for managerial positions can be listed as follows:

1. Ensure your recruitment decisions are impersonal, and for the best interest for the common good and justice.
2. Ensure your recruitment decisions are fair, objective and transparent.

Some of the don'ts of recruitment decisions are as follows:

1. Stereotyping
2. Prejudice
3. Mirroring
4. Laying emphasis on personalities, rather than candidates' capabilities
5. Decisions are not holistic (based on assessment single or some attributes)
6. Spur of the moment decisions
7. Decisions vitiated by halo and horn effects
8. Poor verification of antecedents

The earlier described list of don'ts in recruitment for managerial positions can to a great extent ensure appropriate recruitment and selection processes of any hypothetical organization. Most of the parameters can be objectively measured and assessed, and their effects on the organizations can be predicted using HR analytics. In Chapter 3, we have discussed the usage of HR analytics for recruitment- and selection-related decision-making. There we have explained the process of measuring the above parameters.

ANALYTICS HIGHLIGHT

HR analytics can help HR managers to legitimately position themselves as strategic partners in an organization. HR functions being more and more fact based, organizations can trace HR contributions and can even measure how such contributions could benefit in achieving organizational goals. In most of the organizations, however, HR analytics are used in talent management practices. This is why we often use the terms HR analytics and talent analytics interchangeably. Talent analytics suites are more focused on attraction, recruitment, development and retention of talents. All these also benefit organizations in achieving their goals and objectives. But such outcomes may not be holistic, as all HR decisions need not be talent driven. Complete HR analytics suites cover all HR functions. For example, a decision on the threshold limit of a compensation and benefits programme—which can optimize cost, sustain employee motivation and at the same time their retention—requires inputs from various HR functions, benchmarked data, past trend of the organizations and so on. There are enormous cases in the corporate world where organizations could save substantially on compensation and benefits head while could also retain their employees, motivate them and even could get the enhanced rate of performance from them. Such HR decisions being more and more holistic, it is always better for HR managers to develop their critical thought process and examine all the aspects in terms of data availability. With HR analytics, organizations can get better scientific insights (being data driven), which can help in strategic decisions.

Many HR managers often misconstrue that scorecards, ratios and metrics are synonymous with HR analytics. All these may help in aligning (at least partially) human resources with the business, may enable HR managers to perform gap analysis (again partially), understand the correlations between different variables and even may help them in benchmarking for better decision-making. However, these are not HR analytics. HR analytics can facilitate in analysing people-related data on the important business outcome of organizations. It can pull multiple HR processes

■ **Table 2.2:** Types of HR Analytics

Process Analytics	Integrated Analysis
Recruitment and selection	Talent management
Onboarding	Human resource planning
Performance management	Succession planning
Work-life balancing	HR strategy framing

Source: Author.

together, embed cross-functional inputs with HR decisions and make the decisions more futuristic, holistic and all encompassing. Cause–effect or causation analysis and regression analysis are two important HR decision-making models for HR analytics. However, organizations can design their own algorithms for HR decision-making. People analytics of Google is one such example.

From organizational point of view, we see two types of HR analytics, i.e., process analytics and integrated analytics. Process analytics are those which are process or HR function specific, and more stand alone in nature. Integrated analytics, however, are more holistic and encompassing. Recruitment and selection, onboarding, performance management, work-life balancing and so on are some of the examples of process analytics. On the other hand, talent management, workforce planning, succession planning, HR strategy framing and so on are some the examples of integrated analytics.

In Table 2.2, the types of HR analytics have been demonstrated.

Because of undisputed importance of HR analytics for an effective HR decision-making process, organizations today look for HR managers who possess strong business sense to translate business goals to KPIs and understand how employees' performances can benefit organizations in achieving the business goals. Also, HR managers should have demonstrated capabilities to design research and frame hypothesis, statistical analysis, data analysis and evaluation of results. Again, all these would be meaningless unless preceded by the holistic knowledge of HRM functions.

PREDICTIVE HR ANALYTICS

Predictive HR analytics: It blends data to develop algorithm, based on which HR managers can pre-assess the future events, as consequences of current HR decisions. It can even help in understanding the behavioural changes of employees.

At the outset, let us understand how **predictive HR analytics** works. Predictive HR analytics blends data to develop algorithm, based on which HR managers can pre-assess the future events, as consequences of current HR decisions. It can even help in understanding the behavioural changes of employees. For example, organizations can pre-assess the likely behavioural changes in individual talent when they enforce the culture of collective innovation. Therefore, predictive analytics can add value to HR decision-making. However, organizations worldwide still believe that sole dependency on predictive HR analytics for HR decision-making may not warrant the quality HR decisions. Managerial intuition, instinct or judgement can also play an important role. Hence, blending predictive HR analytics with the gut feeling of the managers can add better value to HR decision-making.

Successful implementation of predictive HR analytics requires organizational adherence to certain well-defined steps as follows:

1. Introduce predictive HR analytics in a phased manner but not simultaneously in all areas. For example, we can first think of introducing it in one small area of HR activity, say implementing it to facilitate workforce planning decisions.
2. List out the actions required for using it, e.g., simple step-by-step guidelines, process of measuring HR decisions, process of optimizing HR decisions and so on.
3. Continue the pursuit of implementation. Difficulty in any stage must not deter implementation. Initial mistakes or failure are quite likely. But relentless effort in implementation is required.

The use of predictive analytics for HR decision-making in organizations is still very limited. Wherever it is used, its use gets restricted to some HR activities only. For example, talent analytics is used for effective talent management in many organizations. Similarly, workforce analytics is used for workforce planning. Predictive decision-making algorithms help in modelling the future behaviour of employees, and with the effect of present HR decisions, its use is likely to increase day by day.

Again predictive analytics, through the process of value addition in HR decision-making, also help in legitimizing the strategic role of human resources. With strategic focus, human resources is becoming more important in predicting the future resource requirement, optimizing costs, provisioning for organizational and employees' capability development and aligning with organizational goals and objectives. In true sense with predictive-analytics-based HR decisions, organizations can get holistic insights and sustain and grow in the long run.

Predictive analytics have become more important in holistic HR decision-making process with deep insights, as the nature of data both within and outside the organizations has significantly changed. Today's employees are connected through social networks. With whom they network, on what topics they post in social media, how frequent they are in social networks and so on are some of the information that may merit consideration while recruiting them, thinking on investing on their development, assessing their probability to stick to a job, their likely performance, their knowledge base, their potentiality and even their likes and dislikes. Although we have many vendors for predictive analytics, more holistic solutions are available from IBM and Oracle.

Many organizations still continue their decision-making process using age-old descriptive analysis tools, such as scorecards, reports, ratios and metrics. But such decisions cannot have a futuristic view. It cannot help us in framing strategies for the future. With predictive analytics, however, we can model our future performance strategies, talent retention strategies and succession plan strategies of an organization. Predictive analytics can also help in resource optimization, can support business strategies or the organizations and so also help human resources to align their decision with the goals and objectives of the organizations.

PRACTICE ASSIGNMENT

We have some examples from the corporate world showing that critical HR decisions are still intuitive than based on predictive modelling. In selecting CEOs in some of the IT majors in India, intuitive decisions have been taken. Identify such cases and detail whether such selection was an appropriate move.

Benefits of Predictive Analytics

Benefits of predictive analytics are not different *per se* from HR analytics, baring the benefit of predictive modelling and designing a decisional algorithm to facilitate HR decisions with a futuristic outlook. Some of the exclusive benefits of predictive analytics can be listed as follows:

1. It can help in recognizing the strengths and weaknesses of the human resources, which facilitates in identifying talent for future leadership roles.
2. Can help in identifying future competency gap and decide strategies to overcome the same.
3. Can help organizations to become future ready building the capabilities of people with critical skill sets, pacing with the change in technology and process.
4. Can help organizations in assessing the attrition rate and can frame strategies in overcoming the same.
5. Can integrate HR decisions with strategies and business goals of the organization.
6. Can minimize the risk of error in HR decision-making for a holistic view.
7. Can factor external data for quality HR decisions.
8. Can help in effective scenario planning.
9. Can reinforce organizational capability with contingency plans.
10. Can develop a robust decision model for HR decision-making.

Reviewing all the earlier listed benefits, it is clear that predictive HR analytics can not only improve the HR decision-making process by adding value, for its obvious deeper insights, but can also help organizations to sustain and grow.

Reviewing organizations, it is evident that predictive analytics for HR decision-making is more evident in talent management functions, in workforce planning, in managing learning and development activities and so on.

In talent management, predictive analytics can help in identifying potentiality, assessing the possible rate of success of such potential employees in their future job roles, predicting the requirements of changing nature of competencies and strengthening the succession planning processes.

For its obvious capability of ramification of HR decisions from different perspectives, predictive HR analytics is no longer a choice but a necessity for HR managers, else they will fail in extending their professional support for the overall improvement of organizations. It is forward looking, based on historical data, including data from outside of the organization. It helps in framing ad hoc questions and answers, perform retrospective and predictive analysis and develop decision-making algorithms.

HR ANALYTICS AND CHANGING ROLE OF HR MANAGERS

Characteristically, human resources today widely vary from the past. Today's human resources are diverse, young and look for more challenging workplaces. The changing pattern of human resources obviously redefined the role of HR managers in organizations. For HR managers, additionally the critical challenge is managing talent. Attracting, developing and retaining talent are not only challenging for HR managers, the requirements, along with other strategic issues, today literally changed the dynamics of HRM functions in organizations. For effective talent management alone, getting answers to questions such as why people leave an organization within a short time, who will be the top performers, what training will be required and who will benefit from training and so on is very important. To get answers to these questions requires HR managers to first develop critical insights and then analyse the data and information using HR analytics. HR decisions being more strategic, with HR analytics, HR managers today can predict the trend on critical HR issues and accordingly can design their interventions to avoid any catastrophe. Hence, today's HR functions are no longer transactional; rather these are more data driven and involve detailed business analysis for better HR insights and predictive HR decisions for strategic HR outcome.

Today's HR managers, therefore, are required to understand which data can give them better HR insights. HR managers also need to understand the availability of such data inside and outside organizations, the integration of such data for developing actionable insights and then making use of these data for strategic and predictive HR decision-making process. With HR analytics, HR managers can take operational HR decisions at the highest level of accuracy and precision. Also, HR managers can create his/her dashboards for better analytical, predictive and strategic decision-making. Depending on the level of IT knowledge, HR managers can create simple dashboards such as bar chats, pie charts, frequency tables and so on or more complex dashboards like scatter plots. Whether simple or complex, dashboards when linked with organizational processes and performances can give better insights into decision-making.

The nature and extent of HR decision-making process that can be facilitated by HR analytics depend on HR managers. However, common HR decision-making processes which can be facilitated by HR analytics are: HRP, performance management, training and development, compensation and benefits programme design and management, talent acquisition, retention, development, mobility of human resources and so on.

A typical job description of HR managers today even includes performing employee-related research, developing models to serve business needs and also focusing on human resources. The collection and analysis of HR data for actionable analysis and reporting to managers and executives are more important part of HR managers' functions in today's organizations. Hence, the responsibilities of HR managers today are: building HR intelligence function, talent acquisition, development and retention with talent analytics, evaluating the effectiveness of any form of HR investment, functioning as HR business partners, providing coaching and training support and so on. However, such responsibilities may change from time to time, depending on the nature of the organization and the scope of HR activities. Intuitive decision vis-a-vis analytics based decision issue is explained in Box 2.4.

Box 2.4   Acquiring Critical Talent Often an Intuitive Decision than Analytics Based

HR managers still believe in intuition-based decision-making, inviting problems for their organization. To ensure HR decisions are more dynamic and encompassing, today intuition-based or metrics-based HR decision-making processes need to be discarded. Instead, HR decisions need to make use of predictive models, so that decisional outcomes can be understood beforehand and appropriate corrective actions can be taken. Wrongdoing in HR decisions is now a luxury, which organizations cannot afford.

However, for Apple hiring the top brass of the company is more a relational than analytics-based decision. At least we could see this when Tim Cook of Apple could afford to wait for 18 months to hire Angela Ahrendts. Tim Cook could successfully persuade Angela to leave her job of a CEO at Burberry and join Apple at a non-CEO position to run Apple's online and offline retailing. Angela's predecessor John Browett was asked to leave Apple, as John said in a conference that he did not fit with the way the company runs its business. At the CEO level, one often takes critical HR decisions without data analysis. The experience often senses better than data.

Such intuitive decision-making process in human resources often can put the organizations in deep trouble. The CEO of Fab.com, Jason Goldberg, reduced his $900-million e-commerce company to a $15-million company when it was up for sale. Such a catastrophic situation in Fab.com is attributable to an intuitive decision-making style, particularly in HR-related processes. Lehman Brothers' collapse is again another lesson for us.

Therefore, organizations need to make use of HR analytics for HR decisions, and with predictive models would try to assess the future implications of present decisions for bringing appropriate changes in the decisions or to minimize the risk of wrong decisions.

Summary

This chapter at the outset reviewed the concept of analytics. The concept of BA is all along prevalent and organizations make use of the same for decision-making in operations and marketing areas. HR analytics, however, is of recent origin. It helps in predictive decision-making, manipulating the big data and assessing the decisional impact before its occurrence.

This chapter then examined the changing pattern of HR decision-making over the years. It elaborated how from intuitive decision-making we gradually embraced matrics-based decision-making, correlational decision-making and finally the analytics-based predictive decision-making process of human resources.

Detailed discussions on analytics have been made for clarity of understanding. In human resources, the analytics-based decision-making process can encompass all functional areas, thereby helping human resources to truly align with the business and strategies of organizations.

After clarifying the concepts of HR analytics, this chapter also discussed the importance and significance of HR analytics, its benefits, steps for implementation and application in predictive HR decision-making process.

In this era of big data, data explosion is a natural phenomenon. HR decisions require cross-functional and also HR data, both from within and outside the organization. With software support, such large volume of data needs to be stored in some databases so that time to time it can be used as input for HR decisions. Such data when properly manipulated can give better insights to HR managers in understanding the veracity of HR decisions, including the future implications. Obviously, the HR decision-making process is getting more and more data driven.

General Review Questions

1. Discuss the concept of HR analytics. How can it benefit an organization?

2. Differentiate between descriptive, correlational and predictive HR decision-making processes.

3. Explain how HR metrics differ from HR analytics.

4. Discuss the importance and significance of HR analytics.

5. Recommend steps that an organization must follow to implement HR analytics.

6. Discuss with examples how in critical HR decision-making, HR analytics can help?

7. Write short notes on the following:

   - HR metrics
   - Incremental approach
   - Big data
   - Intuitive HR decisions
   - Business intelligence

Multiple Choice Questions

1. Indicate which of the following is not an appropriate statement for evidence-based management practices:

    a. It facilitates conscientious decision-making
    b. It ensures effective use of available evidence
    c. It uses data support as evidence
    d. It can be strengthened with HR analytics
    e. None of the above

2. Analytics-based HR decisions are

    a. Evidence based
    b. Value adding
    c. Futuristic
    d. Sustainable
    e. All of the above

3. Predictive decision-making process is

    a. More holistic
    b. Capable to assess the decisional outcomes right in the beginning
    c. Helps managers in calibrating their decisions
    d. Minimizes the adverse effects of decisions, if any
    e. All of the above

4. Identify the incorrect statement out of the following:

    a. HR decisions are not characteristically different from non-HR decisions
    b. Organizational failure is largely attributable to wrong HR decisions
    c. HR decisions are HR managers' judgemental thoughts
    d. HR decisions encompass all stakeholders of an organization
    e. HR analytics is an important tool for HR decision-making

5. Effective HR decision-making process requires the following, except

    a. Integration of critical thoughts and information
    b. Use of professional skill and competence by HR managers
    c. Use of available business information through big-data analysis
    d. Emulating the best practice
    e. Restricting the use of quantitative details

6. HR decision-making process may get constrained for

    a. Organizational systems
    b. Regulatory influences
    c. Social influences
    d. Stakeholders' responses
    e. All of the above

7. Identify the incorrect statement out of the following:

    a. HR analytics facilitate data-driven HR decision-making
    b. HR analytics is a means to an end
    c. Analytics-bound HR decisions are non-strategic in nature
    d. HR analytics can only lend support in strategic workforce planning
    e. None of the above

8. Analytics-based HR decisions can help in the following, except

   a. Making strategic HR decisions less risk-prone
   b. Achieving success in operational HR decision-making
   c. Reducing significantly decisional bias
   d. Helping in the groupthink process
   e. Helping in avoiding wrong decisions

9. Professionally designed HR analytics can make use of

   a. Statistical models to predict the future
   b. Study implications of current HR trends
   c. Take decisions on the critical future organizational issues
   d. Map organizational sustainability, growth, revenues and bottom-line changes
   e. All of the above

10. Characteristically, HR analytics denotes

    a. Consideration of the availability of big data
    b. Use of statistics and research design
    c. Use of relevant data both within and outside the organization
    d. Predictive decision-making
    e. All of the above

11. With predictive analytics, HR decision-making processes have now become more

    a. Encompassing
    b. Integrated
    c. Strategic
    d. Business aligned
    e. All of the above

12. Indicate which of the following is a financial HR decision:

    a. Performance management
    b. Grievance handling
    c. ROI on training
    d. Organizational branding
    e. None of the above

13. Indicate which of the following is not used for descriptive HR decision-making:

    a. Predictive analytics
    b. Metrics
    c. HRIS
    d. Dashboards
    e. HR scorecards

14. Identify the incorrect statement on correlational HR decision-making out of the following:

    a. It assesses the determinants of key variables
    b. It studies relationships between variables
    c. It assesses the goodness of fit
    d. It minimizes the risk of adverse consequences
    e. It helps in the analysis of causation

15. Indicate which of the following is not a predictive HR decision-making tool:

    a. Causation analysis
    b. Regression analysis

    c.   Correlational analysis
    d.   Predictive decision models
    e.   Predictive mathematical algorithm

16. Identify the incorrect statement out of the following:

    a.   Analytics can give better decisional insights than metrics
    b.   Analytics can enhance the power of data
    c.   Analytics can encompass all managerial functions and decision-making processes
    d.   Analytics can only benefit organizations
    e.   With analytics, organizations get the benefit of increased performance results

17. Select the wrong statement on metrics out of the following:

    a.   It can assess the trend of past functions
    b.   It can help us in hypothesizing our future actions
    c.   It can make predictions about the future
    d.   It can report how different business entities are functioning
    e.   None of the above

18. Indicate which of the following is not relevant for big data:

    a.   Big data indicates high volume data
    b.   Big data indicates high varies of data
    c.   Big data indicates high velocity of data
    d.   Untapped big data are junk data
    e.   Big data are used as inputs to analytics

19. HR analytics starts with the following, except

    a.   Identification of key business concerns
    b.   Strategy of the organization
    c.   Control of the organization
    d.   Long-term sustainability issues of the organizations
    e.   None of the above

20. Indicate which of the following is not a characteristic of HR analytics:

    a.   It is time consuming
    b.   It is a quick-fix solution
    c.   It requires cross-functional knowledge
    d.   With it, it is possible to fix responsibilities
    e.   With it, it is possible to make people accountable for their work

21. Indicate which of the following is not a step to implement HR analytics:

    a.   Clarity on HR analytics
    b.   Top management acceptance
    c.   Accelerated approach in implementation
    d.   Designing of common glossaries and definitions on HR analytics
    e.   Developing a cross-functional team

22. Indicate which HR analytics is not a process analytics out of the following:

    a.   Analytics which are standalone in nature
    b.   Recruitment and selection analytics
    c.   Performance management analytics
    d.   Onboarding analytics
    e.   Talent management analytics

23. Characteristically, predictive HR analytics helps in

    a. Blending of data to develop algorithm
    b. Pre-assessment of the future events
    c. Understanding the behavioural changes of employees
    d. Understanding the culture of collective innovation
    e. All of the above

24. Successful implementation of predictive HR analytics requires

    a. Introduction of predictive HR analytics in a phased manner
    b. Listing out of actions required for using it
    c. Continuing the pursuit of implementation
    d. All of the above
    e. None of the above

25. Indicate which of the following is not an exclusive benefit of predictive analytics:

    a. Recognizing the strengths and weaknesses of the human resources
    b. Integrating HR decisions with the strategies and the business goals of the organization
    c. Reinforcing organizational capability with contingency plans
    d. Factoring external for quality HR decisions
    e. None of the above

Critical Review Questions

1. You have been asked by your organization to design an employee engagement programme to reduce the current level of employee attrition. What data analysis may be required to design such a programme? While you answer this, also give your logic for choosing the data.

2. For designing compensation and benefits programme of a knowledge-intensive organization, which proclaims they believe in growing through innovation, list out the nature of data (including external data) that may be required by you. How your listed nature of data can help you in such decision-making?

PRACTITIONER SPEAKS

An HR head of a large organization declared that he uses HR analytics to validate his intuitive HR decision-making. For him, HR analytics is just a process of complicating HR decision-making. With intuitive HR decision-making, he is able to solve critical HR issues. What would be your advice to this HR head, and why?

CASE STUDY

HR Analytics for a Hospitality Chain

In a disparate move to align leadership and culture with the business results, the CEO of a large hospitality chain, spread across 50 countries decided to use HR analytics. After a detailed requirement analysis through high-powered cross-functional team members, the CEO could list the discrete objectives of his intended project as follows:

1. Validate the leadership competency model and its effects on business outcomes.
2. Identify the most impactful leader behaviours on guest loyalty.
3. Quantify the impact of these leadership behaviours on the guest experience and financial performance.

With such mandate of objectives, the CEO of the company started discussions with several software vendors. Analysing the requirement analysis, two software vendors finally agreed to provide analytics solutions. After careful scrutiny of their technical and price bids, the CEO could select one of them and start the process of implementation of HR analytics, across all the establishments of the company.

At the outset, the company came out with their unique leadership competency model. The company intends use of this model in all its establishments, across the globe. With inputs from the vendor, the company could finalize the competencies and the behavioural parameters (in measurable terms). Using the vendor's software solutions, the company then started developing the database. Capturing the data, the company is now able to measure the guest loyalty and revenue per available room. Similarly, the company now predicts the engagement level of employees, and the new recruits, even at the individual level. This helps the company to design its effective employee development plan.

The company believes by alignment of leadership behaviour with the business results it not only could identify the required competencies and behavioural constructs but also could get increased business performance, for obvious improvement in its decision-making processes.

With HR analytics and the opportunity for predictive decision-modelling, the company now strategically emphasizes on developing desired leadership competencies and behaviours in the existing employees, and could make its recruitment process competency driven.

Question: Explain how HR analytics can help the company in aligning leadership behaviour with the business results.

REFERENCES

Bhattacharyya, D. K. (2013). Performance-related pay: Evidence-based studies in Indian central public sector enterprises. *Compensation & Benefits Review, 45*(4), 215–222.

———. (2015). The magnetic organization: Attracting and retaining the best talent. New Delhi: SAGE Publications.

Briner, R. B., Denyer, D., & Rousseau, D. M. (2009). Evidence-based management: Concept Cleanup time? *Academy of Management Perspectives, 23*(4), 19–32.

Charlier, S. D., Brown, K. G., & Rynes, S. L. (2011). Teaching evidence-based management in MBA programs: What evidence is there? *Academy of Management Learning and Education, 10*(2), 222–236.

Locke, E. A. (2009). *Handbook of principles of organizational behavior: Indispensable knowledge for evidence-based management.* New York: John Wiley & Sons.

Pfeffer, J., & Sutton, R. I. (2006). Evidence-based management. *Harvard Business Review, 84*(1), 62–74.

Rousseau, D. M., & Barends, E. G. R. (2011). Becoming an evidence-based HR practitioner. *Human Resource Management Journal, 21*(3), 221–235.

FURTHER READINGS

Cox, T. (1994). *Cultural diversity in organizations: Theory, research and practice.* San Francisco, CA: Berrett Koehler.

Rousseau, D. M. (2006). Is there such a thing as evidence-based management? *Academy of Management Review, 31*(2), 256–269.

———. (2012). Envisioning evidence-based management. In D. M. Rousseau (Ed.), *Handbook of evidence-based management.* New York: Oxford University Press.

Yates, J. F. (2003). *Decision management.* San Francisco, CA: Jossey-Bass.

APPENDIX

Linear Programming, Other Optimization Tools and Predictive Statistics in HR Analytics

For HR analytics, we require the basic knowledge of predictive statistics. Linear decision rules is one such predictive statistics that can balance the output and workforce levels, optimizing costs such as overtime, idle time, inventory costs, hiring costs, layoff costs and so on. This apart, we have a learning curve for predicting productivity. Another important predictive statistics is Markov chain analysis. It is a deterministic, longitudinal potential planning model to assess optimal hiring, promotion, separation and retirement as a function of time and a person's organizational age and grade. Again, it is a deterministic, discrete-time and continuous model for manpower planning, taking into account the effects of learning and turnover rates.

We will not discuss all these predictive statistics, which can immensely help in predictive HR analytics in this chapter. Here, we will focus only on a linear programme as a mathematical technique to select an optimum plan.

Linear programming (LP) helps in getting the best solution to a decisional problem with many interactive variables. Through LP, we try to maximize the profit or contribution margin, and minimize the costs. We always try to achieve an optimum objective (which could be profit maximization or cost minimization). Like any other decisional problem, in LP also we have various constraints, restrictions and possible decisional alternatives. Such constraints describe availabilities, limitations and relationships of resources to alternatives. Some of the characteristic features of LP can be listed as follows:

1. Contribution margin or the cost associated with one unit of product or activity is same for all identical units.
2. Resource inputs for per unit of activity are considered to be the same for all units.
3. All factors and relationships are deterministic.

4. Some inherent constraints in terms of the capacity of a machine, labour availability, time availability, capital availability and so on must exist.
5. With the data fitting in equations, the LP can be solved graphically, when however there are two variables data.
6. With more than two variables, the LP problems are solved using the simplex method.

In HR analytics, LP can be used as an important decisional tool. For example, in manpower planning, we need to consider multiple variables for assessing manpower requirements. Assuming the relations among the objective and constraint variables as linear, LP helps us to take the decisions on manpower optimization.

In LP language, we can formulate a liner programme to decide on manpower planning as follows:

- Decision variables—optimum number of manpower
- Objective function—effect of decision variable on the cost
- Constraints—effective resource utilization for decision variables
- Data—quantified relationship between objective and constraint.

Before we understand the manpower planning decision through LP, let us first go through some basic LP problems and solutions.

Example 1: Your company produces three products: A, B and C. The contribution margin for each product is as follows:

Product	Contribution Margin (₹)
A	2
B	5
C	4

The production requirement of your company along with the information pertaining to the departmental capacities is as follows:

Department	Production (Hours)	Requirement	By	Product/Departmental Capacity (Hours)
	A	B	C	
Assembling	2	3	2	30,000
Painting	1	2	2	38,000
Finishing	2	3	1	28,000

Formulate the objective function and the constraints.

Solution:

Objective:

CM = 2A + 5B + 4C

Constraints:

Assembling: 2A + 3B + 2C ≤ 30,000
Painting: 1A + 2B + 2C ≤ 38,000
Finishing: 2A + 3B + 1C ≤ 28,000

Example 2: Formulate the problem with the objective and constraints as follows:

- Your company seeks to minimize the total cost of materials A and B.
- The per kilogram cost of A is ₹25 and B is ₹10.
- Combining products A and B, we get the materials which weigh 50 kg.
- At least 20 kg of A and not more than 40 kg of B can be used.

Solution:

C = 25A + 10B
Subject to: A + B = 50; A ≥ 20; B ≤ 40

Problem on Minimization

$$180x + 160y$$

Subject to:

$$6x + y \geq 12$$
$$3x + y \geq 8$$
$$4x + 6y \geq 24$$
$$x \leq 5$$
$$y \leq 5$$
$$x, y \geq 0.$$

Here, we have only two variables. The graphical representation of the LP problem, clearly demonstrating the feasible region of solutions, within the given constraints can be presented as shown in the following figure:

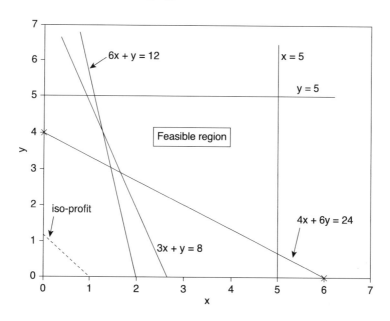

Here, all inequality constraints have been turned into equalities, drawing the corresponding lines on the graph (constraint $6x + y \geq 12$ becomes the line $6x + y = 12$ on the graph). After drawing the line, we can work out which side of the line corresponds to feasible solutions to the original inequality constraint (here, all feasible solutions to $6x + y \geq 12$ lie to the right of the line $6x + y = 12$).

The optimal solution to the LP problem can be determined by plotting $(180x + 160y) = K$ (K constant) for varying K values (iso-profit lines). One such line $(180x + 160y = 180)$ is shown as dotted in the diagram. The smallest value of K (considering a minimization problem), i.e., $180x + 160y = K$, goes through a point in the feasible region and is the value of the optimal solution. The optimal solution to the LP, therefore, occurs at the vertex of the feasible region formed by the intersection of $3x + y = 8$ and $4x + 6y = 24$. It is important to understand that values of x and y need to be determined through simultaneous equations, and not from the graph. The equations represented here

$$3x + y = 8$$
$$4x + 6y = 24$$

have been used to get $x = 12/7 = 1.71$ and $y = 20/7 = 2.86$, and hence, the value of the objective function is given by $180x + 160y = 180(12/7) + 160(20/7) = ₹765.71$.

Hence, the optimal solution costs ₹765.71.

Again, a graphical approach to solve LP problems can be relevant only in cases where we have two variables. But in cases where we have more than two variables, we use the simplex method to solve LP problems.

Simplex Method of LP

With more than two variables, we use the simplex algorithm. In this case, the optimal solution to LP occurred at a vertex (corner) of the feasible region. This is the key to the simplex algorithm for solving LP problems. It starts at one vertex of the feasible region and moves to another, until it reaches the optimal solution. Thus, the simplex method is an iterative process which approaches an optimum solution in such a way that an objective function of maximization or minimization is fully reached. Iteration in this process reduces the distance (mathematically and graphically) from the objective function. It is an application of a function repeatedly, i.e., from the output of one iteration to the input of another iteration. In other words, we can call it also approximate numerical solutions to certain mathematical problems. In the simplex method, the steps to solve a problem of cost-minimization problem are similar to the steps taken in the contribution margin and maximization margin. Using slack variables, at the outset, we try to arrive at the first feasible solution. Apart from slack variables we also make use of an artificial variable with two restrictions or constraints, i.e., equal-to-type and greater-than-or-equal-to type. Artificial variables are of value only as computational devices in maximization and minimization problems. In this minimization problem, an artificial variable, a_1, is introduced in the first constraint, which is of the equal-to type. Thus, the simplex method is an iterative step-wise process to achieve the optimum solution to reach the objective function of maximization or minimization. A problem formulation of the simplex method can be written as follows:

Maximize $x_1 + 3x_2 - 3x_3$
Subject to $3x_1 - x_2 - 2x_3 \leq 7$

$$2x_1 - 4x_2 + 4x_3 \leq 3$$
$$x_1 - 2x_3 \leq 4$$
$$2x_1 + 2x_2 + x_3 \leq 8$$
$$3x_1 \leq 5$$
$$x_1; x_2; x_3 \geq 0.$$

From the above discussions, we can summarize the essential components of the simplex method as follows:

- The objective row indicates the coefficients of the objective function.
- The variable row, including the slack variables, indicates the variables of the problem.
- The problem row indicates the variable constraints within one row.
- Variables which are not included in the constraint are assigned zero coefficients.

In human resources, the LP objective is primarily resource minimization. For some typical nature of HR problems, we can use transportation and assignment problems rather than the general LP problems. For HR analytics, the two major HR-related problems have been selected here: one on maximization and the other on minimization or optimization.

Example on Maximization

A multi-product company produces products A, B and C with per unit profit of ₹10, ₹6 and ₹4, respectively. From the company's records, it is evident that they require 1 man-hour planning, 10 man-hour labour and 2 man-hour support services time to produce 1 unit of product A. For product B, such time requirement is 1, 4 and 2 hours, and for product B, such requirement is 1, 5 and 6 hours, respectively. Based on the manpower availability, the company can make available 100 hours for planning, 600 hours of direct labour and 200 hours for support services time. As a manpower planner suggest the best solution for a profitable product mix.

Let us first tabulate the available data.

Job Nature	Product A	Product B	Product C	Time Availability (Hours)
Planning	1	1	1	100
Direct labour	10	4	5	600
Support services	2	2	6	300
Profit (₹)	10	6	4	

Our task or objective here is to maximize $10x + 6y + 4z$,

where x, y and z represent products A, B and C.

Subject to (constraints) $1x + 1y + 1z \leq 100$, and $x \geq 0$
$10x + 4y + 5y \leq 500$ and $y \geq 0$
$2x + 2y + 6z \leq 300$ and $z \geq 0.$

To convert inequalities to equalities we use slack or surplus variables in LP. Slack variables are introduced in less than or equal to constraints, while surplus variables are used in greater than or equal to constraints. In this problem, we have huge unused capacity; hence, we need to use a slack variable or else we cannot account for the idle time.

Introducing the slack variable, we can write our problem as follows:

Maximize $10x + 6y + 4z$

Subject to:
$$x + y + z + s_1 = 100$$
$$10x + 4y + r_5z + s_2 = 600$$
$$2x + 2y + 6z + s_3 = 300,$$

where

$x \geq 0, y \geq, 0, z \geq 0, s_1 \geq 0, s_2 \geq 0$ and $s_3 \geq 0$.

Solving this, we find that the most profitable mix is y, i.e., product B (400/6), followed by x, i.e., product A (100/3), and the maximum profit is ₹733—i.e., one-third.

Problem on Resource Minimization or Optimization

This problem has been explained using Microsoft Excel problem solver explained in the appendix of Chapter 8.

In the succeeding chapters, we have discussed other predictive statistical tools.

CHAPTER 3

INTRODUCTION TO HR ANALYTICS

LEARNING OBJECTIVES:

After reading this chapter, you will be able to understand:
- Concept of HR analytics
- Process of aligning business to human resources
- History of HR analytics
- Predictive analytics
- Importance and benefits of HR analytics
- HR analytics framework and models

INTRODUCTORY CASE

HR Datafication is not HR or Predictive Analytics: Lessons from SAS

HR and predictive analytics based on the analysis of the past trend measure a decisional issue with extra-organizational and cross-functional data to predict the probability of the occurrence of an event in future. It helps in initiating appropriate initiatives right in the beginning, so that the adverse effect of a decision can be suitably addressed. Thus, HR or predictive analytics per se cannot by default ensure success and positive outcome from a decision; it can only facilitate in correcting the possible adverse effects of a decision. Making best use of predictive analytics SAS is able to limit its talent attrition to 3–5 percent against industry average of 16 percent. Predictive analytics help SAS to constantly monitor talent retention, predicting factors that may inhibit it and initiate timely HR initiatives crafted in line with the best business practices to address those factors. Based on the results of predictive analytics, SAS initiated investment in training in the past, focusing on leadership development aspects, and also accentuated the pace of coaching conversations for employees with the managers. In the process, employees felt more engaged and could make their informed choice of long tenure with the organization, which resulted in their retention. Likewise, SAS also continuously improved its performance management systems, to make it more objective, traceable and development focused.

Leveraging SAS's experience, we could understand right in the beginning that organizations must not start using HR and predictive analytics, rather first embrace data-driven decision-making, start with simple algorithms using some statistics and then gradually shift to decision-making based on predictive analytics. SAS follows an iterative approach to make the best use of predictive analytics, ensuring people can visualize first and then gradually become predictive to measure the future trend.

The process of visualization can enable employees to see the results and the positive changes, which can reinforce their urge to use predictive analytics for better decision-making. This helps in understanding the business, improves the decision-making process, enhances company's insights into talent management issues and facilitates strategic workforce planning. Incidentally, SAS also is a known vendor for predictive analytics solutions.

INTRODUCTION

The use of descriptive and historic metrics in human resources is an age-old practice in organizations. Time to hire, cost per hire, number of participants in a training programme, employee satisfaction survey reports and others alike are some of the examples of these types of metrics. In contrast, HR and **predictive analytics** help organizations in measuring the future outcomes and, hence, can be considered as the most effective decision-making tool. Complexities of businesses today require the alignment of HR decisions with the strategies and business goals of organizations. Rather than analysing the past and present, human resources requires a forward-looking approach to predict the future and base their decisions on such prediction. Sullivan (2000) has appropriately differentiated between a metric and a predictive metric. While a metric tells us about a problem, a predictive metric tells us what should be our action plan for the same. The effective use of predictive analytics can be seen in the case of Google, who could develop its own algorithms for predicting the likely performance of an employee throughout his/her work-life cycle. Likewise, Google could develop a series of algorithms for a critical HR decision-making process, which have direct bearing with their success.

Predictive analytics: It helps organizations in measuring the future outcomes of a decision, hence can provide the opportunity to bring desired change in the decision for reducing adverse effect on an organization.

The HR decision-making process today is moving from reactive to predictive. **Reactive decision-making** denotes decisions based on historical inputs and actual crises situations. HR decisions based on dashboards are reactive in nature, while a **predictive decision-making** process indicates decisions based on future outcomes. Predictive HR analytics establish statistical relationships between proposed HR decisions and organizational success or failure. In the process, it helps in framing suitable strategies for organizational sustenance and growth. As possible effects of HR decisions can be predictive, HR managers can take suitable corrective measures well in advance, without actually waiting for the situations to occur (which is a reactive approach).

Reactive decision-making: It denotes decisions based on historical inputs and actual crisis situation. HR decisions based on dashboards are reactive in nature.

Predictive decision-making process: It is the process of holistic assessment of the decisional outcomes right in the beginning to calibrate decisions for minimizing adverse effect of decisional impact to benefit both the employees and the organizations.

Some of the important challenges before the HR functions today are: cost optimization, achievement of operational efficiency, supporting organizations to improve top (sales revenue) and bottom line (profit), building organizational and individual employees' capabilities to respond to changes, lending support in mergers and acquisitions, lending support for new product or new service development and so on. And all these actions require the availability of agile and competent manpower, and linking of human resources with the strategies and business goals of the organizations.

In critical HR functions, HR managers today face the challenges of answering a series of questions before actually taking any HR decisions. For example, any decision on talent management requires HR managers to decide first the possible sources of talent acquisition, match profiles with the job, make the best use of talent to maximize value and retain talent. In general, for HRM, which we call traditional administration function, HR managers may require data that can be used in building employees' capabilities, in reducing the employees' fraud and in leveraging employees' social network information. Likewise, for performance, training and development, there may be need for data for suitable HR decisions that can support organizational strategies and help in achieving business goals.

In all these cases, **HR analytics** can be of immense help to the organizations.

Even though some technology vendors use HR analytics and predictive analytics as two different solutions, in reality today in HR functions we use predictive decisional models for quality decisions with a forward-looking approach. For the purpose of this chapter, we have considered HR analytics and predictive analytics as one and the same.

HR analytics: It is defined as the application of analytic logic for the HRM function.

CONCEPTS AND DEFINITIONS

HR analytics is defined as the application of an analytic logic for a HRM function, so that it can benefit organizations in improving the performance of employees, help in rationalizing HR decision-making process and also improve ROI from human resources. From employees' point of view, HR analytics provide opportunity to assess how employees contribute to the organizations and assess the extent to which they can meet their career expectations. Critical HR decisions such as retention, potential talent, motivation, performance improvement, employees' capability and so on when backed by HR analytics, organizations can substantially reduce the risk of wrong decisions, and in the process, can improve the quality and process of HR decisions. Moreover, HR analytics can help organizational HR decision-making more strategic and business aligned.

HR analytics includes the use of statistics, developing queries and research design, fitting data (big data) to research designs, evaluating the results and then translating them into meaningful decisions. Behavioural modelling, predictive modelling, impact analysis, cost–benefit analysis, ROI and others, i.e., all the possible tools for analyses, are used in HR analytics, so that the HR decision-making process can move beyond HR metrics, HR scorecards and dashboards. Although ROI, impact analysis and cost–benefit analysis can help in HR analytics, these are more descriptive in nature and also time consuming. In contrast, behavioural modelling, predictive modelling and impact analysis can truly make HR analytics more meaningful, and decisions based on these can be better approximated addressing the strategies and business goals of the organizations. Let us understand this from Figure 3.1. However, this framework is not exhaustive, and it changes with the goals and objectives of an organization.

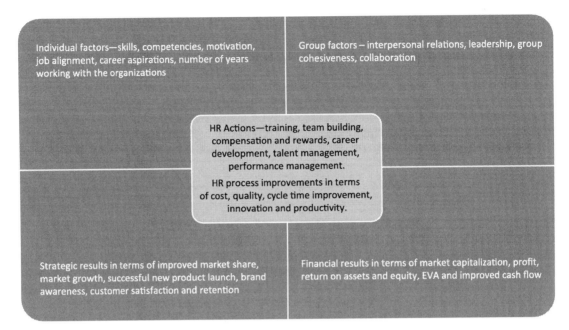

The framework contains the following boxes:

- Individual factors—skills, competencies, motivation, job alignment, career aspirations, number of years working with the organizations
- Group factors – interpersonal relations, leadership, group cohesiveness, collaboration
- HR Actions—training, team building, compensation and rewards, career development, talent management, performance management.
  HR process improvements in terms of cost, quality, cycle time improvement, innovation and productivity.
- Strategic results in terms of improved market share, market growth, successful new product launch, brand awareness, customer satisfaction and retention
- Financial results in terms of market capitalization, profit, return on assets and equity, EVA and improved cash flow

■ **Figure 3.1:** Framework of HR Analytics
Source: Author.

Talent management: It is the function talent attraction, talent recruitment and selection, talent development and talent retention for sustenance and growth of an organization.

Therefore, HR analytics correlate organizational HR or people data with business data to assess how HR function can exert impact on strategies and business results. Based on such impact analysis, while on the one hand the quality of HR decisions can be improved, on the other, organizations can balance their strategies and business plans more in terms of HR capabilities. All HR-decision making processes can be made more effective with appropriate and timely interventions, thus facilitating meaningful HR partnership with the organizations.

With HR analytics, organizations try to assess complex relationships between various HR variables and understand how such relationships relate to strategies and business goals. For example, the recruitment or selection based on HR analytics can help organizations to select the right-fit, who can not only perform but also are likely to continue with the organization for long term. Such recruitment and selection obviously meets the need for **talent management** practices, which ensures sustenance and long-term growth of the organizations. Similarly, HR analytics can help in operationalizing competency-based HR practices, duly assessing the need for changing competency sets and meeting such competency needs with suitable HR initiatives. With an identified competency set organizations can make their future decision-making process competency driven. Likewise, analytics based decisions on compensation design, training plan, designing of performance management systems, talent management practices and so on can ensure better results than traditional metrics-driven or intuitive decision-making process.

Thus, effective HR analytics require modelling of data for measuring and assessing data, which can drive the performance of an organization. It helps in defining HR issues in organizational business and strategies and accordingly can provide successful solutions from HR perspective that can help in realizing organizational business goals and strategic intents. With cross-functional inputs, HR analytics can transform the HR decision-making process into one more holistic and scientific, addressing the issues pertaining to decisional errors.

ALIGNING HUMAN RESOURCES TO BUSINESS THROUGH HR ANALYTICS

Over the years HR functions in organizations have evolved from traditional administrative jobs to strategic jobs, making best use of technology-enabled HR processes, and use of analytics. Talent management, cost optimization, performance improvement, employee engagement and so on can be done more effectively when it is reinforced by HR analytics. With analytics, human resources is now capable to showcase its measurable value, and in the process it facilitates in understanding how human resources aligns with the strategies and business goals of organizations. For example, with HR analytics it is possible to track not only the costs of recruitment but also important details which may have significant bearing with the business and strategies of organizations, such as cycle time to hire, attrition rate in new hire, costs of training and onboarding, diversity inclusivity through recruitment, culture-fit of new hire, performance trend of new hire and so on. With predictive ability, HR analytics can facilitate in reinforcing recruitment functions through appropriate interventions before organizations experience recruitment failure and consequent adverse effect on their business goals and strategies.

Simple cause and effect relationships between HR functions and business goals substantially reduce the risk of bad investments in HR initiatives and focus on those HR initiatives which can have significant positive impact on business results. For example, human resources can avoid investment in training that has poor training transferability, or when post-training performance of employees does not show any incremental change. Similarly, implementing an incentive scheme which has signifi-cant drag on a company's compensation and benefits budget without, however, any positive effect on employees' motivation and performance, can be avoided when such decisions are reinforced by HR analytics.

With predictive modelling, HR analytics can align with the business and strategies of the organizations, in manpower planning, talent manage-ment, change management, redundancy planning, cascading effects of employees' satisfaction with customers' satisfaction and positive change in business results. Manpower or HRP ensures the availability of right manpower at right time, based on the current trend and future business goals. The demographic data of existing employees' attrition rate, normal manpower wastage and so on when analysed against future business goals of the organizations can help develop a predictive model of manpower forecasting. Based on this predictive model, we can rationalize category-wise manpower requirement and accordingly plan for redundancies or new recruitment (including internal recruitment). In many organizations that are set for new technology in future, such a predictive model of manpower forecasting helps in making their available manpower future-ready through appropriate training and development. Public-sector steel manufacturing units under the Steel Authority of India Limited (SAIL) significantly invested in training and development to build their employees' capabilities for future jobs, which are significantly different than what they are doing at present, because of new technology. Similarly, Hindustan Unilever Limited (HUL), and so also many large manufacturing and service organizations that have their global presence, invest in building future leaders and glopats (global patriates, i.e., employees' who will move around the world, wherever organizations have their business presence, both on short-term and long-term assignments), based on such predictive manpower forecasting model.

In talent management the function, i.e., talent attraction, talent recruitment and selection, talent development and talent retention, building the future talent pipeline is one of the important priorities of organizations that aspire for sustenance and growth. Many technology vendors and consulting organizations provide customized solutions in the form of talent analytics, which are predictive and can help in effective talent management analysing the available data on employees. And then, suggesting appropriate decisions, such as attracting talent from target organizations, identifying potential talent in existing employees, developing such identified potential employees, framing appropriate strategies on talent retention and so on.

Similarly, interpreting employees' performance data and assessing their satisfaction level, HR analytics can also help in predicting how its cascading effect can churn to customers' satisfaction and customers' retention, and corresponding growth in sales revenue.

All these, however significant, depend on how the queries are generated, i.e., the questions are framed, organized, related and modelled. HR analytics require re-engineered data-driven HR functions both for cause and effect relationships between different HR functions and predictive modelling. The effective use of HR analytics can make human resources a strategic business partner.

Despite its importance and potentiality to align with business goals and strategies of the organizations, even on date very limited number of organizations make its effective use. A *Harvard Business Review* research report (2014) indicates that even those organizations which make use of HR analytics limit their utilization intermittently largely on tactical decisions.

STEPS FOR ALIGNMENT OF HR ANALYTICS WITH BUSINESS GOALS AND STRATEGIES

Alignment of HR analytics with business goals and strategies of organizations requires adherence to certain steps. Such steps which are commonly followed in organizations can be listed as follows:

1. Framing of queries or questions: Right at the beginning, HR managers need to frame their queries or questions, i.e., what needs assessment or measurement. For example, if the purpose is to assess or measure underlying reasons for talent retention, or possible action plans to avoid talent attrition, HR managers require following certain specific queries:

   a. What motivated talented employees to continue with the organization?
   b. What could perpetuate such continuance with the organization or minimize their possibility of attrition?
   c. What could be the possible reasons in the case of those talents who had left the organization in the past?
   d. Are the retained talents represented mostly by in-house incubated or developed employees?
   e. Does our employee feel engaged with the organization?
   f. Do we provide career development opportunities to our employees in general?
   g. How inclusive we are in our talent development practices?

   The earlier documented list of queries is not exhaustive, as the nature of queries for a particular issue may widely vary with the organization and nature of job. For example, in P&G and in HUL, we find some middle-level managerial talents voluntarily leaving their job, primarily for two important reasons: first, for both the companies' ongoing product restructuring, which results in orphaning many brands, and second, for a perceived feeling by such middle-level managers that they have nothing to contribute or achieve in their organizations. The nature of queries for talent attrition in such a situation will obviously be different.

2. Understanding appropriate data and metrics: Based on the nature of queries, HR managers need to understand what could be the appropriate nature of data, analysing or measuring which answer to the queries can be obtained. For example, if the nature of query is analysing or measuring inclusivity or otherwise in talent development practices, the nature of data would be company's training expenses, average duration or training man-days, number of employees covered, basis of selecting employees' for the training programmes and so on. These apart, data on other human resource development (HRD) related activities such as coaching and mentoring, OD and so on could be possible data or metrics that could answer whether talent development practices in organizations are inclusive or exclusive. We know exclusivity in talent development practices, i.e., restricting

talent development opportunities only for those who are identified as potential talent, often sparks attrition among those who are apparently talented but feel deprived from development opportunity in an organization. Characteristically, organizations that follow exclusivity in talent development restrict their process of identification of potential talent with forced choice performance measurement systems, i.e., use of a bell curve, which distributes hyper performers in a predetermined lower percentage of total employees, mostly 10 percent. Thus, based on the nature of problems or queries, appropriate metrics and nature of data need to be selected.

3. Building an appropriate platform for HR analytics: Appropriate HR analytics platform depends on the specific business and strategic needs of the organizations. Commonly, HR analytics platform is built on integrating various enterprise resource planning (ERP) modules, CRM modules, sales, finance and operational data and so on. All these we can name as other functional analytics. This, however, again depends on whether a specific organization has these modules currently in use. For example, many organizations do not have various ERP or functional modules; they may have one or two. In such cases, the scope of building HR analytics platform holistically may get restricted, as cross-functional data may not be available for better predictability and cause–effect relationships. To illustrate the absence of the CRM module, HR analytics cannot predict customer retention relating employee satisfaction data, and thus, may fail to predict incremental change in sales revenue due to increased level of employees' satisfaction.

4. Gradual enhancement of HR analytics capabilities: Once implemented, organizations must continue to focus on the developing capabilities of HR analytics, systematically investing on technology, training and enhancing the quality of HR decisions with more and more cross-functional inputs. To transform HR decision–making process hundred percent analytics driven culture of the organization needs change. Change in the culture of organization requires commitment from top management. Else, HR analytics will continue to focus on intermittent tactical issues, rather than alignment with the strategies and business goals of the organizations.

5. Disseminating the importance and value of HR analytics: Successful implementation of HR analytics, aligning it with the strategies and business goals of the organizations, also requires communication and dissemination of its importance and value to all stakeholders. Employees in general must feel well informed about its importance and how it adds value to the quality of HR decisions, how it positions human resources into the role of a business partner in organization and how human resources can provide cross-functional synergy, when business decisions embed human resources.

As explained earlier, steps are commonly followed in organizations for better alignment of HR analytics with strategies and business goals. However, it largely varies with the nature of organization, level of technology used in HR decision-making processes, top management commitment to HR analytics and so on.

CHECKLISTS FOR STRATEGIES AND BUSINESS-ALIGNED HR ANALYTICS

Possible checklists for successful alignment of HR analytics with the strategies and business goals of the organizations are:

1. Understanding work to be done
2. Understanding existing processes and structures
3. Understanding important roles of various functions
4. Understanding how far such roles can get influenced with the human resources quality
5. Developing of behavioural and predictive models
6. Understanding the changed performance standards
7. Understanding the process of dissemination of information on HR analytics to all stakeholders
8. Building capabilities of concerned employees to gradually change to data-driven decision-making process
9. Understanding the process of data integration for HR analytics
10. Building the required platform for HR analytics
11. Developing a dedicated task force to work on HR analytics, represented by employees with adequate functional, statistical and business knowledge

Once again such a checklist is not exhaustive, rather tentative, and can help organizations to understand how HR analytics align with their strategies and business goals. One such example is illustrated in Box 3.1 in the context of Maersk Group.

Box 3.1 Maersk's Journey Through HR Analytics

Maersk Group, the Denmark-headquartered global conglomerate in shipping, logistics and oil and gas, operates from 130 countries with headcounts of 89,000 and turnover of USD 3.1 billion. Maersk makes use of HR analytics for HR decision-making process. For effective use of HR analytics, the group at the outset identifies key business issues and their strategies, and then starts teaming up internally. With such identification, it then makes use of its internal knowledge base to develop a model. When internal knowledge is not adequate, the group refers to theories, does research and even consults experts. All this can be managed in-house, as Maersk is one of the largest groups with long-standing legacy of existence. After these exercises, they go for data analysis and base their HR decisions on information. In simple terms, Maersk makes use of metrics, statistics and research methodology to establish linkage with its key issues and from there it goes for using predictive analytics to predict future events and translate the same into recommendations. Some of the areas of human resources where the group has used predictive analytics are employee engagement, managerial commitment, training and safety.

PRACTICE ASSIGNMENT

Identify how HR analytics can help in business and strategic decision-making with specific reference to any organization?

HISTORY OF HR ANALYTICS

To understand the history and process of development of HR analytics, it is essential at the outset to mention about various HR valuation models, which are in use from early 1990s onwards. Such valuation models not only try to measure human resources for organizations but also legitimize the use of various ratios and values for a critical HR decision-making process. For example, balanced scorecard pioneered by Kaplan and Norton (1992) can not only measure performance data but can also provide valuable insights into employees' potentiality, which can substantially influence talent management related decision-making. Similar efforts on monetary valuation models pioneered by Sullivan (2000), intellectual asset valuation by Anderson and McLean (2000), return on assets and economic value added (EVA) by Stewart (1997) and so on help us not only in approximate valuation of human resources in organizations but also in terms of using vital data for critical HR decisions.

HRIS (human resource information system): It is descriptive analytics used by HR managers as a reporting tool for the past and the current happenings. HRIS is not forward looking, hence cannot visualize the future outcomes, or future decisional implications.

HRIS is a descriptive analytics used by HR managers as a reporting tool for the past and the current happenings. It is not forward looking; hence, it cannot visualize the future outcomes or future decisional implications. As a result, with HRIS HR managers cannot align the HR decision-making process with organizational strategies and business goals. With business complexities, the pattern of HR decision-making has been changed. It has now become more dynamic, forward looking and strategic encompassing all functional areas of organizations. Another inherent problem with descriptive decision-making tools like HRIS is that these can only see the situation from the macro perspective, while the modern HR decision-making process requires in-depth analysis even at micro levels for predicting the behaviour of different variables, their interrelationships and how it impacts business of the organization. This can only be done with predictive analytics through the process of identifying the unexplored pattern of the data with appropriate models.

Measures in any form, at the first instance, help us to compare or benchmark. For human resources, obviously measures help us to understand the relative value of data, which ensures better approximation of our decision-making process. With analytics, we can perform multiple measures interpreting interrelationships between data. In the process, our HR decisions also become more encompassing, sophisticated, strategic and business aligned. HR analytics over the years not only helps in measuring but also leads to associating. Over the years it transcended from causation to prediction.

The history or process of development of HR analytics over the years traced back first with various HR valuation models and various measurement tools based on data collection, primarily with the use of statistics. Initial focus was on descriptive methods, surveys and collated data from HR functions, based on which HR managers used to develop metrics and use the same for HR decision-making. With Fitz-enz and Mattox III's (2014) revolutionary publication on 'Predictive Analysis for Human

Resources', we could understand how HR decision-making processes can be made more encompassing, scientific, strategic and business aligned. Although, HR analytics roots are credited to Fitz-enz (1984), its use and applicability has been popularized only after 2014 publications. Today, HR analytics have become a legitimate strategic tool for HR decision-making process, which can substantially reduce the chances of wrong decisions that may have a potential negative effect on achieving the strategic intents and business goals.

Many organizations use the terms HR analytics and talent analytics interchangeably. Today, however, more appropriately it is called people analytics. People analytics require use of big-data in HR as people or employees of the organization have enduring effect on holistic organizational performance, and their assessment requires cross-functional data. Because of this, in people analytics, organizations involve not only HR professionals but also statisticians, engineers and mathematicians.

Bersin (Deloitte) suggested a people analytics model which integrates HR functions with sales, customer retention, accidents and frauds and quality issues, and then performs the management of data to get new insights into better decision-making.

Major technology vendors such as IBM, SAP, Oracle, Visier and Evolv today offer HR analytics solutions to organizations, which can be customized by the HR managers, pacing with their needs, to get edge in decision-making and to emerge as a legitimate business partner for the organization.

APPLICATIONS OF HR AND PREDICTIVE ANALYTICS

HR and predictive analytics help organization in getting forward-looking data on critical HRM functions, based on which statistical models can be developed to predict future trends. Although it is difficult to prepare a detailed list of areas of application of HR and predictive analytics, based on the organizational practices, we can indicate some of their key applications area as follows:

1. Preparing manpower inventory and segmenting employees: Effective talent management precedes this information, as based on this information organizations can classify their manpower and take appropriate steps for talent development. Vital manpower inventory data are basic biographical details of the employees plus their performance trend, experience, training, health records, cross-functional exposure, leadership abilities and so on. With some learning algorithms, organizations can predict the nature of training programmes matching with the identified training needs, assess how diversity inclusive programme can help in bringing diversity inclusive culture in workplace and so on. Leveraging demographics data of employees, organizations can frame strategies befitting for different employee segments and in the process can achieve increased level of employee satisfaction.

2. Preparing attrition risk score: Based on the data on employees, attrition risk score can be prepared even to the extent of identifying which employee or employees is/are more prone to leave the job. This can enable HR managers to initiate appropriate action plans to put the attrition under control, particularly for those who are hyper performers.

3. Prepare loyalty score: Data analysis with predictive models can also help preparing a loyalty score for employees, based on which organizations can take decisions on investing on employees with high loyalty score, prepare their long-term retention plan through career development and so on. Employees with low loyalty score can be studied and suitable HR initiatives can be taken so that such employees in large numbers feel increasingly engaged with the organizations and raise their loyalty and commitment to organizations.

   Both for attrition risk score and loyalty score computation, HR managers can make use of employees' demographic data, performance results, compensation and rewards data, training data, interpersonal relationships or behavioural data and so on.

4. Manpower planning, recruitment and manpower redundancy data: Based on future business plans, human resources needs to assess the availability of manpower and plan for the recruitment, so also for redundancy. This can be facilitated by predictive analytics, based on the relevant manpower data and future business plans. For example, projected attrition score can tell us the availability of manpower in different categories. Manpower inventory can tell us about talent pipeline and in-house availability of required manpower. With projected attrition score, it is also possible to predict the degree and extent of manpower redundancy, which helps human resources to prepare strategic road map well in advance for effective redundancy management.

5. Recruitment and selection based on profile matching: Recruitment and selection activity is not only for manpower replacement against employees' attrition but is also an ongoing strategically important function, as with right-fit recruitment and selection it is possible to meet the talents. Recruitment algorithms are developed based on the host of information on potential candidates, such as their performance records in previous organizations, their participation in social network and so on. This information is an addition to their actual performance in the recruitment and selection process. Through predictive modelling statistical relationships between employees' potentiality and organizational requirements can be established and accordingly a selection decision can be taken. Powerful predictive models can even leverage extra-organizational data about the candidates to arrive at a recruitment and selection decision.

6. Mapping employees' emotion and sentiments: This information is very important for critical HR decisions, such as organizational change, policy changes, change in the compensation and rewards

plan, organizational restructuring and so on. Data for such analysis are collated from several sources, such as employee survey, peer feedback, feedback from immediate supervisor, feedback from customers, employees' social media data and so on. Based on these data predictive models are developed to track and analyse employees' emotion.

7. Potential fraud and risk mapping of employees: HR and predictive analytics also help in identifying employees who are potential fraud and risk for organizations. Such employees not only raise the bar of organizational security but also continue to resist any organizational plan to change. Depending on the risk scores, HR managers have to initiate suitable actions, either in the form of their transformation through training or plan for their gradual withdrawal from an organization. This group of employees is not deadwood, a term we use to indicate poor performers; these are people with negative attitudinal problems and are difficult to transform.

The aforementioned areas of HR and predictive analytics have been prepared based on the standard HR and predictive analytics solutions of leading technology vendors, and also keeping in mind commonly measured HR functions, which have a potential effect on an HR decision-making process.

IMPORTANCE AND BENEFITS OF HR ANALYTICS

We are now clear in our understanding that HR analytics is a process of collation, integration and measurement of data that are appropriate for specific HR decisions, and then designing of the predictive models for assessing the future outcomes. Although it is predictive in nature, but HR analytics also does not discredit the importance and significance of descriptive data and other research inputs. Such data and inputs can also help in predictive modelling, when we apply statistical tools and research methodology with it.

The importance and benefits of HR analytics can be better understood when we have before us examples of world-class organizations that are using it. One such example is Google. Many such organizations use the term HR analytics and talent analytics synonymously. Hence, most of the benefits from organizations' point of view encompass talent management. Also, we see the benefits from HR analytics extend to a strategic HR decision-making process. It can legitimize the role of human resources as a business partner and align human resources with the business goals of the organizations.

Some of the commonly known benefits of HR analytics can be listed as follows:

1. Helping organizations in effective talent management
2. Rationalizing manpower requirements
3. Facilitating in making available right people at right time

4. Improving business performance through quality HR decision-making
5. Planning for effective career development of employees
6. Improving talent retention
7. Strengthening organizational competitive strength making available quality manpower
8. Ensuring right-fit recruitment and selection
9. Helping in identifying factors that can contribute to increased employee satisfaction and performance
10. Helping in identification of KPIs that can contribute to business
11. Help organizations to achieve strategic and business goals

This list of benefits is not exhaustive, rather it is tentative and commonly seen when organizations make use of HR analytics.

HR ANALYTICS FRAMEWORK AND MODELS

Frameworks and models of HR analytics are classifiable broadly into three types: the first one are those which are provided by technology vendors, the second one are normative, as these are professional models of the organizations, while the third one are empirical, designed based on the research.

LAMP framework or model of HR analytics: LAMP represents four critical components of HR measurement, which are essential to drive an organization and to achieve organizational effectiveness. It stands for logic, analytics, measures and process.

The LAMP framework or model of HR analytics has been designed by Boudreau and Ramstad (2004). LAMP represents four critical components of HR measurement, which are essential to drive organizations and to achieve organizational effectiveness. LAMP stands for logic, analytics, measures and process. As per this model, logic is understood in terms of analysis of impact, effectiveness and efficiency. Analytics help in finding answers in the data and are primarily drawn on statistics and research design. Measures are the process of counting, and it could be scorecards, dashboards and so on. The processing part of the model reinforces our actionable insights and helps in developing required strategies for effective decision-making.

Some of the models available through technology vendors cover HR analytics from different functional aspects of human resources. These are offered as individual modules, and all these are integrated with the analytics for decision-making.

For HR analytics, we also use the predictive models that analyse the past transaction data to predict the future, isolating patterns. Predictive models can relate between multiple data sets and guide HR managers for strategic initiatives to achieve business goals of organizations. When HR managers focus on identifying group relationships, they use descriptive models. A single relationship from multidimensional perspectives can be taken using only predictive modelling, whereas arranging employees into different groups in terms of performance level requires descriptive modelling.

We have two types of predictive models: smooth forecast models and scoring models. A smooth forecast model helps us in understanding how multiple variables relate to a particular event, measuring which HR managers can predict a specific numerical outcome. For example, if an HR strategy is to ensure the attrition rate should be less than 5 percent in the following year, smooth forecast models can help in arriving at such an outcome after analysing all the factors which can have possible impact on employees' attrition in organizations. Scoring models are also known as binary or winners and losers models. It is typically used in those types of decision-making which answer in two forms, say the outcome is 0 or 1. Say for example that we need to measure employees into 'learning' and 'not learning' category after a specific training programme. Here, this type of predictive model can be fitted.

In addition to the aforementioned, some organizations continue to use various HCM software, SaaS (software as a service) software, Evolv, SAP's SuccessFactors and so on. Previously, we have also mentioned names of some vendors. All these software have their specific HR analytics or predictive analytics models.

PRACTICE ASSIGNMENT

Indicate one critical HR function which can be effective with HR and predictive analytics. Develop your answer with specific reference to an organization.

Summary

Critical HR decisions which have significant bearing on organizational strategies and business goals today need to be driven by HR and predictive analytics. HR analytics collate, integrate and measure data for understanding the trend of HR functions, such as recruitment, onboarding, compensation and rewards, talent management and retention, employees' career development and so on. Using HR analytics, organizations can understand how HR decision-making process in the organization can be improved. However, an HR decision-making process can be further improved when predictive analytics are used, as it can enhance organizational power of predictability of future and adjustment of HR decisions that can enhance the chances of more positive results.

HR analytics, and so also predictive analytics as a tool for decision-making, evolved through a process, i.e., from descriptive to metrics to dashboards, scorecards and HRIS, to in its present form. Many organizations still make use of HR analytics for measuring the past and the present. Such organizations are not forward looking.

Successful implementation of HR analytics and so also predictive analytics in HR decision-making requires the selection of appropriate technology vendors, investment commitment in human resources, commitment from top management and training of employees. It requires helping employees' gradually adopt this, first through visualization, i.e., understanding how analytics-based HR decisions could result in improving the quality of HR decisions, and then gradually shifting to a predictive approach to decision-making.

General Review Questions

1. Explain the concept of HR analytics. How does it help in HR decision-making?

2. Discuss the process of aligning business to human resources. Why such alignment is necessary for HR analytics?

3. Write a note on the history of HR analytics.

4. What is predictive analytics? Is it different from HR analytics?

5. Discuss the importance and benefits of HR analytics.

6. Write a brief note on HR analytics framework and models.

7. Write short notes on the following:

   - Historic metrics in human resources
   - Reactive decision-making
   - Predictive decision-making
   - Cause and effect relationships
   - Talent management
   - HRIS
   - LAMP framework

Multiple Choice Questions

1. Indicate which of the following is not a descriptive metrics of human resources:

   a. Time to hire
   b. Cost per hire
   c. Risk of attrition
   d. Number of participants in a training programme
   e. Employee satisfaction survey reports

2. Predictive metrics help us to

   a. Measure future outcomes
   b. Base our decisions on prediction
   c. Draw action plan for a problem
   d. Develop algorithms for predicting likely performance of an employee in future
   e. All of the above

3. Indicate which of the following is not categorized as reactive HR decision-making:

   a. Decisions based on historical inputs
   b. Decisions based on actual crisis situation
   c. Decisions based on dashboards
   d. Decisions based on future outcomes
   e. None of the above

4. Any decisions on talent management requires HR managers to answer following questions, except

   a. What are the possible sources of talent acquisition
   b. How can we match profiles with the job

    c.   How can we make best use of talent to maximize value
    d.   How can we retain talent
    e.   How can we exert maximum from the talent

5. Identify which of the following statement is not relevant for HR analytics:

    a.   Application of analytic logic for an HRM function
    b.   It benefits organizations in improving the performance of employees
    c.   It can help in rationalizing an HR decision-making process
    d.   It can transform HR function to the job of a statistician
    e.   It can improve ROI from human resources

6. In all HR functions, HR analytics can play an important role, except

    a.   Talent management
    b.   Employee motivation
    c.   Employee discipline
    d.   Performance management
    e.   Making HR decisions more strategy and business aligned

7. HR analytics involves all the following, except

    a.   Knowledge of statistics
    b.   Developing queries and research design
    c.   Using intuitive ideas
    d.   Fitting data to research design
    e.   Translating results into meaningful decisions

8. Which of the following is not a possible tool for HR analytics:

    a.   Behavioural modelling
    b.   Predictive modelling
    c.   Impact analysis
    d.   Cost–benefit analysis
    e.   None of the above

9. HR analytics can operationalize competency-based HR practices by

    a.   Assessing the need for changing competency sets
    b.   Meeting such competency needs with suitable HR initiatives
    c.   Making future decision-making process competency driven
    d.   All of the above
    e.   None of the above

10. With HR analytics, it is possible to track the following, except

    a.   Cycle time to hire
    b.   Probable attrition rate in new hire
    c.   Diversity neutrality
    d.   Culture-fit of new hire
    e.   Performance trend of new hire

11. Function of talent management involves

    a.   Talent attraction
    b.   Talent recruitment and selection
    c.   Talent development
    d.   Talent retention
    e.   All of the above

12. Identify which of the following is not a step for alignment of HR analytics with business goals and strategies:

    a. Framing of queries or questions
    b. Understanding appropriate data and metrics
    c. Building appropriate platform for HR analytics
    d. Gradual enhancement of HR analytics capabilities
    e. None of the above

13. Identify which of the following is not a right statement about HRIS:

    a. It is descriptive analytics
    b. It is used by HR managers as a reporting tool for the past and the current happenings
    c. It is not forward looking
    d. It can visualize the future outcomes
    e. It cannot align the HR decision-making process with organizational strategies and business goals

14. With analytics, HR decisions become

    a. Encompassing
    b. Sophisticated
    c. Strategic
    d. Business aligned
    e. All of the above

15. Indicate which of the following is not an area of application of HR analytics:

    a. Preparing manpower inventory and segmenting employees
    b. Preparing attrition risk score
    c. Preparing loyalty score
    d. Benchmarking HR practices
    e. Recruitment and selection based on profile matching

16. Mapping employees' emotion and sentiments is necessary for the following, other than

    a. Organizational change
    b. Organizational policy changes
    c. Change in the compensation and rewards plan
    d. Organizational restructuring
    e. None of the above

17. Which of the following is not a point for the LAMP framework:

    a. Logic
    b. Analytics
    c. Measures
    d. Predictive
    e. Process

18. The smooth forecast model denotes the following, except

    a. It is a predictive model
    b. It can explain how multiple variables relate to a particular event
    c. It can measure how HR managers can predict a specific numerical outcome
    d. It can help in arriving at an outcome after analysing all the factors of a decisional issue
    e. It can answer in two forms: 0 or 1

Critical Review Question

1. Visit the website of a company that uses HR analytics for HR decision-making. Collect some details about their analytics-driven HR functions and prepare a note.

> **PRACTITIONER SPEAKS**
>
> For a specific HR function like employee engagement, explain how HR analytics can help a particular organization. While you develop the answer ensure that all aspects of employee engagement are covered.

CASE STUDY

Strategic HR Analytics—Lessons from Walmart

Walmart today with the sales revenue of USD 482 billion is managing 22 lakh employees and 260 lakh customers, spreading across 28 countries and sustaining over half a century. The company manages its human resources with a data-driven decision-making process, and hence, the use of HR analytics is more a legitimate requirement. For example, workforce planning systems in Walmart are so designed today that Walmart managers can assess the overall impact on sales revenue with even one hour engagement of a headcount at the store level. With HR analytics the company not only manages its HR operational issues with the forward-looking approach but can even significantly improve the culture of innovation in the workplace. Today, the company is able to assess what needs to be measured in human resources and how the same could be measured, and what could be the actionable strategies (based on the measurement results) for achieving the business objectives.

Walmart considers its HR analytics as strategic analytics and it encompasses all the functions as follows:

1. Assessment of business needs
2. Establishment of logic for the business needs
3. Review of relevant data availability both within and outside organizations
4. Collection of additional information
5. Identification of commonalities across various data sets
6. Framing strategy and action plans for implementation.

Strategic HR analytics in Walmart build actionable insights which influence the decision-making process in human resources. Actionable insights have both quantitative and qualitative workflows. Quantitative workflows are broken into data, exploratory analysis and statistical models. Qualitative workflows encapsulate employees' (Walmart calls them associates) voice (focus group discussions, engagement surveys and so on), market research information, inputs from advance research and others. Actionable insights get further reinforced when quantitative and qualitative workflows are integrated. This helps Walmart's human resources to come out with actionable strategies.

Walmart's strategic HR analytics rest on four pillars which are capable of modelling and data mining, research and social media data integration, visualization and building prototype and finally, testing and learning. Each pillar is taken care of by a dedicated team of professionals, who continuously strive for improving strategic HR analytics in line with the business goals. More thrust is given on understanding employees' capabilities, drawing actionable strategies to manage employee turnover, absenteeism, leadership development and so on.

Strategic HR analytics of Walmart is supported by SAS, Alteryx, Tableau and SPSS.

Question: Based on this case study, list out the essential features of strategic HR analytics of Walmart.

REFERENCES

Andersen, R., & McLean, R. (2000). Accounting for the creation of value: ongoing research project sponsored by the Canadian Institute of Chartered Accountants. Burnby, BC, Canada.

Boudreau, J., & Ramstad, P. (2004). Talentship and human resource measurement and analysis: From ROI to strategic organizational change (Center for Effective Organizations Working Paper No. G04-17). Los Angeles, USA: Marshall School of Business, University of Southern California.

Fitz-enz, J. (1984). *How to measure human resources management.* New York: McGraw-Hill.

Fitz-enz, J. & Mattox III, J. R. (2014). *Predictive Analytics for Human Resources, New Delhi.* New Delhi: Wiley India.

Harvard Business Review. (2014). HR joins the analytics revolution. Available at: https://hbr.org/resources/pdfs/comm/visier/18765_HBR_Visier_Report_July2014.pdf (accessed on 31 December 2014).

Kaplan, R. S., & Norton, D. P. (1992). The balanced scorecard—Measures that drive performance. *Harvard Business Review*, 70(1), 71–79.

Stewart, T. A. (1997). Intellectual capital: The new wealth of organisations. New York, NY: Doubleday.

Sullivan, P. (2000). Value driven intellectual capital: How to convert intangible corporate assets into market value. New York, NY: John Wiley & Sons.

FURTHER READINGS

Lawler, E., Levenson, A., & Boudreau, J. (2004). HR metrics and analytics: Use and impact. *Human Resource Planning, 27*(4), 2004.

Levenson, Alec. (2005). Harnessing the power of HR analytics. *Strategic HR Review, 4*(3), 28–31.

APPENDIX

Regression Analyses

For predictive HR decision modelling, we use regression analyses. In HRP, information on the number of people employed in other comparable organizations in similar nature of work may be of interest to us. For such purpose, we select random samples of people and their level of productivity, and use the same as the means to predict the number of people actually required by us. This technique may not be foolproof as experience, performance levels, size of organization, salary and revenue and so on, can play important roles in manpower determination.

Regression analyses allow us to consider all these factors in deciding the requirement of manpower in an organization. Linear regression allows us to make predictions of any dependent variable (y) based on any independent variable (x). Multiple regressions allow us to make predictions of any dependent variable (y) based on several independent variables (x).

Linear Regression

In linear regression, right in the beginning we use the straight-line model. This model does plotting of x value on the x-axis (horizontal line) and y value on the y-axis (vertical line). Each x value and its related y value make up the coordinates of each point. After all the points have been plotted on a graph, the result is known as a scatter diagram, as shown in the following figure:

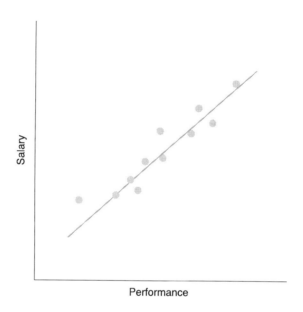

Performance

In this case, we are studying how the salary level significantly changes performance in an organization. Obviously, this information can be construed as important for HRP. Therefore, using a scatter diagram, we try to visualize the relationships, if any, between the x and y variables. Since this relationship is linear we can predict values of y from various values of x.

Least-squares Model

This method finds the straight line that best fits the data. Underlying principle here is that a line of best fit to describe best relationships between two variables is a line for which the sum of the squares of the deviations between values on the straight line and the actual values will be the least or minimum. The line of best fit is computed mathematically, and it will always pass through the average of the x and y data. We can express this with the following equation:

$$y = \beta_0 + \beta_{1x} + \beta$$

y	dependent variable
x	independent variable or predictor (used as a predictor of y)
β	random error or residual (actual y value – mean of y)
β_0	y-intercept
β_1	slope

With this equation we can predict any y value when we know the value of x. This equation can be graphically presented as shown in the following figure:

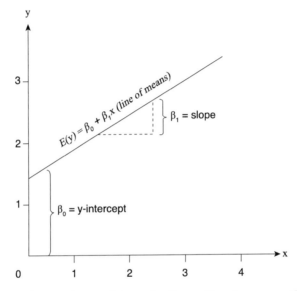

One can visually approximate the position of a line of least squares through data plots by calculating the means of both axes. Regression lines always pass through these two means on any data plot.

We can express mathematically least-square estimates as follows:

Slope: $\hat{\beta}_1 = \dfrac{SS_{xy}}{SS_{xx}}$ y-intercept: $\hat{\beta}_0 = \bar{y} - \hat{\beta}_1 \bar{x}$

where

$$SS_{xy} = \sum_{i=1}^{n} x_i y_i - \frac{\left(\sum_{i=1}^{n} x_i\right)\left(\sum_{i=1}^{n} y_i\right)}{n}$$

$$SS_{xx} = \sum_{i=1}^{n} x_i^2 - \frac{\left(\sum_{i=1}^{n} x_i\right)^2}{n}$$

n = Sample size
SS = Sum of squares
With higher correlation (r) between x and y we can get the better line of fit.

Line of Best Fit

We use the line of best fit to get the best estimate of y based on any given value of x. Quantitatively we can calculate it assessing the extent to which the data points deviate from the line. Such error or deviation explains the vertical distance between the data point and the line. By calculating error or deviation for each data point and then squaring and adding them together, we get sum of squared errors (SSE). The line with the smallest SSE is considered to be the line of best fit. We have illustrated this in the following figure:

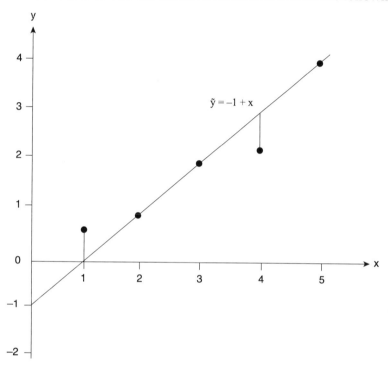

$\tilde{y}$ denotes the value of y predicted from a visually fitted model.

As indicated earlier, the best-fit line is the line with the least SSE, and this can measure the extent to which the data points deviate from the line.

Based on the above graph, we can summarize as follows:

x	y	$\tilde{y} = -1 + x$	$(y - \tilde{y})$	$(y - \tilde{y})^2$
1	1	0	$(1 - 0) = 1$	1
2	1	1	$(1 - 1) = 0$	0
3	2	2	$(2 - 2) = 0$	0
4	2	3	$(2 - 3) = -1$	1
5	4	4	$(4 - 4) = 0$	0
			sum of errors = 0	sum of squared errors (SSE) = 2

Here, we see the sum of errors equals 0, and the SSE equals 2. If we draw different lines through the graph shown we will get different values for the sum or errors and for the SSE. However, the line with the smallest SSE would be the regression line.

In Chapter 7, we have solved a regression analysis using SPSS.

CHAPTER 4

HR BUSINESS PROCESS AND HR ANALYTICS

LEARNING OBJECTIVES:

After reading this chapter, you will be able to understand:

- Concepts of HR business process
- Statistics and statistical modelling for HR research and HR decision-making
- HR research tools and techniques
- Data analysis for human resources
- HRIS for HR decision-making
- HR metrics
- HR scorecard
- HR analytics as a tool for HR decision-making

INTRODUCTORY CASE

HR Metrics: Finding Answer to Why?

While developing HR metrics, most of the companies feel that more the number of metrics, the better it is, as then the measurement of human resources from all dimensions, both in length and breadth, would be possible. Also, companies lack the logic for HR metrics, resulting which they develop metrics in vacuum. Such directionless and meaningless approach to prepare HR metrics ultimately defeats the purpose of measurement. While developing HR metrics, it is always desirable to embrace a collaborative approach. Collaboration among cross-functional employees and even with the top management is important, as the top management can give a strategic direction and suggest which strategic measures can help them to assess business health. Similarly, developing unnecessarily large number of metrics complicates the process of measurement. Also, it may not be possible to use all such metrics in real-life situations. Although we do not have any definitive answer, about eight to ten metrics can be considered as optimum.

An effective approach to develop HR metrics is to focus on the measurement on people which relates to the performance of an organization. For example, good diversity management practices, which can be measured in terms of diversity-related metrics, can help an organization to be innovative and perform better. In contrast, poor diversity management practices not only have adverse effects on the organizational performance but can also enhance the organizational cost of litigation.

Another approach to prepare HR metrics is developing it based on stakeholders' interests, primarily in the context of shareholders' value.

INTRODUCTION

The term human resources emerged as a business process once HR business partnership was globally accepted in principle subsequent to the scholarly contributions of Ulrich (1997) and further refinement by Beer (1997), Brown et al. (2004) and Ulrich and Brockbank (2005). With these researches today we can understand four key roles of human resources, i.e., strategic (embedding the business partnership role), administrative, employee champion and change agent (Keegan and Francis, 2010).

The role of human resources as a strategic partner requires it to help line management achieve their goals, both in terms of strategy framing and strategy execution (Ulrich and Brockbank, 2005). As a change agent, human resources is responsible to manage cultural and transformational changes in organizations. In its administrative role, human resources contributes to achieve organizational efficiency through the process of reengineering of HR function and HR processes developing shared services. Employee championship role, as propounded by Ulrich (1997), focuses on managing HR operations to elicit employees' contributions to organizational business. Later, the employee championship role of human resources extended to the role of a consensus negotiator (Torrington et al., 2005), regulator (Storey, 1992) and contract manager (Tyson, 1995). Such plurality in managing the employee championship role gradually needed trade-offs between employee needs and organizational needs, which in turn matured the concept of HR business partnership.

After the theoretical analysis of previous researches and studies, once we are convinced that HR business partnership role, in fact, necessitated to manage human resources as a business process function, it is now important to streamline HR activities. Not that all activities of human resources can be managed as a business process, particularly the compliance and some operational monitoring and control activities. Most of the HR business process vendors that provide support to organizations to manage their HR activities as a business process consider that the following HR activities can be directly attributable to HR business processes, as these can significantly influence organizational business and strategies. These are:

a. HRP and recruitment
b. Employee development and succession planning
c. Employee development and learning management
d. Talent management
e. Performance management systems
f. Reporting of core human resources
g. Compensation and reward management.

In line with Cakar et al. (2003), the business process approach to human resources primarily rests on three arguments as follows:

a. Human resources is a support process for organizations; hence, all other processes of organizations are customers to HR business.

b. In the processing of extending support to HR customers, human resources automatically maximizes its contributions to business objectives and strategies of the organizations.

c. Like all other business processes, an HR process also continuously evolves and it consists of several sub-processes, i.e., it frames strategy, implements strategy and monitors its impact on organizational business.

Using some of the basic tools such as job redesign, competency mapping and so on we can align our HR support process with the business process of an organization.

In this chapter, we have delineated, at the outset, HR measurement issues through HR research, use of statistics, HR metrics, HR scorecards and HR dashboards, and then discussed how the use of HR analytics can improve such measurements and contribute to organizational effectiveness. With HR analytics, organizations can objectively take HR decisions, frame strategies and align with the business goals.

STATISTICS AND STATISTICAL MODELLING FOR HR RESEARCH AND HR DECISION-MAKING

To make sense of data, HR managers use statistical analysis which involves collection, analysis, interpretation and presentation of data for decision-making and also for predicting the future. For managerial decisions, we use both descriptive and inferential statistics. **Descriptive statistics** help in describing the existing data, using measures such as average, sum and so on. **Inferential statistics** helps in finding patterns and relationships in data. Obviously, this involves statistical testing, using various statistical models.

> **Descriptive statistics:** It helps in describing the existing data, using measures such as average, sum and so on.

> **Inferential statistics:** It helps in finding patterns and relationships in data. Obviously, this involves statistical testing, using various statistical models.

HR research helps us in understanding how organizations are structured and function, how decisions are made, what factors affect organizational operations and, finally, what strategies are important for gaining sustainable competitive advantages. Sometimes this research is carried out for descriptive purposes, such as to assess why operations costs of some operations are higher over others. Obviously, this requires the collection and analysis of data. Also, such research may be normative, prescriptive and strategic. Irrespective of research scoping, data collection, analysis, statistical modelling and use of HR analytics for predictive decision-making are required.

In all functional areas of human resources, we use statistics for various researches, which can help in improving future HR decisions. For example, research in recruitment and selection can significantly help in future decision-making on issues such as how best we can attract talents, what can ensure better diversity, how we can optimize recruitment costs and so on. An extended recruitment research even can provide direction for successful onboarding, workforce planning and so on. Even in compensation and benefits management practices, we can make use of statistics for various researches to improve our future decision-making process. Likewise, in performance management, training and development, employee motivation and also in many SHRM issues, we can use statistics. For doing HR research with statistics, we need to have data; hence, the data identification process is critical. In all HRM areas, such as descriptive, conceptual and normative, we can make use of statistics for necessary research. Briefly descriptive human resources considers getting facts right, conceptual aspects consider how facts relate to each other, while normative aspects consider things that we should do for obtaining a specified goal.

Resource-based view:
It assumes physical, organizational and human resources differences between organizations, which make differences in their potentiality.

Behavioural perspective:
It focuses on HR practices that can best shape employees' behaviour for achieving goals and objectives of organizations.

Again HR research issues encompass **resource-based views** and behavioural perspectives. A resource-based view assumes physical, organizational and HR differences between organizations, which mark the differences in their potentiality. **Behavioural perspectives** focus on HR practices that can best shape employees' behaviour for achieving goals and objectives of organizations. Carrying out HR research from both these two perspectives requires extensive use of statistics and data-driven research.

Another important area that HR research focuses on is SHRM, which thrusts on competency-based approach for sustaining competitive advantage for organizations. To assess the social and economic dimensions of SHRM, understanding relationships of SHRM with business performance, relationships between SHRM and development of organizational capability and so on, we make use of statistical models and predictive HR analytics for our research.

Table 4.1 maps the possible HR research areas based on statistics, statistical modelling and subsequent HR analytics for predictive decision-making.

■ **Table 4.1:** HR Research Areas

HR Functions	Research Areas
Recruitment and selection	Outsourcing or direct recruitment, contractual or on permanent payroll, multi-skill attributes or specialization are some of the issues considered at this level.
Career development	Career mapping, succession planning and management development, integrating career development with OD initiatives, are the factors considered in this area.
Performance management	Designing appropriate tools and aligning such appraisal with training needs, promotion, transfer and relocation are the issues that deserve attention at this stage.
Training and development	Developing in-house training, ROI models for evaluating training, training budgets and so on are considered for this research.
Compensation and benefits plan	Designing compensation and incentive schemes, suitable to attract talent and retain them, non-wage labour cost aspects and so on.
HRP	Developing an HRIS, aligning HRP with corporate strategies and skill and competency mapping are important aspects of strategic HRP.

Source: Author.

HR RESEARCH TOOLS AND TECHNIQUES

HR research can be either quantitative or qualitative. Quantitative data are gathered through experimental/clinical trials, observations and recording of events, collection of data from databases such as ERP and management information systems (MIS), survey reports and so on. Qualitative research covers historical data analysis and even collection of narrative data for understanding the phenomena through discourse analysis.

Statistical analysis helps in all types of research, such as descriptive, correlational, casual-comparative and experimental. Descriptive researches engage in data collection and testing of hypotheses, say for measuring the satisfaction level of employees. **Correlational research** helps us in determining relationships among variables to establish cause–effect relationships, so as to study how a new incentive scheme correlates with employees' performance. **Casual-comparative research** helps in comparing two relationships, e.g., determining the cause of differences between two groups of employees. **Experimental researches** study the cause–effect relationships by comparison, i.e., manipulating one variable while controlling the others. Irrespective of the type of HR research we can use statistics and statistical modelling for better research results.

Correlational research: It helps us in determining relationships among variables to establish cause–effect relationships, say to study how a new incentive scheme correlates with employees' performances.

Casual-comparative research: It helps in comparing two relationships, say determining the cause of differences between two groups of employees.

Experimental research: It studies cause–effect relationships by comparison, manipulating one variable, while controlling other variables.

Again in HR research and decisions, we make use of different levels of measurements: nominal, ordinal, interval and ratio. Nominal measurement involves classification of objects in two or more categories; hence, we call it categorical measurement. Ordinal measurement classifies objects in order from the highest to the lowest, from the most to the least. It can indicate one object is better than the other, but cannot say how better it is. Interval measurement combines both the characteristics of nominal and ordinal measurements. Employees' performances are measured using a measurement tool which can have a scale with arbitrary maximum and minimum scores (say a zero point). Ratio measurement along with the properties of interval measurement can analyse differences in scores and the relative magnitude of scores. All these measurements require the use of different scales and then make use of statistics for better inferences.

DATA ANALYSIS FOR HUMAN RESOURCES

After data collection for HR research and HR decisions, we need to organize and summarize data primarily with two statistical techniques, i.e., measurement of central tendency and measurement of dispersion. Central tendency is measured calculating mean, mode and median. Mean is the average, mode is the value that occurs most and median is the mid-value, mid-point or the 50th percentile. **Dispersion** or variability is measured using range, quartile deviation and standard deviation. The range measures the difference between the highest and the lowest scores in a data set and quartile deviation is the difference between the upper quartile and the lower quartile in a data set. For example, if the upper quartile of a data set is in the 90th percentile, it means there are 90 percent scores below that point. It can also be interpreted as: The 90th percentile is in the top

Dispersion: It is also known as variability and is measured using range, quartile deviation and standard deviation. Range measures the difference between the highest and the lowest score in a data set. Quartile deviation is the difference between the upper quartile and the lower quartile in a data set. Standard deviation is the square root of the variance and it is the distance of each score from the mean.

10 percent bracket. Standard deviation is the square root of the variance and it is the distance of each score from the mean.

The measurement of the relative position indicates the performance score of an employee in relation to others. This helps in understanding how well an employee has performed compared to others. Two most frequently used measures of relative positions are percentile ranks and standard scores. A percentile rank indicates the percentage of scores that fall at or below a given score. If a score of 65 corresponds to the 80th percentile, it means that 80 percent of the scores in the distribution are lower than 65. A standard score is a derived score that expresses how far a given raw score is from some reference point, typically the mean, in terms of standard deviation units. The most commonly reported and used standard scores are z-scores, t-scores and stanines. The z-score expresses how far a score is from the mean in terms of standard deviation units. The t-score is an expression of the z-score in a different form. Stanines are standard scores that divide a distribution into nine parts. These stand for a standard nine and may be used as a criterion for selecting employees for special programmes.

This introductory discussion, therefore, helps us to understand the importance of statistics in HR research, and so also in an HR decision-making process. HR decisions become more and more scientific with the use of statistical tools. Preliminary statistical analysis further requires us using some statistical models and then making use of HR analytics for predictive HR decisions.

PARAMETRIC AND NON-PARAMETRIC TESTS

Depending on the nature of data, and the pattern of HR decisions, we can use parametric or non-parametric statistical tests. Characteristically, data sets for both these tests are different. For parametric tests, data have at least one interval level measurement, populations from where samples are drawn are normal, variances of the populations are expected to be equal and the sample size is large. For non-parametric tests, however, data sets are not from normal populations. Hence, we also call these tests non-normal data analysis, or distribution free tests.

HRIS FOR HR DECISION-MAKING

HRIS can be used as decision support systems (DSS) for human resources. We define it as the composite of databases for collecting, recording, storing, managing, delivering, presenting and manipulating data for human resources (Broderick & Boudreau, 1992). The initial thrust of HRIS was to use it as an automated tool to keep records of employees, including computerization of payrolls. However, with the present improved versions, HRIS also supports the HR decision-making process at the strategic level. For example, one of the important areas of HRIS application is effective HRP. HRP ensures right people at the right time, pacing with organizational strategies and business plans. Making data available on recruitment, selection, training and development, career planning, compensation, productivity and performance, attrition, motivation and also from skill inventory, HRIS helps in effective HRP. In addition to strategic HR decision-making, HRIS also helps in routine or operational HR decision-making process.

Often we confuse HRIS as standard or customized HR software that can help in the HR decision-making process, along with HR record-keeping and payroll preparation. But, HRIS today is capable of including even organizational policies and procedures, and data. It can now provide service in the form of information that helps in the decision-making process and is even capable of extracting data from other functional departments to fit them to the process. Simultaneously, it can also help in decision-making processes of other functional departments, such as finance, marketing, operations and so on.

For a finance manager, data on aggregate compensation cost may not be the right input for preparing a compensation budget. But when such compensation data are simulated with attrition rate, like the increase or decrease of dearness allowance (DA), absenteeism, loss of man-days, increments, incentive, promotion, redundancy and so on, it can provide a better estimate. This can be best ensured with HRIS. Likewise for marketing department, HRIS can help in critical decision-making, such as sales performance, availability of sales force, sales competency and so on, by providing the required data.

Objectives of HRIS

Based on the earlier discussions, we can see that HRIS can serve the following objectives:

- Planning and policy formulation. HRIS supports planning and policy formulations both at macro and micro levels.
- Monitoring and evaluation. It helps in monitoring and evaluation of HR activities, such as performance monitoring, evaluation and so on.
- Providing inputs to strategic decision-making. Human resources has to take strategic decisions from time to time on manpower restructuring and rightsizing, competency mapping, change of organizational culture and so on, apart from other HR activities such as enforcing cost control, managing all operational HR issues and so on. For all HR-related strategic decisions, HRIS can help making the required data available.

Therefore, from the earlier discussions, it is clear that HRIS can provide critical inputs in all spheres of HR activities and in the HR decision-making process.

HRIS can be in the form of specific modules or sub-systems, e.g., recruitment, HRP, training, performance management, payroll, job analysis and

■ **Table 4.2:** HRIS Modules

Recruitment Management	Training and Development
• Applicant/Vacancy details	• Course specification
• Shortlisting	• Course scheduling
• Job/Person specifications	• Evaluations
• Skills matching	• Mail merge facility
• Mail merge facility	• Cost analysis
• Standard reports	• In-house faculty database
• Cost analysis	• External faculty database
• Internal job posting	
• Interview scheduling	
• Internet job posting	

Source: Author.

so on, or it can be an integrated DSS. We have hundreds of HRIS products available in the market. It is advisable for human resources to make brief review on the available HRIS products, matching with their requirements, and then select an appropriate one. Most of the HRIS products are customizable.

In Table 4.2, the contents of some specific HRIS modules have been presented.

Similarly, we have separate HRIS modules for all HR functions. HRIS today is recognized as an important DSS for HR decision-making process.

HR METRICS

HR metrics: It measures all HR operational and strategic areas, interpreting which HR managers can take effective HR decisions.

For measuring HR performances, **HR metrics** are used. HR metrics can report present, on-going and year-on-year information on HR performances, even in strategic areas such as employee attrition, employee engagement and performance, incentives and employees' performance, training and employees' performance and so on. HR metrics can be developed for all HR operational and strategic areas, interpreting which HR managers can take effective HR decisions. It helps in setting targets for human resources and measuring the performance of an HR department. While developing HR metrics, it is important to see which metrics can be better aligned with the business goals and strategies of the organization. Such metrics can report meaningful HR information, based on which appropriate HR decisions can be taken. For example, human resources can assess the trend in training expenditures and accordingly can try to analyse how such training expenditures relate to employees' performances.

Most of the HR metrics that we see today can be credited to Fitz-enz (1984) and later to Fitz-enz and Davidson (2002). All these metrics were developed jointly by Saratoga Institute and Society for Human Resource Management. Kaplan and Norton (1996), however, refurbished our thought process on HR metrics introducing a balanced scorecard. Balanced scorecards design performance indicators from four generic perspectives, i.e., financial, customer, business process, and learning and growth. We will not discuss balanced scorecards in detail, as it is not within the scope of this book.

During the same period, Huselid (1995) introduced the concept of high-performance work systems that could establish how systematic HRM can make significant differences in organizational effectiveness. Further, Becker et al. (2001) could improve this concept to develop HR scorecards, which we have discussed in detail in the succeeding paragraph.

Most of the HR metrics focus on data on cost and benefits, rather than intelligently reporting on insights on HR functions that can help in taking critical business and strategic decisions. Such common metrics aggregate the observation to the level of organization. This can only be improved when HR managers take an initiative to align HR metrics to business goals and strategies of organizations and see the information from a holistic perspective.

HR metrics and HR analytics are not one and the same. HR metrics are data that can provide some descriptive details about some HR processes, e.g., the success of a training programme. Therefore, characteristically, HR metrics can report on organizational HR activities. HR analytics on the other hand combines data with metrics and can examine the relationships or the changes in HR metrics. From this perspective, HR analytics has significant influence on decision-making. Also, HR analytics can help in predicting the future outcome of a decision, which helps in taking precautionary steps, when decisional negativity has potential adverse effects on an organization.

RECRUITMENT METRICS

We can develop metrics for all HR functions. However, here we have elaborated some recruitment metrics to provide guidelines on the way HR metrics are prepared.

For talent attraction and sourcing, recruitment function in any organization is strategically important. Some of the recruitment metrics that can help in measuring recruitment efficiency are listed as follows:

1. Recruiting cost ratio: This is an important metrics, as it has direct relationships with the recruitment efficiency. To calculate this ratio, we require the actual costs of manpower hiring and the compensation costs of new employees during the period of their onboarding. In addition, we also factor new recruitees' cost of underperformance during the initial period of their job placement, say up to six months.

This, however, varies with the nature of job. Ideally, this is manpower replacement cost. It is calculated using the following formula:

RCR = [(Total hiring costs/Total compensation cost for the period of onboarding) + Cost of underperformance during the initial period of job placement] × 100.

2. Recruiting efficiency ratio: This metrics is prepared to measure the extent of talented people attracted for a job vacancy. Simply, it is the ratio of talented people recruited over the total number of people recruited in an organization.

3. New hire performance ratio: This ratio helps in recruitment validation and can be measured in terms of the performance results of new recruitees after onboarding and subsequent to job placement.

4. Recruitment success ratio: It is measured in terms of percentage of successful recruitment over the total number of candidates interviewed. It can measure the efficiency of a screening process or of shortlisting candidates for an interview.

5. Time to hire ratio: It is measured in terms of cycle time required from initial HRP to actual recruitment in terms of job placement.

Apart from these, organizations can have several other types of recruitment ratios depending on their specific requirements. For example, some organizations measure the success of sourcing channels, the retention ratio of new recruitees, the gender-mix ratio and others alike.

METRICS FOR TRAINING AND DEVELOPMENT FUNCTION

In managing the training and development function, we use various metrics. These metrics help in measuring the efficiency of the training and development function in an organization. Some of these metrics are internal accession rate, internal addition and replacement rate, headcount trained rate and so on. All these metrics can be combined to build the total career path ratio, i.e., employee promotion as the percentage of employee movement within an organization. Other than promotion of employees, movement can also happen due to transfer, redeployment and so on. Another important training and development metrics is regular employees' headcount trained ratio, which indicates the number of employees who are being trained as the percentage of regular headcount. Apart from these, we have the training investment factor ratio (represented in terms of average training cost per employee), the training transfer ratio (indicated in terms of the rate of utilization of training inputs for an actual job) and so on.

HR metrics, therefore, provide some standards of measurement, based on which the HR performance can be measured and the measurement results can be used for better HR decision-making.

PRACTICE ASSIGNMENT

Is HR analytics a sub-set of HRIS? Give your answer with examples. Like recruitment metrics, develop some metrics for performance management function.

HR SCORECARD

An HR scorecard provides a framework for measuring human resources. It is designed with the balanced scorecard measurement framework. This framework, as we know, is developed based on four perspectives, i.e., financial, internal process, customer, and learning and growth. Often organizations hurriedly go for measurement. But quantifying HR measurables primarily requires understanding what needs to be measured. That will justify the logic behind developing a scorecard. Before we design an HR scorecard, it is also important to draw tentative lists of operating metrics, so that the scorecard can effectively help in the HR decision-making process. It is unwise to put all measures in one scorecard, rather it has to be structured using a sequence such as value-based HR metrics, HR outcome measures, operational HR metrics and HR analytics. With this sequence, we can use an HR scorecard meaningfully and provide support to the HR decision-making process.

HR scorecard: It is a framework for measuring human resources.

Some of the other contextual issues for an HR scorecard are: value drivers, value propositions, human resources' value, its contribution, measurable HR functions, activity- and value-driven metrics, human capital metrics and so on. All these issues are directly attributable to organizational business. Hence, designing an HR scorecard factoring such contextual issues can make it more meaningful. We try to get results from an HR scorecard in three important dimensions including the business values of human resources, HR processes and employees to an organization. Preparing an HR scorecard with value-based metrics may not be a straightforward journey, but it needs to be scaled up gradually, foremost with HR operational and efficiency metrics.

It is said an HR scorecard is an organic design, as it evolves through the changes in business—one that changes with the business. Obviously for this reason, a scorecard has to be continuously reviewed and updated, ensuring it generates reports with relevant metrics. Old metrics are gradually discontinued. This can make an HR scorecard relevant to organizational business needs, rather than reporting of some operational and efficiency metrics.

Therefore, an HR scorecard aligns HR support with organizational business and strategies. It demonstrates HR value contribution in achieving organizational business and strategic intents. It helps in strategic alignment of HR functions by mapping critical HR supports such as performance management systems, innovation, training and development and so on. An HR scorecard creates strategic alignment between human resources and the organization at all levels.

For developing an HR scorecard, we need to follow a certain sequence of actions as follows:

   a.   Develop a strategy
   b.   Map the strategy
   c.   Establish measures for each strategy

d. Cascade it to a scorecard
e. Implement the scorecard.

All the earlier listed actions can help us in developing a suitable HR scorecard that can benefit organizations in multiple ways. Some of these benefits are presented as follows:

- Helps in framing an HR strategy in alignment with the organizational strategy
- Helps in getting clarity on the vision and mission of the organization
- Creates a sense of ownership of the strategy
- Improves communication of strategy
- Prioritizes HR initiatives aligning activities to business goals
- Supports functions to identify and communicate unique strategies
- Creates a framework for prioritization of initiatives
- Aligns measurement with business goals
- Measures human resources' strategic contribution in candid terms
- Provides real-time graphical display of KPIs.

Table 4.3 presents a sample HR scorecard.

■ **Table 4.3:** Sample Scorecard for an HR Manager

Sl. No.	Key Result Areas (KRAs)	KPIs	Weight of KPIs	Target Score	Actual Score	Final Score
1.	Recruitment and selection	Cost of recruitment				
		Lead time for recruitment				
2.	Performance management	Percentage of employees reaching expected performance levels				
		Percentage of hyper performers				
3.	Training and development	Per employee man-days of training				
		Post-training performance increase				
4.	Employee attrition	Percentage of employees who leave the organization				
		Percentage of talented employees who leave the organizations				
5.	Compensation and benefits plan	Average cost of compensation and benefits				
		Average cost of deferred compensation and benefits				

Source: Author.

Again, the earlier described list of benefits is not exhaustive. It can vary from one organization to another. For example, the HR scorecard of Tata Steel focuses on four clear business perspectives, i.e., capital management, customer management, product and process management, and talent management. These help the company to derive the benefits in alignment with their business goals.

HR DASHBOARDS

From an HR scorecard, we can deduce **HR dashboards** primarily for monitoring and measurement of HR activities based on various operating metrics. Hence, dashboard per se is not an HR scorecard, nor is it aligned with the business and strategies of organizations. It primarily focuses on short-term or operational goals, helps in visualization of the performance and reports immediately the deviation for interventions. With charts and diagrams, HR managers can track and monitor the performance. Dashboard development requires metrics in KPIs format.

> **HR dashboards:** These are developed after an HR scorecard to monitor and measure HR activities based on various operating metrics.

HR ANALYTICS AS A BETTER TOOL FOR HR DECISIONS

HR analytics today is the most important strategic tool for the HR decision-making process. While HR metrics and tools such as HR scorecards and HR dashboards can monitor and control HR operational functions, HR analytics, making use of HR metrics, can develop algorithms for HR decisions in alignment with the business goals and strategies of organizations. HR analytics gather HR data from multiple sources and then develop algorithms for predictive HR decisions. Today, most of the organizations across the globe manage their human resources or HC with strategic focus using HR analytics. Some of the strategic benefits of HR analytics are: managing talent attrition, anticipating performance, effectively managing compensation and benefits programme, improving employee motivation and morale and so on.

Beginning of HR analytics can be credited to Jac Fitz-enz, when in 1984 he could develop ideas of measuring HRM services with metrics. Although our initial focus was on measuring employee performances, with the passage of time HR analytics has developed (rather evolved) for managing the entire gamut of HRM or HC management strategically. Organizations using HR analytics as a strategic tool can not only measure but also improve critical HR issues, such as employee satisfaction, retention, compensation design, workforce planning, performance management and identification of employees for a future leadership role. HR analytics gather workforce data, prepare algorithms and feed the same in advanced computer models to get insights into the past, present and future trends for critical decision-making. For example, a typical decision to change incentive plan may be tested in advance using HR analytics, in terms of its positive or negative effect on talent retention. Such impact analysis in advance, therefore, ensures a better HR decision-making process. With improved HR decisions, organizations also benefit, as human resources can be made more business aligned.

With HR analytics, HR managers can analyse data to draw hiring strategies, highlight business opportunities and forge the best career paths for top performers. Today, HR analytics can gauge talent availability, predict talent retention and can objectively determine the implications of all HR decisions in advance. In August 2012, IBM bought talent management software provider Kenexa for a whopping $1.3 billion. SAP (with SuccessFactors) and Oracle (with Taleo) also made acquisitions to enter this field while smaller players such as Visier and Evolv gain ground with highly scalable, cloud-based tools. Therefore, HR analytics is an evolving and expanding field of HR decision-making process.

Two prominent examples of an HR decision-making process using HR analytics have been explained as follows:

1. **Talent retention:** This is one of the critical areas where HR analytics is now used for better decision-making. Often organizations feel that with hike in compensation and benefits, they would be able to retain talent. But this is an absolute misnomer. With HR metrics, HR scorecards and HR dashboards can assist here only by indicating the turnover rate, voluntary resignation rate or involuntary separation rate and so on. But we cannot understand these trends over time: across various departments or divisions or units in the organization, and between various group and levels of employees. Such insights cannot be obtained only through metrics; this requires HR analytics, usage of various predictive models and so on. With metrics, we can develop algorithms to determine what can help organization to improve talent retention.

2. **Performance-related pay (PRP):** This important area also requires help of HR analytics. PRP-related decisions rationalize distribution between fixed and variable pay, decide on important KPIs for performance measurement, allocate weights between individual and group performances, rationalize the total cost of compensation and so on. All these decisions on performance alignment with pay cannot be taken based on HR metrics alone. HR metrics in this case can only help us to document the pay differentials, i.e., the differences in pay between employees. But for aligning the business value with the pay, we require HR analytics. Also, with HR analytics, it is possible to optimize the pay at risk, balancing between fixed and variable pay.

In fact, for any HR-related decisions, wherever prediction is necessary, we see the importance of HR analytics. In other words, while HR metrics report transactional outcomes, HR analytics rationalizes HR decisions with fewer consequences of decisional error.

COMPELLING REASONS FOR HR ANALYTICS

Some of the compelling reasons for HR analytics can be elaborated as follows:

1. **Recognition of human resources' strategic and business roles:** For playing effective strategic and business roles, human resources has to make use of HR analytics, so that HR decisions do not just get rationalized with past data but can even become predictive. HR analysis today is predictive in nature, and this facilitates a more futuristic decision-making process, taking into account the decisional implications and its adjustment time to time. With past data, human resources can extrapolate using various models, and can predict implications of decisions, and thus can minimize the risk of wrong decisions that are not aligned with the strategic and business roles of organizations.

2. **Demand for ROI:** All HR decisions one way or the other bring incremental change in the performance and productivity of organizations. Measuring such incremental change within terms of the ROI is possible with HR analytics. Moreover, use of HR analytics requires investment; obviously, pay back from investment can be measured once we measure the ROI. Some of the incremental changes, after making use of HR analytics, other than employees' performance and productivity, are: market capitalization, customers' satisfaction, talent retention and so on. Even because of decisional accuracy, we have seen more objective performance evaluation, better transparency in management and increased employees' happiness and engagement.

3. **Meaningful utilization of HR data:** HR record-keeping as a system is prevalent in organizations for quite some time. So far, such HR data were kept more for compliance reasons. Now, human resources can also make best use of these data to get greater insights into organizational work, and accordingly can make HR decisions more business focused and strategic.

4. **Need for driving business-focused results:** Putting analytics in the context of business goals and outcomes, human resources can become strategic, proactive and predictive. This makes the holistic understanding of business possible and can focus on all HR activities towards business success.

5. **Achieving team effectiveness:** With HR analytics, as we can connect HR activities with HR outcomes, we can make our teams more focused on the right things, which can make visible improvement in business results.

6. **Gaining better relationships:** Capabilities of HR analytics for assessing business impact helps in aligning human resources with other activities of organizations, and in the process, it can improve the quality of HR decisions.

7. **Efficient executive reporting:** HR analytics being helpful in reporting HR activities in terms of business outcomes can make executive reporting systems and so also communication more efficient.

8. **Enhancing credibility and influence of human resources in organizations:** With HR analytics HR managers can enhance their decision-making skills and can quickly communicate their decisions to the top management with details of results outcomes. Obviously, this enhances their credibility and increases their influence in the organizations.

An HR analytics model developed based on the industry practices is presented in Box 4.1.

Box 4.1   HR Analytics Model

Objectives and Business Goals

Articulate and prioritize business objectives, goals and desired outcomes.

Metrics

Identify metrics that align to objectives.

Segmentation

Segment metrics by key demographics (job, location, performance, tenure and so on).

Insight

Identify meaningful patterns, areas of opportunity, hotspots and anomalies that are out of alignment with objectives.

Action

Take action to drive improvement and achieve business outcomes.

PRACTICE ASSIGNMENT

Discuss with examples how human resources is a business process for an organization?

Summary

HR business partnership role is now acknowledged in the corporate world. This necessitated the need for managing human resources as a business process function.

To make sense of data, HR managers use statistical analysis, which involves collection, analysis, interpretation and presentation of data for decision-making and also for predicting the future.

HR research helps us in understanding how organizations are structured and functions; how decisions are made; what factors affect organizational operations and finally what strategies are important for gaining sustainable competitive advantages.

HR research can be either quantitative or qualitative. Quantitative data are gathered through experimental/clinical trials, observations and recording of events, collection of data from databases such as ERP and MIS, survey reports and so on. Qualitative research covers historical data analysis and even collection of narrative data for understanding phenomena through discourse analysis.

After data collection for HR research and HR decisions, we need to organize and summarize data primarily with two statistical techniques, i.e., measurement of central tendency and measurement of dispersion.

HRIS can be used as DSS for human resources. We define it as the composite of databases for collecting, recording, storing, managing, delivering, presenting and manipulating data for human resources.

For measuring HR performances, HR metrics are used. HR metrics can report present, ongoing and year-on-year information on HR performances, even in strategic areas such as employee attrition, employee engagement and performance, incentives and employees' performance, training and employees' performance and so on.

HR scorecard provides a framework for measuring human resources. It is designed with the balanced scorecard measurement framework of the organization.

HR analytics, making use of HR metrics, can develop algorithms for HR decisions in alignment with the business goals and strategies of the organizations. HR analytics gather HR data from multiple sources, and then develop algorithms for predictive HR decisions.

General Review Questions

1. Discuss why human resources is a business process.

2. Explain how HR research results can help in HR decision-making process. Give your answer with some examples.

3. What are the different HR research tools and techniques?

4. Discuss the use of statistics and statistical modelling for an HR decision-making process.

5. Why data analysis is important for human resources? How data analysis relates to an HR decision-making process?

6. Define HRIS. Explain how HRIS can help in HR decision-making.

7. Elaborate on HR metrics. Develop some HR metrics for compensation and benefits management function.

8. Explain how an HR scorecard is developed in an organization. Design a scorecard for talent management function.

9. What is HR analytics? How it is different from HR metrics?

10. Write short notes on the following:
    - Dashboard
    - Employee champion role of human resources
    - Change agent role of human resources
    - Business partnership role of human resources
    - Quartile deviation
    - New hire performance ratio

Multiple Choice Questions

1. Key roles of human resources include the following, except

   a. Strategic
   b. Political
   c. Administrative
   d. Employee champion
   e. Change agent

2. Identify the incorrect statement out of the following:

   a. Strategic role of human resources requires helps in strategy framing and strategy execution
   b. Change agent role of human research manages cultural and transformational changes in organizations
   c. Administrative role contributes to achieve organizational efficiency
   d. Political role helps in conflict resolution
   e. Employee championship role helps in trading off between employee needs and organizational needs

3. HR activities as a business process consider

   a. HRP and recruitment
   b. Employee development and succession planning
   c. Employee development and learning management
   d. Only (a) and (b)
   e. All (a), (b) and (c)

4. Identify the incorrect statement out of the following:

   a. Human resources is a support process for organizations
   b. All other processes of organizations are not customers to HR business
   c. Human resources automatically maximizes its contributions to business objectives
   d. It contributes to strategies of organizations
   e. Like all other business processes, the HR process also continuously evolves

5. Statistical analysis for human resources involves the following, other than

   a. Data collection
   b. Data analysis
   c. Data interpretation
   d. Data presentation
   e. Data manipulation

6. Indicate which of the following is not a part of inferential statistics:

   a. Finding patterns and relationships in data
   b. Describing the existing data using measures such as average, sum and so on.
   c. Statistical testing
   d. Using various statistical models
   e. None of the above

7. Research in recruitment and selection can significantly help in future decision-making on following issues, other than

   a. How best can we attract talents
   b. What can ensure better diversity

    c.   How can we optimize recruitment costs
    d.   How likely the recruited person will be in generation Z
    e.   How likely the recruited person will perform

8. In career development research, we consider the following, except

    a.   Career mapping
    b.   Job sculpting
    c.   Succession planning
    d.   Future leadership development
    e.   Integrating career development with OD initiatives

9. Quantitative HR data are gathered through

    a.   Experimental/clinical trials
    b.   Observations and recording of events
    c.   Collection of data from databases
    d.   Collection of data from survey reports
    e.   All of the above

10. Qualitative HR data denote

    a.   Historical data analysis
    b.   Collection of narrative data
    c.   Data through discourse analysis
    d.   All of the above
    e.   None of the above

11. Indicate which of the following is not a measurement level:

    a.   Nominal
    b.   Diagonal
    c.   Ordinal
    d.   Interval
    e.   Ratio

12. Identify the incorrect statement out of the following:

    a.   Nominal measurement is the study of a single object
    b.   It is the classification of objects in two or more categories
    c.   Nominal measurement is a categorical measurement
    d.   Ordinal measurement classifies objects in order from the highest to the lowest, from the most to the least
    e.   Interval measurement combines the characteristics of both nominal and ordinal measurements

13. Indicate which of the following is the measurement of dispersion:

    a.   Mean
    b.   Median
    c.   Range
    d.   Mode
    e.   Standard Deviation

14. Indicate which of the following is the measurement of central tendency:

    a.   Quartile deviation
    b.   Standard deviation
    c.   Square root of the variance
    d.   Mid-value
    e.   Range

15. Identify the incorrect statement out of the following:

   a. Measurement of the relative position indicates the performance score of an employee in relation to others
   b. It helps in understanding how well an employee has performed compared to others
   c. Two most frequently used measures of relative positions are percentile ranks and standard error
   d. A percentile rank indicates the percentage of scores that fall at or below a given score
   e. If a score of 65 corresponds to the 80th percentile, it means that 80 percent of the scores in the distribution are lower than 65

16. Most commonly reported and used standard scores are

   a. z-scores
   b. t-scores
   c. stanines
   d. Only (a) and (b)
   e. All (a), (b) and (c)

17. Indicate which of the following is not an objective of HRIS:

   a. Planning and policy formulation
   b. Monitoring and evaluation
   c. Providing inputs to strategic decision-making
   d. Data analysis and interpretation
   e. None of the above

18. Indicate which of the following is not a part of recruitment metrics:

   a. Recruiting cost ratio
   b. Recruiting efficiency ratio
   c. New hire performance ratio
   d. Recruitment success ratio
   e. None of the above

19. Identify which of the following is not a perspective of balanced scorecard:

   a. Financial
   b. External process
   c. Internal process
   d. Customer
   e. Learning and growth

20. Indicate which of the following is not a relevant statement for an HR scorecard:

   a. It provides a frame for measuring human resources
   b. It is independent of balanced scorecard
   c. Value-based HR metrics can be a part of an HR scorecard
   d. HR outcome measures can be a part of an HR scorecard
   e. Operational HR metrics can be a part of an HR scorecard

21. Indicate which of the following is not a sequence of actions for developing an HR scorecard:

   a. Develop a strategy
   b. Map the strategy
   c. Establish measures for each strategy
   d. Cascade it to a scorecard
   e. None of the above

22. Indicate which of the following is not a compelling reason for HR analytics:

   a. Recognition of strategic and business roles of human resources
   b. Demand for an ROI
   c. Achieving individual excellence
   d. Meaningful utilization of HR data
   e. Enhancing credibility and influence of human resources in organizations

Critical Review Question

1. Identify a hypothetical HR research issue. Explain how you will collect data for the proposed research. How you will analyse and draw inferences? In what way your research results can help in HR decision-making in the hypothetical organization.

PRACTITIONER SPEAKS

You want to design an HR dashboard on performance management issues for the sales force of your organization. Based on your identified list of issues, choose at least two important issues and design an illustrative dashboard.

CASE STUDY

HR Scorecard of Verizon

With 173,300 employees, the US-based communications major Verizon today operates from 150 countries. One of the topmost companies in diversity inclusive employment practices, Verizon built its HR scorecard keeping pace with its business strategies. To ensure an HR scorecard encapsulates compelling strategic and critical business issues, Verizon had prepared its own checklists with series of questions. The process of HR scorecard development was started by the company well before 1998, primarily to articulate how HR activities can be aligned with the business strategy. Since then, the company continues with its HR scorecard development process building some measurement indicators for understanding human resources' contribution to business strategies. In between, Verizon's business landscape was changing from monopoly to competition, which required the total transformation of the business process. Some of the issues that influenced organizational transformation, in addition to transition from monopoly to competition, were as follows: technology, stakeholders' interest, new market opportunities, increasing customers' expectations, mergers and acquisitions, challenge of talent attraction and retention and so on. All these changes, the company felt have people dimensions; hence, they need to be addressed with people-imperative strategies.

The process of development of an HR scorecard started with the assessment of skills and competencies so as to know what would be the requirements for the present year and for 3–5 years down the line. The leadership development process was accelerated with the identification of potential future leaders and building their capabilities for future leadership roles. For this purpose, the company segmented its competency development programme in three different types: current, enhanced and new. Current competencies are those that already exist. Enhanced competencies are those that exist but require sharpening. New competencies are those which are required for future leadership roles.

Such competency requirements have been tabulated for better clarity in the following table:

Current Competencies	Enhanced Competencies	New Competencies
Network management	Leadership	Shared mindset
Customer support	Partnering with unions	Marketing and distribution
International management	Customer relationship management	Data management
Financial control	Team work	Alliance management
Operational control	Innovation	Integration capability

With such stratification of competencies, the company meaningfully developed a scorecard in alignment with its business and strategies.

Question: Emulating the example of Verizon, illustrate the case of a large manufacturing organization (chosen by you) in designing a business-focused HR scorecard for some identified new set of competencies.

REFERENCES

Becker, B. E., Huselid, M. A., & Ulrich, D. (2001). *The HR scorecard: Linking people, strategy and performance.* Boston, MA: Harvard Business School Press.

Beer, M. (1997). The transformation of the human resource function: Resolving the tension between a traditional administrative role and a new strategic role. *Human Resource Management, 36*(1), 49–56.

Broderick, R., & Boudreau, J. W. (1992). Human resource management, information technology and the competitive edge. *Academy of Management Executive, 6*(2), 7–17.

Brown, D., Caldwell, R., White, K., Atkinson, H., Tansley, T., Goodge, P., & Emmott, M. (2004). *Business partnering, a new direction for HR.* London: CIPD.

Cakar, F., Bititci, Umit S., & MacBryde, J. (2003). A business process approach to human resource management. *Business Process Management Journal, 9*(2), 190–207.

Fitz-enz, J. (1984). How to measure Human Resources Management. New York: McGraw-Hill.

Fitz-enz, J. & Davidson, B. (2002). *How to measure human resources management* (3rd ed.). New York: McGraw-Hill.

Huselid, M. A. (1995). The impact of human resource management practices on turnover, productivity, and corporate performance. *Academy of Management Journal, 38*(3), 635–672.

Kaplan, R. S., & Norton, D. P. (1996). *The balanced score card: Translating strategy into action.* Boston, MA: Harvard Business School Press.

Keegan, A., & Francis, H. (2010). Practitioner talk: The changing text space of HRM and emergency of HR business partnership. *The International Journal of Human Resource Management, 21*(6), 873–898.

Storey, J. (1992). *Developments in the management of human resources*. Oxford: Blackwell.

Torrington, D., Hall, L., & Taylor, S. (2005). *Human resource management* (6th ed.). Upper Saddle River, NJ: Prentice Hall.

Tyson, S. (1995). *Human resource strategy*. Upper Saddle River, NJ: Prentice Hall.

Ulrich, D. (1997). *Human resource champions: The next agenda for adding value and delivering results.* Cambridge, MA: Harvard Business School Press.

Ulrich, D., & Brockbank, W. (2005). *The HR value proposition.* Cambridge, MA: Harvard Business School Press.

FURTHER READING

Fitz-enz, J. (1995). *How to measure human resources management* (2nd ed.). New York: McGraw-Hill.

APPENDIX

Predictive Statistical Tools

In this section, we have discussed on two important predictive statistical tools which can be commonly used in HR analytics for predictive decision modelling. These are:

Learning curve

The learning curve concept was developed by T. P. Wright (1936). It is believed that by doing same job repetitively, employees and so also organizations become efficient over time, which obviously exerts influence on HR decisions. Using the learning curve, we can measure the change in the productivity level for future production. With this understanding we can calculate change in per unit man-hour requirement for the future units, and can accordingly predict the future labour cost. For example, an 80-percent learning curve indicates:

- The first unit takes 8 labour hours.
- The second unit takes 80 percent of 8 hours, i.e., 6.4 hours.

Likewise, labour hours will proportionately decrease for subsequent units.

In HR analytics, a learning curve can predict the proportionate reduction in headcounts or man-hours and consequent reduction in labour costs. We have certain assumptions of a learning curve. These are:

- Reduction in time in completing a task will decrease in direct proportion to the number of times the task is done.
- Decrease in time will decrease at a decreasing rate.
- Decrease in time will show a predictable pattern.

The usual learning curve model is $Y = ax^b$, where
Y = average time per unit of x units
a = time taken for the first unit
x = cumulative number of units
b = learning coefficient.

Illustration

A company manufacturing transmission towers has experienced an 85 percent learning curve. The company would like to compute the labour hours required to manufacture the 50th unit when it takes 3,000 hours for manufacturing the first unit.

Solution

$Y = 3000 \ (50)^b$
'b' coefficient is = –0.23446, i.e. (log 0.85/log 2 = –0.07058/0.30103)
Hence, $Y = 3000 \times 50 – 0.23446$
Log 3000 – 0.23446 (log 50) = 3.07878
Antilog of 3.07879 is 1198.8918 hours.

Hence, labour hours required for manufacturing the 50th unit would be 1,199 hours, considering the learning curve rate of 85 percent. Obviously, for this reason, manpower requirement will also vary and so also the labour cost will decrease considerably.

Using Excel, SPSS and other analytics solutions, learning curve results can be obtained at a faster rate.

Net Present Value (NPV) Methods

Using the learning curve as the base, we can account for the value-adding capabilities of human resources. However, to do the same, we need to consider the discounted cash flow method with the application of the NPV technique. This helps us to price the human assets. From the basic logic of financial management, we know that the higher the NPV of an individual employee, the better the ROI. Hence, if an employee with higher NPV leaves the job, the company suffers the risk of notional loss, as replacement may not contribute the matching NPV. In such cases, the company tries to retain, as retention is more cost-effective. To understand the relative worth of employees, we consider the time value of money, based on discounted cash flow, using the formula as follows:

$$NPV = \sum_{t=0}^{N} (C_t) \div (1 + r)^t$$

where N = work cycle span of employees (in years) after recruitment,
t = timing of cash flow (year);
r = interest rate, or discount rate;
and C_t = cash flow in year t.

Now fitting data in the equation, we can predict the NPV. The NPV, using the expected values (EV), helps us understand the cost–benefit analysis of our retention strategies, based on which we can decide whether we should retain employees or not, when they decide to resign.

Like a learning curve the NPV for calculating the EV of employees can be obtained using different HR analytics solutions.

CHAPTER 5

FORECASTING AND MEASURING HR VALUE PROPOSITIONS WITH HR ANALYTICS

LEARNING OBJECTIVES:

After reading this chapter, you will be able to understand:

- Concepts of value propositions and HR decisions
- Sustainability in HR decisions
- HR analytics and HR value propositions
- HR optimization through HR analytics
- HR forecasting, HR plan and HR analytics
- Predictive HR analytics

INTRODUCTORY CASE

Making Effective Use of Predictive HR Analytics: Lessons from Starwood

Starwood, a US-based hotel and leisure company with headcounts of 188,000, operates from 100 countries and has 1,300 properties. For Starwood, the challenge was to relate their leadership and culture to their business results. This necessitated the validation of their leadership competency model and studying how this model can influence business outcomes. The idea behind this was to identify impactful leadership behaviours that can positively contribute to enhance guest loyalty and company's business performance. The company could achieve this with HR predictive analytics designing the leadership competencies model, encapsulating behavioural attributes and designing a 360-degree feedback software. This software could help the company to account for behavioural performance in terms of three important parameters, i.e., employee engagement, guest loyalty and revenue per available room. After collating the data, with statistical analysis, the company could successfully come out with a desired leadership team profile. Such leadership team profile was used by the company for incubating in-house leaders and also for future hiring decisions. Lessons learnt by the company in this process were relationships between leadership behaviour with the employee engagement and guest loyalty. With higher guest loyalty, they also could enhance the revenue per room.

INTRODUCTION

Linking HR strategies to organizational strategies and ultimately to business goals of organizations is a step towards making HR functions more relevant for organizations. Through a strategy, we articulate a plan for the optimization of results, including human resources for achieving organizational goals. This requires HR managers to acquire knowledge in understanding the process of internalizing business goals and objectives as their own objectives, thorough the understanding of organizational strategies, and design HR practices with a business focus: understanding of key business drivers, customers' needs and expectations (more importantly customers' value propositions) and looking at the business from 'outside in' (Ulrich & Brockbank, 2005). With such understanding, HR managers can link HR strategy and HR practices with the organizational business and gradually can develop human resources' **value propositions**. The journey of HR analytics starts from here, as HR managers need to speak business with numbers, the financial implications of HR decisions and so on through operational measurements. Obviously, all of these can be done by HR managers once it is possible to measure customers' satisfaction, financial results, operations, organizational change process and so on, relating the same with HR value proposition.

Value proposition:
It indicates a clear statement on the specific differentiating value of a service or product. Through a value proposition statement, an organization can communicate to its stakeholders' unique value-generating features.

Based on our inputs from previous chapters, now it is clear that HR analytics does not collate employee data for decision-making. HR analytics requires gaining insights into different HR processes of organizations and their alignment with business, with ultimate focus on the improvement of HR processes and the overall performance of organizations. For better insights, in this chapter, we have first clarified HR value propositions and HR sustainability, and then discussed how we can strengthen these two with HR analytics, which ultimately contributes to organizational success.

VALUE PROPOSITION AND HR DECISIONS

Value proposition indicates a clear statement on the specific differentiating value of a service or product. Through a value proposition statement, an organization can communicate to its stakeholders' unique value-generating features. The concept of value proposition enunciates its key role in business strategy (Payne & Frow, 2014). Kaplan and Norton (2001) argued that value proposition is the core essence of strategy. Likewise, we see the contribution of various other research scholars, such as Lehmann and Winer (2008) and Collis and Rukstad (2008), could also see value proposition as core strategy. Also, through the statement on value proposition, companies can describe their distinctive competitive advantages. For customers, it is a promise of value combining benefits and price (Lanning & Michaels, 1988). Through a value proposition statement, companies also clarify how they are achieving differentiation from their competitors. While developing a value proposition statement, companies can make use of either of the approaches: benefits, favourable differences and resonating focuses (Anderson et al., 2006). Benefits denote benefits to the customers; favourable differences denote differentiating benefits that a company offers over its competitors, while resonating focuses indicate company's most-valued key benefits from the customers' point of view. From marketing and customers' focused approach to value proposition, gradually we could see its application to all other stakeholders (Bhattacharya & Korschun, 2008).

In HRM value propositions focus on attraction and retention of talent (Chambers et al., 1988; Heger, 2007). Value propositions of HRM also enable employees to assess comparative benefits that they can enjoy over other organizations in terms of compensation and benefits, corporate brand value and so on (Bell, 2005).

In human resources, companies' value proposition helps in attracting talent. Unless human resources creates value proposition for the employees to make them understand how their organization is different from others, there may be the problem of retention of employees, more particularly the talented employees. For a job offer, value proposition from human resources' side could be a competitive compensation, enabling work culture, opportunity to acquire new knowledge, opportunity for career development and so on.

Ulrich and Brockbank (2005) could observe that human resources can add value when human resources extends help to employees in reaching their goals. Having employee-friendly policies, well-designed career development programmes and market competitive compensation designs are not enough. HR value proposition requires proactive HR practices that can generate values to the employees and other stakeholders. Once human resources is able to create value propositions, it can increase the influence on organizations and that can also enhance human resources' legitimacy for business partnership role. This can create a 'line of sight' for human resources with all stakeholders of an organization. In fact, the future role of human resources is becoming more focused on value creation; hence, mere concentration on transactional work cannot legitimize human resources' business partnership role. With value propositions, HR deliverables can create competitive advantages for organizations; hence, managing human resources today is more challenging for its critical impact on stakeholders' value. HR value propositions are essentially intangibles and their impact on the business performance of organizations is clearly seen. These are research and development, innovation and creativity, leadership, organizational brand identity, tacit knowledge, employee commitment and loyalty and so on.

Ulrich and Brockbank (2005) argue that, in future, human resources has to focus on more value-generating pursuits, with specific transformation in the following areas:

1. Beginning HR work with a business focus and emphasizing value creation for key stakeholders.
2. Creating a line of sight for human resources, so that all stakeholders can trace human resources in their value consideration.

3. Positioning human resources as a source of competitive advantage in terms of building of individual and organizational capabilities that are better than organizational competitors.
4. Aligning human resources with the needs of internal and external stakeholders.
5. Acquiring required knowledge and skills essential for linking human resources to stakeholders' value. This requires appropriate articulation as to how human resources adds value.
6. Spelling out as to how human resources has unique value propositions that align with the employees' commitment, customers' loyalty and shareholders' returns.

Likewise, we also see HR value proposition can be enhanced when we systematically map it to develop an HR mental model. This can make human resources more visible and credible to stakeholders, and can objectively assess human resources' value addition to business. Some of the identified HR competencies that can make a difference in adding stakeholder value are capability to frame a culture-based HR strategy, change management, business decision-making, designing of organizational structure, managing learning and development and so on.

ANALYTICS HIGHLIGHT

For HRD, one of the strategic functions of human resources, the business process models start with strategy framing, aligning with the goals and objectives of an organization. After strategy framing, HRD business process focuses on training needs assessment (TNA) to draw the training calendar in various functions. An HRD business process, thereafter, accounts for the budgeting to assess whether training programmes listed in the training calendar can be offered or not. Accordingly, HRD business process finalizes the training calendar trading off between the needs and the budget constraints. Finally, the HRD business process implements the envisaged strategy drawn right in the beginning.

Based on the earlier discussions, we can understand that value propositions no longer emphasize single customers' or marketing perspective. Value propositions need to be seen from all stakeholders' perspectives. It is co-created, reciprocal and dynamic (Ballantyne et al., 2011; Kowalkowski et al., 2012).

With the establishment of the importance of HR value proposition, organizations increasingly felt the need for measurable tools that can help in identifying or tracing HR values for stakeholders to understand. For human resources also, business partnership role is challenging, and this cannot be legitimized unless human resources is able to showcase its importance with some meaningful value proposition statements. All these necessitated the need for HR analytics.

SUSTAINABILITY IN HR DECISIONS

It has already been acknowledged by several researchers (Arthur, 1994; Boselie, 2010; Delery and Doty, 1996; Guthrie, 2001; Huselid, 1995) that HRM practices are positively linked with organizational performance. However, some researchers viewed that HRM practices are more focused on enhancing financial outcomes (Boudreau, 2003). This obviously reduced HRM practices as a ploy exploiting human resources, rather than developing and reproducing (Mariappanadar, 2012). In this context, we find the relevance of sustainability approaches in managing human resources in organizations. Sustainability acknowledges the need for triple bottom line effect, i.e., economic, ecological and social aspects (Elkington, 1997). Ehnert (2009), for the first time, acknowledged the need for sustainability in HRM practices. This is embedded in two arguments as propounded by Ehnert and Harry (2012). The first argument emphasizes the need for HRM's social consideration, as organization operates in a given economic and social environment, while the second argument centres around the premises that HRM has to embed sustainability approach in managing human resources with an approach of reproducibility because of scarcity of human resources. In line with Ehnert (2011), **HRM sustainability** has to be seen in three different contexts, i.e., sustainable work systems, sustainable resource management and sustainable HRM. Sustainable work systems acknowledge sustainability as the social responsibility. Sustainable work systems need to focus on HRD rather than human resource exploitation. Sustainable resource management intends to guide us to the ways and means of managing scarce resources. Finally, sustainable HRM sees sustainability in the context of mutual benefits for all stakeholders.

HRM sustainability: Sustainable HRM sees sustainability in the context of mutual benefits of all stakeholders. It emphasizes the reproducibility of human resources through its nurturing and development.

Acknowledging HRM is a means and the end to realizing organizational strategic objectives (Huselid et al., 2005), Taylor et al. (2012) argued sustainability is important for HRM on two important counts. First, with sustainability approach, HRM can have direct influence on the employees' attitude and actions in achieving sustainability goals, i.e., treating HRM as a means. Second, with the embedded concept of sustainability in HRM, organizations can ensure long-term physical, social and economic well-being of human resources, i.e., considering HRM as an end.

Organizations go for sustainable HRM practices primarily for three important reasons (Ehnert, 2009), i.e., normative, efficiency-oriented and substance-oriented. The normative approach acknowledges the importance of relationships between the business and society. Efficiency-oriented approach integrates organizational resources (including human resources) with social and economic objectives, while the substance-oriented approach understands decision-making processes differentiating between consumption and reproduction of human resources.

Based on aforementioned arguments, we can say human resources today needs to look into the overall business sustainability for adding value to organizations. But this can only be made possible when an HR decision-making process gets powered by HR analytics.

HR ANALYTICS AND HR VALUE PROPOSITIONS

HR analytics is defined as the application of data mining and techniques of business analytics in HRM practices, more particularly in an HR decision-making process. It helps in managing human resources with a business focus, and thus, can help organizations to achieve strategic and business goals. For effective use of HR analytics, human resources has to decide, first, the nature of data that need to be collected, fitting such data to algorithms and models for predicting how a specific HR decision can benefit organizations in terms of achieving business results, optimizing the ROI on human resources. Often, we see organizations restrict their data search only to employee efficiency, which is not correct. It may be one of the requirements of HR analytics, but more holistically, the scope of data collection for HR analytics may even extend beyond HR functions for getting better insights into HR processes so that HR processes, and so also HR decisions, can be more organizational, and business and strategy aligned. Along with the data (which may be even cross-functional), HR analytics require the use of software for developing predictive decision models and algorithm. We have many software vendors for HR analytics. Again software alone cannot ensure effective use of HR analysis; with software, HR managers need to develop the skill on mining and interpreting data. They need not be data scientists but at least must have understanding of the process of data mining and data interpretation. Many large organizations separately engage data scientists to be involved in HR analytics for HR department. But in mid-size and smaller organizations, requirements are different.

Often we use the term big data to characterize HR analytics. Big data, according to Gartner (2012), is high-volume, high-velocity and high-variety data, processing which we can enhance our decisions, get better insights into organizational functions and even can go for process optimization. We process big data using HR analytics. From this perspective, HR analytics is a tool for analysing big data.

The use of HR analytics, and even the age-old HR metrics today in organizations, encompasses all HR decision-making processes such as recruitment and selection, compensation and benefits plan, succession planning, training and development, talent management, performance management, employee engagement and retention and so on. But we see that in talent management the use of HR analytics is more, because organizations today manage their human resources as HC (more with an investment focus), which could make HR functions more development driven.

Often, we use the term talent analytics, instead of HR analytics. In Chapter 6, we have discussed about talent analytics.

HR analytics can effectively contribute to HR value propositions, as it can help in objectively measuring the value of human resources to organizations. Without HR analytics, human resources still contribute to organizational value, but the line of sight gets lost. Some of the important HR value propositions that can be objectively measured by HR analytics are as follows:

1. Effective talent management, in terms of talent attraction, recruitment, development and retention, for enhanced organizational performance
2. Effective HRP
3. Effective management of employee attrition, duly identifying the reasons and initiating the corrective actions
4. Effective career planning and development
5. Effective management of recruitment function
6. Effective performance management
7. Effective management of compensation and benefits programme
8. Effectively positioning human resources as an important enabler for driving business performance

The aforementioned list is not exhaustive, rather tentative. Literally, HR analytics can manage all HR costs and investment functions, provide inputs for strategy framing and contribute in achieving business goals.

Commonly known HR analytics suites are talent analytics, workforce analytics and planning, and so on. **Talent analytics suite** includes all talent management functions, such as recruitment, succession planning, development and retention. Workforce analytics suite usually covers recruitment methods and decisions, organizational structure optimization, job satisfaction measurement, employee motivation and future leadership development actions. In general, this suite helps in achieving excellence in work systems. **Workforce analytics suite** and planning suite essentially help in HRP.

Talent analytics suite: It includes all talent management functions, such as recruitment, succession planning, development and retention.

Workforce analytics suite: It usually covers recruitment methods and decisions, organizational structure optimization, job satisfaction measurement, employee motivation and future leadership development actions.

Irrespective of the nature of HR analytics suites, the primary role of HR analytics is to get human resources recognized as a strategic enabler. Obviously, this needs human resources to build their capabilities in terms of defining and communicating their value, i.e., preparing solid statements on HR value propositions.

HR OPTIMIZATION THROUGH HR ANALYTICS

With HR analytics, we can also achieve HR optimization with a holistic understanding of the organizational strategy, processes, structure, skills and performance measures. HR optimization can significantly add value to the organization. To develop an HR optimization plan with the use of

HR analytics, we require developing and analysing a potential methodology, deciding on the future plan for HR optimization, drawing plan for implementation and provisioning for review and monitoring for future improvement right in the beginning.

Some of the areas of HR optimization through HR analytics are as follows:

- Defining human resources' vision and mission aligning with the business goals and overall strategy of the organizations
- Unleashing the value of HC
- Unleashing talent and leveraging potentiality of employees
- Strengthening human resources' role as a strategic advisor in organizational business
- Focusing more on business partnership role
- Benchmarking and calibrating HR practices in line with the best-practice organizations
- Developing a world-class HR service delivery model

All these are the important areas of focus for achieving HR optimization at the organization level. These are in addition to cost optimization in all HR operations and processes, as this also forms important part of HR value propositions.

HR FORECASTING, HR PLAN AND HR ANALYTICS

HR forecasting: It focuses on measuring the implications of human resources on organizational strategy. HR forecasting is done considering the effects of various economic, technological and organizational forces on the human resources and this requires some structured steps such as framing a business strategy, relating business strategy with various HR scenarios, assessing demand and supply of human resources, assessing the cultural issues, developing the HR forecast and, finally, translating HR forecast into an HR plan.

HR forecasting primarily focuses on measuring implications of human resources on organizational strategy. HR forecasting is done considering the effects of various economic, technological and organizational forces on the human resources, and this requires some structured steps such as framing a business strategy, relating business strategy with various HR scenarios, assessing demand and supply of human resources, assessing the cultural issues, developing the HR forecast and, finally, translating HR forecast into an HR plan. Thus, an HR plan is the end result of HR forecast, and once the plan is developed, human resources has to allocate resources to execute plan. With HR plan, HR managers weigh various strategic options, analysing various HR data and information, ranging from data on manpower, HR costs, talent retention and information on culture, training and learning and so on. Also, the HR plan needs to be dynamic, as it is based on the organizational strategy, and organizational strategy is also influenced by various unpredictabilities. These require the use of HR analytics as it has the feature of predictability.

HR plan, being inseparable from organizational business plan, has to be systematically reviewed and changed. Some of the components of HR plan are as follows:

1. HR plan for the headcounts. This is a quantitative plan which optimizes headcounts with the business strategy of an organization.
2. HR plan for organizational design and development. Such a plan considers options of organizational structures, both for the present

and future, and plan for various organizational development initiatives to support such structure.

3.   HR acquisitions plan. This plan helps in framing recruitment strategies, which even extends to internal recruitment plans, redeployment plans, relocation plans, retention plans, redundancy plans and so on.

4.   HR development plan. It helps in designing the training and development plan, measuring the ROI from employee development programmes and so on.

5.   HR compensation and reward plan. This helps in aligning compensation and reward with performance to value meritocracy; benchmarking and calibrating compensation and reward time to time; and budgeting for the compensation and reward.

6.   HR engagement plan. It helps to ensure the engagement of human resources with the organization and involves a plan for the employee attitudinal survey and so on.

This is a tentative list of HR forecasts and plans, depending on the nature of organizations and the strategic requirement; we may have different other types of HR plans and forecasts as well.

ANALYTICS HIGHLIGHT

We do not have any single approach to develop a strategic HRP model. It is absolutely organization specific. However, some of the generic steps for a strategic HRP model can be listed as follows:

1. Understanding strategic direction of the organization
2. Developing HRIS
3. Planning for the human resources
4. Understanding the possible sources of acquisition of human resources
5. Investing on developing human resources
6. Sustaining the culture of performance

Some of the reasons for HR plans and forecasts are appropriate accounting of employees' contributions to organizational success, aligning HR strategies with the organizational strategies, HRP and developing business-focused plan for HRM. With effective HR plans and forecasts, organizations can optimize HR utilization, ensure high degree of commitment from human resources and effectively train human resources to help them sustain in future.

With HR analytics, HR plans and forecasts can be done more effectively.

PRACTICE ASSIGNMENT

Discuss how HR optimization can be achieved through HR analytics with specific reference to any organization.

PREDICTIVE HR ANALYTICS

Predictive HR analytics, through statistical relationships, can align HR actions with the achievement or otherwise of the organizational strategic goals. This helps HR managers to evaluate the future implications of their decisions and accordingly develop a long-term strategy. Predictive HR analytics, unlike HR analytics, per se, can base HR decisions envisaging the future risks and can, therefore, enhance human resources' importance in organizations. Human resources also can increase value propositions and emerge as a strategic business partner for organizations. Like general HR analytics suites, mentioned earlier, here also we find important predictive analytics suites for human resources, such as talent acquisition and resource management, workforce administration, performance and learning and so on.

The use of predictive analytics in business decisions for hedging risk and achieving better customer relationship management have been all along there in organizations. Customer retention, sales forecasting, pricing, supply chain management, credit score analysis and cash flow analysis are some of the known fields for predictive analytics. In human resources, predictive analytics requires data that are business aligned, as this can then help in assessing the business implications of HR decisions and improving the quality of HR decisions to reinforce strategic business outcomes of organizations. HR decisions with predictive analytics are based on predictive models that are again developed using statistical techniques. Some of the key areas where human resources can take decisions based on predictive modelling are as follows:

- **Segmenting and profiling of employees:** This helps in understanding the employees better. Based on this analysis, we can also assess the type of future requirement of manpower. With predictive analytics, we can identify specific employees with appropriate skill sets and deploy them in appropriate jobs. Combining the demographic data with the respective job roles, we can segment employees and understand how such employee segments help in achieving future expectations of organizations, can know to what extent this employee segment can contribute in some new project assignment, with what type of training this segment of employees can assume future leadership roles and so on.
- **Analysis of employee loyalty and attrition:** With predictive models, we can measure the attrition of risk of a particular employee and initiate appropriate action right in the beginning so that such identified employees gradually become loyal to the organization. The attrition risk score of individual employees can be estimated with predictive models of attrition. This can help organizations prevent the potential attrition of high-performing employees, ensure business continuation and identify loyal employees. For such predictive models, we require demographic data of employees and data on their performance, compensation and benefits, social media participation, recognition, training, behavioural data, employee's

attitudinal survey and so on. With the identification of the reasons for attrition, it is possible for human resources to initiate an appropriate action to stop its occurrence. Integrating attrition risk scores with the employee's performance data, human resources can identify potential risks for on time interventions. Transforming such employees to commit for the organization and become loyal require human resources again to draw a suitable employee engagement programme.

- **Analysis of recruitment needs:** Through predictive analytics, HR managers can draw recruitment plans, design suitable onboarding programmes, draw plan for job placement, training and other supports. All these are necessary for manpower resource optimization. Accurate forecasting of manpower needs can ensure effective sourcing of manpower, keeping pace both with the present and future needs. Predictive analytics can estimate future needs, factoring projected or predicted rate of attrition and the business growth. Data required for this type of predictive analysis are attrition risk score, forecasted business growth, number of employees, their performance trend and productivity level and so on. Fitting all these data in the predictive models, HR managers can come out with appropriate estimate, matching with organizational needs. Since the predictive analysis can even estimate attrition at the individual employee level, it also helps in drawing a manpower replacement plan well in advance.

Along with the recruitment needs analysis, predictive analytics can also help in appropriate profile selection. This requires analysis of existing employees' data on performance, productivity, attrition risk scores and value. With such analysis, human resources can design suitable profiles, and matching with the same, they can take effective recruitment decisions. With appropriate profiles selection, the risk of wrong recruitment can be suitably reduced.

In addition to the aforementioned details, predictive analytics can help in employee sentiment analysis, employee risk analysis and so on. Employee sentiment analysis is considered more powerful in terms of accuracy than employee survey. This analysis is done collating information from different sources. It helps in adopting suitable HR initiatives to keep employees engaged and committed with organizations. Employee risk analysis is done encapsulating information on employees' activities, demographics, social media reports, privileged data accessibility and so on. Such analysis helps in initiating suitable strategies in advance to avoid any eventual fraud in future. The use of predictive HR analytics in managing talent attrition is explained in Box 5.1.

Box 5.1   Predictive HR Analytics in Managing Talent Attrition

Talent retention is a major challenge for today's organizations. With predictive analytics Xerox Corporation could improve employee engagement and ensure talent retention. The company admits that they could reduce attrition by 20 percent with predictive analytics, as they could understand the appropriate characteristics of a good employee right at the stage of sourcing. Xerox could observe employees with creative personalities who are likely to stay longer rather than those who possess inquisitive personalities. For Xerox, the average employee training cost calculated is USD 5,000 after recruitment. Hence, with their retention, the company could substantially save costs also.

Therefore, predictive analytics in human resources can help in solving many business problems, in addition to optimization of HR costs and driving a culture of high performance. With the increased level of employee engagement and satisfaction, organizations significantly benefit in terms of customer satisfaction, retention and business growth.

Summary

Linking HR strategies to organizational strategies and ultimately with the business goals of organizations is a step towards making HR functions more relevant for organizations.

HR analytics requires gaining insights into different HR processes of organizations and their alignment with the business, with ultimate focus on the improvement of HR processes and the overall performance of organizations.

In HRM, value propositions focus on attraction and retention of talent. Value propositions of HRM also enable employees to assess comparative benefits that they can enjoy over other organizations in terms of compensation and benefits, corporate brand value and so on.

Sustainability, HRM practices emphasize the need for HRM's social consideration, as an organization operates in a given economic and social environment. On the other hand, the second argument centres around the premise that HRM has to embed a sustainability approach in managing human resources with an approach of reproducibility because of scarcity of human resources.

For effective use of HR analytics, human resources has to decide, first, the nature of data that need to be collected and then fit such data to algorithms and models for predicting how a specific HR decision can benefit organizations in terms of achieving business results, optimizing the ROI on human resources.

With HR analytics, we can also achieve HR optimization with a holistic understanding of the organizational strategy, processes, structure, skills and performance measures. HR optimization can significantly add value to the organization.

With an HR plan, HR managers weigh various strategic options, analysing various HR data and information, ranging from data on manpower, HR costs, talent retention and information on culture, training and learning and so on.

Predictive HR analytics through statistical relationships can align HR actions with the achievement of the organizational strategic goals. This helps HR managers to evaluate the future implications of their decisions and accordingly develop long-term strategy.

General Review Questions

1. Explain the concept of value propositions in the context of HR decision-making.
2. Discuss how HR analytics can help in assessing HR value propositions.
3. How can HR optimization be achieved through HR analytics?
4. Differentiate between HR forecasting and HR plan. How can HR analytics help in developing an HR plan?
5. Write a detailed note on predictive HR analytics.
6. Write short notes on the following:
   - HR value propositions
   - HRD business process
   - Sustainable HR decisions
   - Big data
   - HR optimization
   - Predictive analytics

Multiple Choice Questions

1. Developing human resources' value propositions requires
   a. Understanding of key business drivers
   b. Understanding customers' needs and expectations
   c. Looking at the business from 'outside in'
   d. All of the above
   e. None of the above

2. Identify which of the following statement is not relevant for value proposition:
   a. It indicates specific differentiating value of a product or service
   b. It helps an organization in communicating to its stakeholders' unique value-generating features
   c. It enunciates its key role in business strategy
   d. It describes distinctive competitive advantages for the organization
   e. It cannot achieve differentiation from competitors

3. In HRM, value propositions focus on
   a. Attraction and retention of talent
   b. Assessment of comparative benefits over other organizations
   c. Corporate brand value
   d. All of the above
   e. None of the above

4. From the recruitment point of view, value proposition from human resources' side does not include
   a. Competitive compensation
   b. Enabling work culture
   c. Employment tenure
   d. Opportunity to acquire new knowledge
   e. Opportunity for career development

5. Identify the wrong statement. Human resources can add value when

   a. It extends help to employees in reaching their goals
   b. It offers market competitive compensation
   c. It adopts proactive HR practices
   d. It can create a 'line of sight' for the human resources with all the stakeholders' of organizations
   e. Its deliverables can create competitive advantages for organizations

6. According to Ulrich and Brockbank, future human resources has to focus on the following value-generating pursuits, except

   a. Beginning HR work with a business focus
   b. Creating a line of sight for human resources
   c. Positioning human resources as a source of competitive advantage
   d. Aligning human resources with the needs of internal and external stakeholders
   e. Reducing HR costs

7. Value proposition

   a. Is seen from all stakeholders' perspectives
   b. Is co-created
   c. Is reciprocal
   d. Is dynamic
   e. All of the above

8. Sustainability acknowledges the following bottom line effects, except

   a. Economic
   b. Ecological
   c. Developmental
   d. Social
   e. None of the above

9. Organizations go for sustainable HRM practices primarily for the following reasons, except

   a. Normative
   b. Efficiency oriented
   c. Substance oriented
   d. Reproducibility of human resources
   e. Increased profitability

10. According to Gartner, big data is

   a. High-volume data
   b. High-variety data
   c. High-velocity data
   d. All of the above
   e. None of the above

11. HR analytics can measure the following HR value propositions, except

   a. Effective talent management
   b. Effective handling of employee discipline issues
   c. Effective management of employee attrition
   d. Effective career planning and development
   e. Effective management of recruitment function

12. The commonly known HR analytics suites are

    a.   Talent analytics
    b.   Workforce analytics
    c.   Workforce analytics and planning
    d.   All of the above
    e.   None of the above

13. Following are some of the areas of HR optimization through HR analytics, except

    a.   Defining human resources' vision and mission aligning with business goals and overall strategy of organizations
    b.   Unleashing the value of HC
    c.   Unleashing talent and leveraging potentiality of employees
    d.   Strengthening human resources' role as strategic advisor in organizational business
    e.   Focusing on HR costs

14. HR forecasting requires some structured steps, other than

    a.   Framing a business strategy
    b.   Relating business strategy with various HR scenarios
    c.   Assessing demand and supply of human resources
    d.   Assessing HR plan
    e.   Assessing cultural issues

15. Through an HR plan, HR managers weigh various strategic options, other than

    a.   Analysing various HR data and information
    b.   Analysing HR costs
    c.   Analysing information on culture
    d.   Preparing HR budgets
    e.   Analysing training and learning

16. Which of the following is not a component of an HR plan:

    a.   Employee development
    b.   Employee compensation and reward
    c.   New product development
    d.   Organizational design and development
    e.   Employee engagement

17. A typical HR plan helps an organization in which of the following:

    a.   Planning for human resources
    b.   Planning for manpower sourcing
    c.   Planning for developing human resources
    d.   All of the above
    e.   None of the above

18. Important predictive analytics suites for human resources consist of

    a.   Talent acquisition and resource management
    b.   Workforce administration
    c.   Performance and learning
    d.   All of the above
    e.   None of the above

19. HR decisions based on predictive modelling can help organizations in the following, except

   a. Segmenting and profiling of employees
   b. Analysing employee loyalty and attrition
   c. Predicting critical illness of the employees
   d. Predicting recruitment needs
   e. Analysing employee sentiment

20. Identify which of the following statement is incorrect:

   a. Linking HR strategies with organizational strategies can make HR functions more relevant for organizations
   b. HR analytics requires gaining insights into different HR processes of organizations
   c. In HRM, value propositions focus on attraction and retention of talent
   d. Sustainability in HRM practices emphasizes the need for HRM's social consideration
   e. None of the above

Critical Review Question

1. Study the use of HR analytics in an organization. Review how an HR decision-making process of this organization could be improved by the use of HR analytics?

PRACTITIONER SPEAKS

With HR analytics explain how your company can measure HR value propositions. Frame your answer selecting at least two important HR value propositions for your organization.

CASE STUDY

HP's Flight Risk Score Through Predictive Analytics

HP with 302,000 headcounts operating from several countries can be better defined as information technology major. Using predictive analytics, HP could come out with a predictive model to pre-assess which employee is likely to leave the job. This has been named as 'flight risk score'. With this score value, human resources can infer which employees are planning to resign and accordingly can initiate an appropriate action to retain them. This way HP could also reduce the cost of new sourcing of manpower and the cost of training. Potential savings that the company could make from the flight risk score goes beyond USD 300 million. Like a tracking signal, when the flight risk scores reach 40 percent, the managers are warned to get ready for intervention plans, as the probability of employees leaving the organization increases with higher score values. The company could see that with 75 percent flight risk scores employees are almost sure to quit.

Flight risk scores assessment process started by the company with mathematical calculation of each employee's loyalty, based on two years' data on compensation, raises, job ratings, job rotations and so on. Tracking these data for each employee, the company could identify possible defectors. Interestingly, HP could observe addressing the issues of defectors with promotion did not always work in the company, and this was more relevant for the sales people, although the effect of promotions for retention of other cadre of employees was positive. For sales people, compensation could work as a possible mediating factor for retention.

Further study of modalities could confirm that with higher compensation, more raises and better performance ratings, employees are likely to continue with their jobs.

Question: Emulating HP's example of 'flight risk score', explain how a large manufacturing organization in India can predict their talent attrition.

REFERENCES

Anderson, J., Narus, J., & Van Rossum, W. (2006). Customer value propositions in business markets. *Harvard Business Review, 84*(3), 91–99.

Arthur, J. B. (1994). Effects of human resource systems on manufacturing performance and turnover. *Academy of Management Journal, 37*(3), 670–687.

Ballantyne, D., Frow, P., Varey, R., & Payne, A.F. (2011). Value propositions as communication practice: Taking a wider view. *Industrial Marketing Management, 40*(2), 202–210.

Bell, A. (2005). The employee value propositions redefined. *Strategic HR Review, 4*(4), 3–13.

Bhattacharya, C. B., & Korschun, D. (2008). Stakeholder marketing: Beyond the four Ps and the customer. *Journal of Public Policy & Marketing, 27*(1), 113–116.

Boselie, P. (2010). High performance work practices in the health care sector: A Dutch case study. *International Journal of Manpower, 31*(1), 42–58.

Boudreau, J. W. (2003). Sustainability and the talentship paradigm: Strategic human resource management beyond the bottom line (CAHRS Working Paper No. 03-21). Ithaca, NY: School of Industrial and Labor Relations, Center for Advanced Human Resource Studies, Cornell University.

Chambers, E., Foulon, M., Handfield-Jones, H., Hankin, S., Michaels III, E. (1998). The war for talent. *McKinsey Quarterly, 1*(3), 44–57.

Collis, D. J., & Rukstad, G. (2008). Can you say what your strategy is? *Harvard Business Review, 86*(4), 82–90.

Delery, J. E., & Doty, D. H. (1996). Modes of theorizing in strategic human resource management: Tests of universalistic, contingency, and configurational performance predictions. *Academy of Management Journal, 39*(4), 802–835.

Ehnert, I. (2009). Sustainable human resource management: A conceptual and exploratory analysis from a paradox perspective. Heidelberg: Physica-Verlag.

———. (2011). Sustainability and human resource management. In A. Wilkinson & K. Townsend (Eds.),*The future of employment relations* (pp. 215–237). Hampshire: Palgrave Macmillan.

Ehnert, I., & Harry, W. (2012). Recent developments and future prospects on sustainable human resource management: Introduction to the special issue. *Management Review, 23*(3), 221–238.

Elkington, J. (1997). Cannibals with forks: The triple bottom line of the 21st century. Oxford: Capstone.

Guthrie, J. P. (2001). High involvement work practices, turnover and productivity: Evidence from New Zealand. *Academy of Management Journal, 38*(3), 635–672.

Heger, B. (2007). Linking the employment VP (EVP) to employee engagement and business outcomes: Preliminary findings from a linkage research pilot study. *Organization Development Journal, 25*(2), 121–132.

Huselid, M. (1995). The impact of human resource management practices on turnover, productivity, and corporate financial performance. *Academy of Management Journal, 38*(3), 635–672.

Huselid, M. A., Becker, B. E., & Beatty, R. W. (2005). *The workforce scorecard: Managing human capital to execute strategy.* Boston, MA: Harvard Business School Press.

Kaplan, R., & Norton, D. (2001). Transforming the balanced scorecard from performance measurement to strategic management: Part I. *Accounting Horizons, 15*(1), 87–105.

Kowalkowski, C., Ridell, O. P., Röndell, J. G., & Sörhammar, D. (2012). The co-creative practice of forming a value proposition. *Journal of Marketing Management, 28*(13 and 14), 1553–1570.

Laney, D. (2012). Deja VVVu: Others Claiming Gartner's Construct for Big Data. Available at: http://blogs.gartner.com/doug-laney/deja-vvvue-others-claiming-gartners-volume-velocity-variety-construct-for-big-data/ (accessed on 15 February 2016).

Lanning, M., & Michaels, E. (1988, July). A business is a value delivery system (McKinsey Staff Paper No. 41).

Lehmann, D. R., & Winer, R. S. (2008). Analysis for marketing planning (7th ed.). Boston, MA: McGraw-Hill.

Payne, A., & Frow, P. (2014). Developing superior value propositions: A strategic marketing imperative. *Journal of Service Management, 25*(2), 213–227.

Taylor, S., Osland, J., & Egri, C. P. (2012). Guest editor's introduction: Introduction to HRM's role in sustainability—Systems, strategies, and practices. *Human Resource Management, 51*(6), 789–798.

Ulrich, D., & Brockbank, W. (2005). *The HR value proposition.* Boston, MA: Harvard Business School Press.

FURTHER READING

Mariappanadar, S. (2012). The harm indicators of negative externality of efficiency focused organizational practices. *International Journal of Social Economics, 39*(3), 209–220.

APPENDIX

Multivariate Statistics in HR Analytics

Multivariate statistics helps us to reduce large data sets to a manageable form. Particularly in understanding patterns and determinants of employees' behaviour, we use multivariate analysis. When HR managers can understand this, they can manipulate complex behavioural attributes of employees and can accordingly calibrate their HR decisions. We can explain this with the following equation:

$$R = f(a,b,c,d,.......n,......x,y,z).$$

Here,

R	=	Response
a,b,c,d	=	Various motivational stimulus
n	=	Number of times stimulus applied
x,y,z	=	Internal condition of motivation.

A careful study of this equation can indicate that we have made use of simultaneous analysis of more than two variables, i.e., we have gone for multiple measurements of behavioural attributes of individual employees who have been chosen for our investigation. Obviously, our equation here takes the following form:

$$R = f(x,y,z...........n).$$

Our assumptions here all variables are random and interrelated, therefore, it is possible to manipulate their effects separately.

For multivariate data analysis, we can use various techniques as follows:

1. **Multiple regressions:** It is used to predict a single dependent variable by a set of independent variables. Unlike correlation, which is an associative technique as it explains how a dependent variable changes or co-varies when an independent variable changes, multiple regressions can predict the dependent variable based on the

level of the independent variable. For example, CEO pay is the dependent variable, while profit for the company is the independent variable. When we get results like; $r = 8$, $r^2 = .64$, it indicate profit of the company can explain 64 percent of the variation in CEO's pay.

2. **Multiple discriminant analysis (MDA):** It is used to predict the likelihood that an individual or an object will belong to a particular class or group. It helps in reducing the differences between variables and can be used in recruitment and selection processes.

3. **Factor analysis:** It is used to predict interrelationships among a large number of variables in terms of common underlying dimensions or factors.

4. **Cluster analysis:** It is used to classify individuals or objects into a small number of mutually exclusive groups based on similarities, i.e., it helps in measuring the degree of association between two individuals or objects. This technique can be used for pay grade determination.

5. **Multivariate analysis of variance (MANOVA):** It is used to predict simultaneous relationships between several independent variables and two or more dependent variables. In human resources, a good example is the study of organizational effectiveness and the quality of work-life in terms of performance achievement of employees.

6. **Multivariate analysis of covariance (MANCOVA):** It is used in conjunction with MANOVA to remove the effect of any uncontrolled independent variables on dependent variables. Therefore, it is better understood in terms of extension of MANOVA. Also, it may have multiple independent variables. For example, organizational effectiveness and the quality of work-life (two dependent variables) can be related to multiple independent variables such as performance achievement, age group, education level, sickness and so on using MANCOVA.

7. **Canonical correlation analysis:** It is used to predict the linear combination of different sets of variables, both dependent and independent, for maximizing the correlation between the two sets. We can use this method in human resources to predict the relationships between HRM practices and operational performance measures.

8. **Multidimensional scaling:** It is used to predict similarity or preferences into distances represented in a multidimensional space. For example, we can study the sustainability of HR systems of an organization in terms of multiple indicators such as investment in HC development, opportunity to acquire new skills, empowerment, autonomous work group and technology-enabled HR processes. Multidimensional scaling technique here can help.

9. **Conjoint analysis:** It is used primarily for developing multi-attribute compositional models. For example, for human resources to study how employees value and trade off different types of compensation and benefits packages, we can use conjoint analysis. This can help in framing suitable HR policies. A good example of this is that in benefits employees may prefer social clubs and entertainment over office café. Conjoint analysis also helps us in cluster analysis by developing needs-based segmentation.

Here, we have only discussed most commonly used multivariate research tools for HR analytics. All these are some of the commonly used multivariate tools that can be used for HR analytics. HR managers need to familiarize themselves with these techniques right in the beginning, before going for using HR analytics solutions to develop predictive decision-making models.

CHAPTER 6

HR ANALYTICS AND DATA

LEARNING OBJECTIVES:

After reading this chapter, you will be able to understand:

- Concepts of HR data
- HR data and data quality
- HR data collection
- Big data for human resources
- Transforming HR data into HR information
- Process of data collection for HR analytics
- Data collection for effective HR measurement
- HR reporting
- Data visualization
- Root cause analysis (RCA)
- Datafication of human resources

INTRODUCTORY CASE

With Data, Alstom Could Achieve Success in its Integration Process

With the motto of sustainable mobility, today Alstom is the world leader in integrated railway systems and so also in transport solutions. Headquartered in France, Alstom operates from 60 countries with a total headcount of 31,000. The company constantly innovates and focuses on value creation for customers. To emerge as a single business entity, the company merged all its activities pertaining to power generation, bringing together power systems and power services. This process required the restructuring of the organization with defined values. Instead of imposing a new set of culture and value, the senior management team of the company focused on buying-in, so that people of the organization can adapt them with the changes.

To strengthen the process of integration, the company renewed its commitment to employee development and developed more effective performance systems with critical understanding of the trends in employee engagement. To ensure employees' buy-in to the vision, focus was on the continuous improvement of the performance management systems (PMS), so as to ensure correct measurement of performance and the culture of organizations. Successful measurement of the way employees look at an organization and how they feel and act for the business of the organization quantitatively could enable the company to get valuable data. These data then help the company to take effective decisions with the futuristic look. Data could also help in designing metrics, balanced scorecards and MIS.

INTRODUCTION

Data are considered as the core essence of business and so also HR decision-making. Without data, organizations feel constrained to take decisions without understanding any underlying reasons, and obviously, this makes the decisions flawed. HR decisions on the one hand influence people and on the other business. These involve many operational, business and strategic issues, which require laying fundamental emphasis on quality and credible data collection, and then interpretation with HR analytics for better insights. We have many solutions available for HR analytics. For human resources, it is important to opt for simple solutions, rather than one that requires complicated mathematical algorithms and high level of knowledge of statistics and programming languages. Again, HR analytics solutions are difficult to choose because people's issues are different in different organizations. People differ in wants, needs, skill and performance. Also, we have many other potential human behaviour variables that can make HR decision-making complicated. All these require reliable data collection.

An HR function also has influence on business decisions. For example, all HR decisions such as employee sourcing, organizational restructuring, employee productivity improvement, performance management, employee engagement, employee redundancy and so on have direct influence on business decisions. From this perspective, HR data for HR analytics are not just available from HR functions but can be collated from all other functions of organizations. For example, we can measure the efficacy of employee engagement in terms of customers' satisfaction. Therefore, HR analytics solutions that can capture accurate information and give rich insights into holistic management of organizations are more preferred. Going by the spirit of the generic meaning, like all other analytics, HR analytics first focus on learning about the parts of HR decisions and then try to understand the interrelationships between the parts for explaining the phenomenon, the nature and the meaning of any decision. Knowledge about data and data collection methods is considered important for HR analytics. Data need not be statistical; they can be gathered by simply talking with people to see how they are doing. Thus, for human resources, talking with employees about their work, experiences and work conditions could also be a source of gathering data. It is important that the data are timely, accurate and credible; else, information and insights based on the data may be flawed. Data should provide insights and obtaining the right data on which we can act on is important. Often, on capturing vast data we feel we can take better decisions, but this may be a distraught. For example, HR managers often feel that better insights into PMS can be obtained when we go for data on employee compensation, on compensation budgets and so on. In this process, HR managers may collect a host of data and ultimately muddle the decision-making process. A good practice is starting with small data and then building on the same. HR data on performance management must help in credibly determining how employees are performing. Likewise, HR data on internal customers, data on other stakeholders, correlation of HC with financial and operational

A hypothesis-based approach to examine a business decision can be alternatively studied using data and analytics. At times we even get better insights into a business problem because of our intuition. With data and analytics, we can adjudge the credibility of our intuitive thought process. A good example is that an HR manager can intuitively understand which potential talent could leave the company in near future. But with data and analytics, such intuitive understanding becomes more authenticated to initiate appropriate action to retain such potential talent.

data, data on employee selection and so on are important and are collected and interpreted to get better insights into better HR decision-making.

With data-driven human resources, globally, organizations are becoming more innovative. Apart from using standard HR analytics solutions available in the market, HR managers are making use of social network analytics for getting better insights into employees' data. Social network analytics can provide data on employees behind the scene relationships that can help in tracking their potential and risk. Thus, with organizational HR and business data and data from social media, we can truly transform our HR functions that are data driven. With data-driven human resources, we can ensure correct, business-aligned and strategic HR decisions.

HR DATA AND DATA QUALITY

HR data: HR data is considered as the core essence of business. Without HR data, organizations feel constrained to take decisions without understanding any underlying reasons, and obviously, this makes HR decisions flawed.

HR data and its quality is an important issue for HR analytics. Many organizations unknowingly get overloaded with data resulting in HR managers' pursuit to count everything and in the process making HR decisions flawed. This requires, at the outset, to ensure the collection of appropriate data and its appropriate use. We use the appropriateness of data in terms of data quality. This can be ensured when we adhere to some important criteria while collecting data. These have been explained as follows:

Degree of comprehensiveness: This can be ascertained understanding whether data can articulate the decisional intents. To clarify, let us assume based on performance evaluation that HR managers want to take decisions on employees' promotions. In this case, comprehensive data are understood answering the following questions:

- How effective is our PMS to measure the performance of employees?
- Can our PMS be efficient enough to capture employees' performance in terms of business uncertainties?
- Can the employees' sustain performance even in uncertainties?
- Can the performance data speak on employees' potentialities?

There may be many other specific issues depending on the specific organizational requirements.

1. **Degree of validity:** Data validity is measured in terms of describing data assertion and is measured in terms of confidence in data

using statistical tools. For example, with what degree of confidence we can say attrition of people is attributable to organizational compensation and benefits programme? Can the data qualify the test of recency?

2. **Degree of reliability:** Data reliability denotes trustworthiness of data. Data become reliable when we get the same result, if we collect it again. Some of the questions to assess the degree of reliability are as follows:

   - Can we get the same result if we collect data again?
   - Were there any untoward or adverse circumstances that can have potential effect on data during data collection?
   - Can the data truly represent the population (when we collect data through a survey)?

3. **Degree of variation:** This can be understood in terms of differentiating characteristics of data. Without such characteristics, decisions may be flawed. A good example of this is: Does an MBA degree from a premier business school make a difference in managerial performance?

4. **Data usefulness:** Understood in terms of usefulness in terms of decision-making. Often HR managers feel burdened with data, which may have little or no relevance.

5. **Data defensibility:** It can be understood in terms of all the earlier stated criteria of data collection. When all these criteria or dimensions of data quality are adhered to, data become defensible, i.e., even if it is challenged, we may defend its accuracy.

All these are also considered as important quality dimensions of HR data. Poor HR data quality can potentially affect the quality of HR decisions. Therefore, before we make use of HR data to draw insights into and to take decisions on, we must have confidence on data accuracy.

HR DATA COLLECTION

Whether it is for descriptive or predictive analytics, HR data collection is important. We already know descriptive analytics helps in understanding the trend in the past and the present, while predictive analytics can tell us what is going to happen in future. Whatever may be the type of analytics, we need data; hence, we need to think on data collection. Most of the organizations have their own systems of HR data collection, data storage and data management. Legal compliance, risk alleviation and operational management are important reasons for data collection. Now the question remains what should be the nature of data collected. Naturally, this varies with the specific needs of organizations, even partly due to the type of industry. However, we can have some common HR data sets, which every organization collects for HR analytics. These are data on employees' attendance, data on diversity management practices, data on employee retention, employee recruitment, skills and competency, performance, training and so on. All these HR data sets help organizations to get specific answers to their queries that help in the HR decision-making process. For example, if an organization finds employee attrition data of some departments are alarming, then with the identification of the reasons, human resources can draw an intervention plan that can help in reducing such attrition rate. Similarly, organization can assess the efficacy of the training function, correlating training with the employees' post-training performance.

ANALYTICS HIGHLIGHT

Effective data collection requires, at the outset, understanding the organization as a system. Systems view of the organization facilitates in understanding the interconnectedness of different parts or sub-systems of the organization. It can help HR managers to relate between employees, their job roles, their skills and competencies and so on. Further, with analytics such relations can even be extended with organizational strategies and businesses.

HR data collection must respect boundaries of employees' privacy. Although we do not have a boundary line on employees' privacy, we can see it in the context of culture, processes and attitudes. A data collection team that is formed to collect data needs to ensure privacy. Data collection efforts need to be supported by some hypothesis to draw a map on whatever is needed. Such hypothesis can also help us with concrete data collection objectives. While collating employees' data, it is important to ensure employees' anonymity. When anonymity is not ensured, it is always important to seek permission of the concerned employees. Also, it is important to screen the confidentiality of information. At this stage, HR managers need to be careful about mistakenly divulging of employees' personal information.

Steps for HR Data Collection

Some of the important steps followed while collecting HR data are as follows:

1. Identification of issues and opportunities for data collection: This requires review of prevalent policies, practices and procedures pertaining to employees of various organizations.
2. Fixing priorities of identified issues and opportunities for data collection: Based on the priorities assigned, data collection goals are set. Specific goals for each issue depend on our queries or hypotheses that can be resolved using our collected data.
3. Planning for approach and methods of data collection: This addresses issues pertaining to how data can be collected, what are the sources that organizations may use for data collection and so on.

4. Collection of data: For better results, it is often desirable to proceed through data collection, after drawing a data collection plan. This is particularly relevant for HR data collection.

5. Data analysis and interpretation: Both qualitative and quantitative data can be analysed developing mathematical algorithms and then using HR analytics solutions for getting better insights. Such insights help in HR decision-making in alignment with the business and strategies of organizations.

6. Framing HR decisions: With insights, HR decisions can be made with a futuristic outlook. Such decisions, however, need to be reviewed time to time, keeping pace with the change in the data set, if any.

It is desirable to prepare a checklist for each such step to ensure the data collection process becomes flawless.

While collecting HR data, HR managers also take into consideration the data source, data context and data quality. When data are collected from best possible sources, data authenticity also enhances. For example, rather than asking managers to provide data on employees, at times it is better to collect data directly from employees themselves. This, however, depends on the nature of data that we are targeting to collect. Similarly, data context is important. For example when we ask employees' about their feelings on compensation level during the actual process of compensation review, employees are likely to vent their dissatisfaction. This is because of potential adverse effect on the data context. With new technology support, we can check the data quality before taking decisions based on the data. A good example for understanding the effect of rater-bias on performance evaluation results may be important before we take any decisions based on the performance results. Without such quality checking of data, HR decisions bound to be flawed.

Therefore, we need to do HR data mapping, linking various data elements through HR analytics for better HR decisions.

BIG DATA FOR HUMAN RESOURCES

Big data denotes gathering data from several data sources and collate the same using HR analytics tool for decision-making. HR data need to be big data for its obvious alignment with the organizational business and strategies. In other words, we can also see big data as integrated data from HR context. Characteristically, big data can integrate marketing data with human resources and operations, or HR data with finance and strategies and so on. With big data, HR decisions can be more holistic. Accuracy and reliability of big data is important. All the points that have been highlighted for HR data quality are also valid here. For successfully managing big data for HR decision-making, it is important to have a well-documented data management plan. This can significantly identify data overlaps and gaps, and so data quality.

HR big data: HR big data denotes gathering data from several data sources and collate the same using the HR analytics tool for decision-making. HR data need to be big data for their obvious alignment with organizational business and strategies.

ANALYTICS HIGHLIGHT

HR data need not always be big data. Only problem HR data encompasses many functions. This requires HR managers to go for data wrangling, i.e., the art of merging, cleansing, visualizing and manipulating data to ensure such data become useful and capable to give better insights.

Big data for human resources helps us in assessing the trends, patterns, correlations and further insights into intricacies of HRM in relation to organizational business and strategies. Even for understanding employee engagement, which is more related to HR decision for HR function, we need big data in terms of performance results, productivity, employees' promotion and transfer data and so on. Thus, big data for human resources facilitates better informed HR decision-making, as it can give better insight into business situations and ensure better HR results in terms of retention, training and HR acquisition.

TRANSFORMING HR DATA INTO HR INFORMATION

HR information: Processing raw data with HR analytics solutions, human resources can transform HR data into HR information. With such information human resources can get the required guidance in taking decisions and in action planning.

For specific nature of HR functions, we find human resources in organizations gets flooded with data not only from internal stakeholders but also from various external reference points, such as different government reports, legal notifications, reports of various professional bodies and so on. Such data are vast and, hence, require processing and raising specific queries that may resolve decisional issues. Processing raw data with HR analytics solutions, human resources can transform HR data into **HR information**. With such information, human resources can get required guidance in taking decisions and in action planning. In many organizations, **HR reports** are generated through HRM systems (HRMS). To transform HR data into HR information, we require HRMS which provides opportunities for data selection and data sorting, mostly raising questions like 'what is' and 'what if'. 'What is' type of questions can be queries to understand the cost of training or the cost of compensation. 'What if' type of questions, on the other hand, try to study the effect when some specific actions are taken, e.g., 'what if' when we reduce incentives payout by 10 percent.

HR reports: Analysing data with HR analytics solutions, we generate various HR reports. Predominantly, HR reports focus on employee data more in the perspective of the cost issues; however, combining these reports with other databases, such as budgets, performance evaluation records, attendance records and so on, human resources can take better business-focused decisions.

We generate HR reports, leveraging HR data, making use of HR analytics. HRMS may not require database queries. It is designed to offer standard outputs with data selection and data-sorting options, to make the HR-report-generation process simple. Future HRMS is expected to even manage unstructured verbal queries, making the HR report generation and decision-making process much simpler.

HR data analysis requires some basic knowledge on statistical skills and knowledge. For example, basic understanding of the facts that having huge numbers of successors for the organizations may not be right, as organizations may not have the capabilities to offer future leadership roles to all these potential employees. Similar understanding on the appropriateness of data presentation through charts, bar diagrams and so on needs to be clear. Likewise, understanding that correlations need not always talk about cause and effect relationships, samples need not be representative of population and so on. All these do not require specialized knowledge of statistics; even with elementary-level statistical knowledge, data analysis can be done intelligently.

PRACTICE ASSIGNMENT

Give some examples of data wrangling with reference to HR data, citing some industry practices.

PROCESS OF DATA COLLECTION FOR HR ANALYTICS

For HR analytics, we require both **qualitative** and **quantitative** data. The process of data collection for these two types of data is different. Qualitative data are in the form of words, and it may even be in the form of numeric information, photographs, videos, sound recordings and so on. Qualitative data need to be understood in specific context, namely underlying reasons for specific workplace behaviour, such as mentoring and coaching and so on. Qualitative data collection is done through observations, personal interviews, focus groups and case studies. Although qualitative data has inherent strength of providing rich descriptive details, often its accuracy is questioned. HR decisions based on past qualitative data may be suicidal.

Quantitative data are essentially in the form of numbers. Surveys, questionnaire administration, statistical reports and so on are potential sources of quantitative data. This type of data is more reliable than qualitative data as it is objective. However, it also suffers from potential weaknesses, such as oversimplification by numbers and rankings, and losing the context of data.

Both these types of data are collected from more than one source. It could be from official data, survey data, focus groups data, interviews data or simply observed data. Each data source has its individual merits and demerits. For example, collection of official data is less time-consuming and cost-effective. But it suffers from major weaknesses in terms of diligence and accuracy, as these depend on reporting by employees who had collected it. Again focus groups data can capture multiple narratives, but it may not allow focus groups participants to express their individual opinions.

However, HR managers cannot alter the data, rather choose the data from both these data types for predictive analysis and for taking futuristic business- and strategy-aligned HR decisions.

Qualitative data: These data are in the form of words, and may even be in form of numeric information. These may be photographs, videos, sound recordings and so on. Qualitative data need to be understood in specific context, namely underlying reasons for specific workplace behaviour, such as mentoring and coaching and so on. Qualitative data collection is done through observations, personal interviews, focus groups and case studies.

Quantitative data: These data are essentially in the form of numbers. Surveys, questionnaire administration, statistical reports and so on are potential sources of quantitative data. This type of data is more reliable than qualitative data, as it is objective. However, it also suffers from potential weaknesses, such as oversimplification by numbers and rankings, and losing the context of data.

DATA COLLECTION FOR EFFECTIVE HR MEASUREMENT

Identification of relevant and easily retrievable data for getting the right insights is considered as an important data collection process to measure HR effectiveness. This requires base-level knowledge of understanding data types and data analysis after collection. Important considerations for data collection are quality and consistency of data, data compatibility with different available systems of the organizations, data accessibility, frequency of data collection, cost of data collection and so on.

Although we do not have any universal approach to generalize data types and sources for human resources, some important types and sources can be listed as follows:

- Employees' data from HRMS or HRIS
- Survey data on employees
- All transactional and process data on human resources
- Organizational business performance data
- Customers' related data
- Financial data.

In the following table, some of the types and sources of HR data have been summarized.

Most of the data mentioned in this table are available with the organization. HR managers need to collate these data for subsequent analysis and HR measurements. Wherever data are not available, HR managers need to embrace the appropriate methods of data collection, such as generating data through surveys, using various reports and databases, social network analysis and so on. But all these require suitable HR analytics solutions. Better results can be obtained when HR managers first make use of data that are available and start the analysis, and then gradually build the

Types of Data	Sources of Data	Data Elements	Data Examples
Employees' data	HRMS, HRIS, HR reports, payroll and surveys	Employment status, job history, demography, attendance records, pay, department, place of posting, education and skills	Demographic data such as age, religion, gender, marital status, dependents and so on
			Employment status data such as full/part time, contractual, pay grade and so on
			Attendance data such as days of absence, days of absence without prior leave approval, days of absence due to sickness and so on
			Pay-related data such as Base pay, bonuses, benefits, perquisites and so on

Types of Data	Sources of Data	Data Elements	Data Examples
Data on HR processes and practices	HRMS, HRIS, PMS, and other HR systems, if any	Recruitment and selection	Attraction of quality candidates for the job positions, cycle time from interview to selection decisions and appointments
		Retention	
		Performance management systems	Voluntary attrition
		Learning and development	Performance ratings
			Promotions
		Knowledge, skills and competencies	Training man-days, participation rate in training, and training evaluations
		Succession planning and future leadership development	Skills audits, competency mapping and assessments
		Talent management	Talent pipeline
		HR services	Grievance handling
			Disciplinary actions and so on
			HR litigation
Data on organizational business	Financial, operational and resource management systems	Financial	Total revenue, total costs, and profits
		Operational	Transactions, KPIs,
		Customers	Work volumes
			Numbers of customers, demographics of customers, customer services, customer complaints
Data from external sources	Public sources	Labour market	Unemployment rate, labour participation rate, rate of compensation and benefits, data on skill shortage and so on
	Private providers	Compensation and benefits plan	
	Consultancies		
	Researchers	Business or industry	Economic trends, economic growth, market trends and so on
	Professional bodies	Benchmarking with peer group companies	
	Industry bodies		Competition data

analysis based on other data that are presently not available with the organization. Also, HR managers need to consider the cost-efficiency issues for data collection. Therefore, effective HR measurement requires credible and relevant quality data and then makes use of HR analytics solutions.

Before the process of data collection starts, it requires a strategy on how different data variables are collected fitting with the structure of the organization. For example, data collection strategy requires the evaluation of available data and how they fit HR measurements, accessibility of such data, operating characteristics of the organization and so on.

HR REPORTING

With data collection, we complete the initial requirements of HR analytics, as these data help us to get insights that ease our decision-making process. Analysing data with HR analytics solutions, we generate various HR reports. Predominantly, HR reports focus on employee data more in the perspective of the cost issues; however, combining these reports with other databases, such as budgets, performance evaluation records, attendance records and so on, human resources can take better business-focused decisions. HR reports also benefit HR managers to showcase the business value of human resources. For example, with a HR report that connects employee satisfaction with customer satisfaction, it is possible to illustrate human resources' contribution to business. Likewise, small savings in HR costs can enhance organizational profitability. Similarly, talent retention can help in successful new product development and so on. Effective HR reports can benefit pulling all employee information into one single view, looking at which HR managers can understand on real-time basis the pulse of HR functions in the organization. A quick glance at HR reports also helps in integrated HR decision-making.

As HR reports are connected with the MIS of the organization, moving the cursor to the specific report contents, we can get detailed insights. For example, using a bar diagram, we can represent last five years' trend in headcounts. Here, we can get the specific number of headcounts for a particular year moving the cursor in the right position of the bar diagram.

Again HR reports may be conflicting with the reports from other functional areas. For example, HR reports may conflict with finance reports because of the difference in the nature of reports in these two functional areas. Such problems can be resolved when an organization standardizes its entire reporting systems. Having understood the importance of HR reports, it is now important to see different types and forms of HR reports. Each type and form has its individual merits and demerits.

Types and Forms of HR Reports

Following is a list describing the various types of reports prepared:

1. Detailed employees' reports: Such reports are mostly prepared for internal use, say finance department. Based on this report, the finance department takes necessary decisions, such as release of monthly compensation, preparing compensation budgets, according monetary sanctions, estimating the welfare expenses and so on. A sample employee report is presented as follows:

Sample Employee Report, July, 2016

Functions	Employee ID	Hiring Date	Number of Years in Same Job Position	Compa-ratio
HR manager	212	2 January 2005	5	1.55
HR manager	213	4 February 2007	3	1.08
HR executive	311	5 February 2012	4	1.02

If you examine this employee report, you could see that the first HR manager who is in the same job position for five years with a compa-ratio of 1.55 needs to be promoted, or we can say that his/her promotion is overdue, while the other HR manager and the HR executive can still continue in the same job position for some more time. As this report only factored into the compa-ratio and not performance measures, we can interpret this likewise. However, higher compa-ratio is an indicator of good performance, else the employees could not have received raise in compensation to reach to the current level of compa-ratio. All these depend on company-specific policies and strategies.

2. Detailed payroll reports: Based on the detailed employees' reports, payrolls are prepared by the finance department, and again forwarded to the HRD for final vetting. Payroll reports are also important for statutory filing of HR information to the concerned bodies. A sample payroll report is presented further:

Compensation Reports of HRD, July, 2016
Annual Compensation by Grade and Level

Grade	Level 1	Level 2	Level 3	Level 4	Level 5
1	15,000	18,000	21,000	23,000	25,000
2	20,000	23,000	25,000	26,000	27,000
3	24,000	27,000	30,000	33,000	35,000
4	30,000	33,000	36,000	39,000	42,000
5	40,000	45,000	50,000	55,000	60,000

Notes: Grades 1–5 are assigned from HR executives (Grade 1) to HR director (Grade 5).
The levels indicate the years of service in the same job and the corresponding pay after annual increment.
The company follows promotion from within and also goes for lateral recruitment, wherever necessary.

3. Detailed leave reports: Leave records are important and have direct linkage to the finance functions of the organization as employees get paid for the unavailed leaves. Also, employees get salary for the leave period, when such leaves are approved and the employees have sufficient leave. Employees' leaves are classified and credited to the respective leave account depending on the nature of the leave.

4. Detailed performance reports: These reports summarize employees' performances, breaking it into convenient slots, e.g., monthly, quarterly, six-monthly and annually. Such reports help in quick understanding of the performance trend, help in understanding which employees need training and development support, help in understanding who are eligible for future promotion and so on. In the following table the annual performance summary report of the sales department of a hypothetical company has been presented:

Annual Performance Summary of Sales Department for Year 2015–2016

Employee Code	Revenue Generated (in Million Rupees)	Target Assigned Current Year (in Million Rupees)	Target Achieved Last Year (in Million Rupees)	Achievement as Percentage to Last Year	Performance Rating
260	2.6	2.01	1.56	167	Outstanding
241	2.01	2.3	1.95	103	Good
171	2.05	2.3	1.87	91	Average
189	2.87	3.09	2.67	107	Very good

5. Detailed training report: This report essentially focuses on documenting the training calendar, with supportive information like target participants, training duration, training faculty and training goals. Also, this report summarizes the average man-days of training, expenses on training as the percentage of total revenue and costs and so on.

6. Dashboards: We have already explained dashboards in Chapter 4. Basically, it is a snapshot of organizational HRIS. Updating dashboards with HR data from time to time ensures real-time monitoring of employees' performances and other HR phenomena. This form of HR report can be prepared with HR analytics solutions and even using Excel. Better visualization of trend enables HR managers to initiate appropriate actions to drive organizational growth. For example, dashboards may have talent retention trend in the company, monitoring which HR managers can initiate the adoption of appropriate strategies for talent retention. A dashboard is also known as visual HR reporting. A sample dashboard is illustrated further:

Head Counts in HR Department as on July, 2016

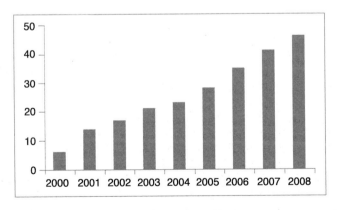

Employees by Functions

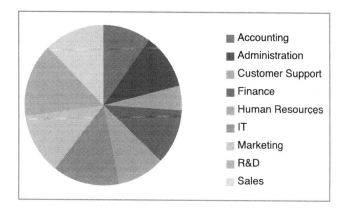

For preparing HR reports, HR managers can make use of MS Excel, or some standard HR analytics solutions.

PRACTICE ASSIGNMENT

Develop one HR report for a training and development function for a hypothetical FMCG company with global presence and headcounts of more than one lakh.

DATA VISUALIZATION OR HR REPORT VISUALIZATION

Data visualization is data presentation in pictorial and graphical form. Data visualization or HR report visualization by placing data in a visual context helps us to quickly understand data patterns, trends and data correlations, which otherwise could have been impossible for a layman to understand. We have many data visualization solutions available in the market. HR managers now need to focus on data visualization beyond traditional charts and graphs which can be developed using Excel. Various data visualization solutions today make innovative data visualization tools such as dials and gauges, maps, sparklines, more elaborate pie and bar charts and so on available. Such visual tools are built with interactive capabilities, helping HR managers to manipulate through data drilling for various analyses to support decision-making.

Data visualization: Data visualization is data presentation in pictorial and graphical forms. Data visualization or HR report visualization by placing data in a visual context helps us to quickly understand data patterns, trends and data correlations.

Some of the essential features of data visualization are that it helps in qualitative understanding of the data, processes, relations and even concepts; helps in manipulation of data visuals and also helps in data measurement and comparison for getting multiple views from multiple perspectives. Irrespective of data characteristics, e.g., numeric, symbolic, discrete, continuous, spatial, relational and so on, data visualization tools can help in data analysis and then facilitate in decision-making. From an organization's point of view, data visualization can quickly identify areas that deserve immediate attention of HR managers, provide clarity

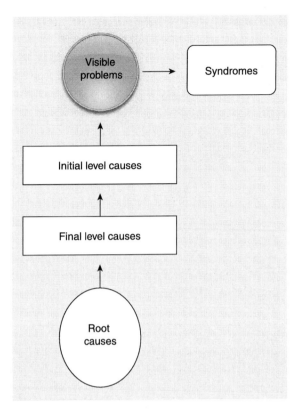

■ Figure 6.1: RCA Flowchart
Source: Author.

on influencing factors for specific data characteristic and predict the likely future. In short, we can say data visualization helps us to comprehend information quickly, understand relationships and patterns, dig in emerging trends, communicate the trend to others and so on. Some software vendors call their data visualization solutions as visual analytics.

Root cause analysis (RCA):
Root causes are defined as the basic reasons attributable to problems. Thus, RCA is the pursuit for the identification of basic reasons for problems.

PERFORMING ROOT CAUSE ANALYSIS

Identifying root causes of problems, **RCA** helps us in problem-solving. With the elimination of the root causes, problems get resolved and decisions can be taken. Root causes are defined as the basic reasons attributable to the problems. Thus, RCA is the pursuit for identification of the basic reasons for problems. RCA is done adopting different approaches, tools and techniques. It is the root cause as its elimination can help in decision-making. Prima facie examination of problems cannot help in identifying root causes, as visible syndromes may only represent initial level causes of problems. This has been explained in Figure 6.1.

It is evident from Figure 6.1 that 'root cause' is the underlying cause of a problem.

RCA is performed primarily with a problem-solving approach. However, we can also follow the under-mentioned approaches for systematic RCA.

1. Analysis of causal factors: This approach makes use of evidence to identify the contributing factors for establishing causal relationships.
2. Change analysis: This approach tries to attribute the root causes to the eventual organizational change process that may encompass human resources, equipment and machines or business processes.
3. Analysis of barriers: This approach examines the control systems to identify the problems and prevents recurrence of such problems in future.
4. Risk tree analysis: Using a tree diagram, this approach looks into what happened and why.
5. Kepner–Tregoe problem-solving and decision-making: This approach analyses the problems from four dimensions, i.e., situation analysis, problem analysis, solution analysis and potential problem analysis, and then identifies solutions to problems.

ANALYTICS HIGHLIGHT

Kepner and Tregoe method of RCA is considered as a generic problem-solving method. The method essentially makes use of questions such as who, what, where, when, why, how and how much. Answers to these questions help in analysing the problem state, solution state, transition state and ways to prevent future recurrence of problems. We also call it 'is/isn't' analysis. As doing RCA using this method, we raise questions such as where lies the problem and where not, when the problem started and when it did not, who encounters problem and who do not and so on.

This method after analysis of the problem, while analysing the solution state, makes use of some set of metrics and then divides the solution state into specific needs and wants. When a solution fails to address needs, we discard it. Wants being measured using metrics, we can reach the solution state providing a number of possible solutions attributing numerical value.

In organizations, RCA is done through a cross-functional team, especially with the help of a quality management expert, with experience in similar nature of work.

RCA helps in the identification of answers to what, how and why something has happened. Thus, it facilitates suitable managerial interventions to eliminate identified problems and prevent its recurrence. It involves data collection, charting of causal factors, identification of root cause and recommendation of action plans to eliminate the root cause. Characteristically, root causes are identifiable and can be fixed with managerial intervention.

DATAFICATION OF HUMAN RESOURCES

It is the process of turning the existing aspects of a phenomenon into data business, i.e., computerization of data and transforming data into

Datafication of human resources: It is the process of turning the existing aspects of a phenomenon into data business, i.e., computerization of data and transforming data into information that has a business value.

information that has a business value. A good example of this is datafication of our social network data by Google, Facebook or LinkedIn. From the introductory case of this chapter, we could see how Alstom datafied its all businesses to converge into one. We also call it our effort to monetize data around business. Let us take an example of talent attrition. To understand the problem better, we may ask basic questions such as who are the employees that are leaving? To find answer to this question we study whatever data we have about these group of employees, their immediate managers or supervisors. With this process of datafication, we develop our talent retention model using HR analytics solutions. Thus, **datafication of human resources** denotes transforming human resources into a data-driven business process in an organization.

Summary

Data are the core essence of business and so also for HR decision-making. Without data, organizations feel constrained to take decisions without understanding any underlying reasons, and obviously, this makes the decisions flawed.

People differ in wants, needs, skill and performance. Also, we have many other potential human behaviour variables that can make HR decision-making complicated. All these require reliable data collection.

HR data and its quality is an important issue for HR analytics. Many organizations unknowingly get overloaded with data, resulting in HR managers' pursuit to count everything and, in the process, making HR decisions flawed. This requires at the outset to ensure the collection of appropriate data, and its appropriate use. We use appropriateness of data in terms of data quality.

Whatever may be the type of analytics, we need data; hence, we need to think on data collection. Most of the organizations have their own systems of HR data collection, data storage and data management. Legal compliance, risk alleviation and operational management are the important reasons for data collection.

HR data encompass many functions. These require HR manager to go for data wrangling, i.e., the art of merging, cleansing, visualizing and manipulating data to ensure such data become useful and capable to give better insights.

To transform HR data into HR information, we require HRMS which provides opportunities for data selection and data sorting, mostly raising questions such as 'what is' and 'what if'.

For HR analytics, we require both qualitative and quantitative data. The process of data collection for these two types of data is different. Qualitative data collection is done through observations, personal interviews, focus groups and case studies. Surveys, questionnaire administration, statistical reports and so on are potential sources of quantitative data.

Identification of relevant and easily retrievable data for getting the right insights is considered as an important data collection process to measure HR effectiveness. This requires base-level knowledge of understanding data types and data analysis after collection.

With data collection, we complete the initial requirements of HR analytics, as these data help us to get insights that ease our decision-making process. Analysing data with HR analytics solutions, we generate various HR reports.

Data visualization is data presentation in pictorial and graphical forms. Data visualization or HR report visualization, by placing data in a visual context, help us to quickly understand data patterns, trends and data correlations, which otherwise could have been impossible for a layman to understand.

RCA helps us in problem-solving. With the elimination of the root causes, problems get resolved and decisions can be taken. Root causes are defined as the basic reasons attributable to the problems. Thus, RCA is the pursuit for the identification of basic reasons for problems. RCA is done adopting different approaches, tools and techniques. It is the root cause as its elimination can help decision-making.

Datafication is the process of turning existing aspects of a phenomenon into data business, i.e., computerization of data and transforming data into information that has a business value.

General Review Questions

1. Explain various concepts of HR data.

2. How can we ensure the quality of HR data?

3. What are your recommended steps for HR data collection?

4. Discuss the process of transforming HR data into HR information.

5. For HR analytics, what process of data collection would you recommend and why?

6. Define effective HR measurement. How can you ensure effective HR measurement in an organization?

7. What is HR reporting? How can HR reports be prepared?

8. Discuss the concept of data visualization.

9. What is RCA? How is it performed?

10. Write short notes on the following:
    - Datafication of human resources
    - Data validity and data reliability
    - Big data for human resources
    - Dashboard
    - Kepner and Tregoe method.

Multiple Choice Questions

1. Identify the incorrect statement out of the following:
    a. HR decisions influence employees of an organization
    b. HR decisions influence business of an organization
    c. HR decisions involve all operational issues
    d. HR decisions require fundamental emphasis on quality and credibility of data
    e. Data and its interpretation with HR analytics ensure better insights

2. While choosing HR analytics solutions, it is important to consider the following, except

    a.   Select those HR analytics that require knowledge of programming languages

    b.   Select those HR analytics which are simple

    c.   Select those HR analytics which are capable to predict future

    d.   Select those HR analytics which match with people issues of an organization

    e.   None of the above

3. Following HR decisions can influence business decisions, except

    a.   Employee sourcing

    b.   Organizational restructuring

    c.   Employee productivity improvement

    d.   Employee engagement

    e.   None of the above

4. Identify which of the following is an incorrect statement on HR analytics:

    a.   HR analytics help us to understand the interrelationships between variables

    b.   HR analytics cannot explain the phenomenon of something

    c.   HR analytics require data and data collection methods

    d.   HR data need not be statistical

    e.   HR data can be collected simply by talking with people

5. It is important that the HR data are

    a.   Timely

    b.   Accurate

    c.   Credible

    d.   Insightful

    e.   All of the above

6. Identify the incorrect statement on good practice for HR analytics out of the following:

    a.   Start with small data and then build on the same

    b.   Start with big data and then build on the same

    c.   Correlate HC with financial and operational data

    d.   Correlate employee selection data with future performance

    e.   Ensure data are credible

7. Data quality can be ensured when we adhere to the following criteria, except

    a.   Degree of comprehensiveness

    b.   Degree of validity

    c.   Degree of reliability

    d.   Degree of usability

    e.   Degree of consensus

8. The degree of comprehensiveness for PMS can be understood in terms of

    a.   Effectiveness of PMS in measuring the performance of employees

    b.   Efficiency of PMS to capture employees' performance in terms of business uncertainties

    c.   Sustainability of employees' performance even in uncertainties

    d.   Credibility of performance data on employees' potentialities

    e.   All of the above

9. Common HR data set for HR analytics are

    a.   Data on employees' attendance

    b.   Data on diversity management practices

    c.   Data on employee retention

    d.   Data on employees' recruitment

    e.   All of the above

10. Understanding an organization as a system is important for effective data collection because

    a.   It can facilitate in understanding interconnectedness of different parts or sub-systems of an organization

    b.   It can help HR managers to relate between employees

    c.   It can help HR managers to relate between job roles

    d.   It can help HR managers to relate between skills and competencies

    e.   All of the above

11. HR data collection must respect boundaries of employees' privacy in terms of the following, except

    a.   Culture

    b.   Processes

    c.   Attitudes

    d.   Food habits

    e.   None of the above

12. Important steps for HR data collection are the following, except

    a.   Identification of issues and opportunities for data collection

    b.   Fixing priorities of identified issues and opportunities for data collection

    c.   Planning for approach and methods of data collection

    d.   Deleting data that are contentious

    e.   Collection of data

13. While collecting HR data, HR managers consider the following, other than

    a.   Data source

    b.   Data context

    c.   Data quality

    d.   All of the above

    e.   None of the above

14. Big data for human resource denotes

    a.   Gathering HR data from several data sources

    b.   Collating HR data using HR analytics tool for decision-making

    c.   Aligning HR data with the organizational business and strategies

    d.   Integrating data from HR context

    e.   All of the above

15. Identify the incorrect statement out of the following:

    a.   HR data need to be always big data

    b.   Big data for HR help us in assessing the trends

    c.   Big data for HR help us in assessing the patterns

    d.   Big data for HR help us in assessing the correlations

    e.   Big data for HR help us in getting insights into intricacies of HRM in relation to organizational business and strategies

16. HR information denotes

    a.   HR data from internal stakeholders

    b.   HR data from various external reference points

    c.   Processed HR data with DSS

    d.   Processed HR data with HR analytics

    e.   Processes HR data with HRIS

17. Identify which of the following is an incorrect statement:

    a. HRMS can even manage unstructured verbal queries
    b. HR data analysis requires advance-level knowledge on statistics
    c. HR data analysis can be done through charts, bar diagrams and so on
    d. Correlations need not talk about cause and effect relationships
    e. Statistical knowledge can help in intelligent data analysis

18. Identify which of the following is not correct for qualitative data:

    a. Qualitative data cannot be in the form numeric information
    b. These are in the form of words
    c. These may be photographs, video or sound recordings
    d. These need to be understood in a specific context
    e. Their collection is done through observations, personal interviews, focus groups and case studies

19. Indicate which of the following is not an important type and source of HR data:

    a. Employees' data from HRMS or HRIS
    b. Survey data of employees
    c. All transactional data of human resources
    d. Machine breakdown data
    e. Organizational business performance data

20. Indicate which of the following statement is not relevant for HR reports:

    a. HR reports are prepared based on the HR analytics
    b. These focus on employee data more in the perspective of costs
    c. These can be business focused when combined with the budgets, performance evaluation records, attendance records and so on
    d. These cannot showcase the business value of human resources
    e. These can connect employee satisfaction with customer satisfaction

21. Indicate which of the following is not important for data visualization:

    a. It is data presentation in pictorial and graphical form
    b. It can be ensured by placing data in a visual context
    c. It helps us in understanding data patterns, trends and data correlations
    d. It cannot facilitate data drilling
    e. It can be supported by Excel

22. RCA helps in the following, other than

    a. Identifying root causes of problems
    b. Problem-solving
    c. It is quantified using the square root of the problem algorithm
    d. It is root cause as its elimination can help in decision-making
    e. It is the basic reason attributable to problems

Critical Review Question

1. Prepare a HR report on PMS of your organization.

Root Cause Analysis Application

A multinational manufacturing company uses behavioural event interviewing (BEI) for several decades to ensure the quality of their hires. However, recently with the recruitment of generation Y and partly also generation Z candidates, the company observes that more than 50 percent of the hiring decisions are wrong. New recruits in large numbers leave the organization within a year. Also, some of the new recruits underperform.

The analysis of the problem could identify for the following reasons:

- Sourcing issue (not the interview technique)
- Mismatched job allocation
- Inadequate antecedents check

Using the Kepner and Tregoe method of RCA, recommend your proposed solutions.

CASE STUDY

Data-driven Teamwork:
Experience of Indian Real Estate Major

On-time completion of projects within budget constraint can be considered as the core business objective of the real estate major having presence in all metropolitan cities of India. Within this core business objective, the company always endeavours to improve the cash flow and achieve incremental profit. Such approach, the company believes can motivate employees and enhance their performance. However, results are not always forthcoming. The company often observes project delay for unexplainable reasons, as employees cannot fix the reasons for the delay. Lack of ownership and poor accountability has been identified as the root cause of the problem. This requires teambuilding, rather than typical matrix structure with dual reporting. This is a shift from command and control to collaboration. Successfully driving the culture of teamwork in the organization, across all its work sites, requires participation of all cross-sections of employees of the organization. Concerted efforts of all to chase business goals inevitably raises motivation of all employees of the organization. This also helps in improving the quality, reducing the cycle time of projects, reducing the costs and enhancing profit. Also, it can build employees' capabilities to manage more projects successfully.

However, the culture of teamwork cannot be embedded with organizational management systems, unless people are made to understand the plan and other details to work together. This requires use of data for helping people to objectively understand the situation.

To start with, the company formed a cross-functional team with mix of managers and functional experts. This cross-functional team was entrusted the responsibility to drive the change, so that organizations can institutionalize team culture. This cross-functional team was entrusted with the responsibility of identifying prohibiting factors for poor ownership and accountability among employees. Interestingly, prohibiting factors that the company could identify are frequent changes in project plans, requiring rework and duplication of work and reactive style of managing the project, as employees feel they can not foresee future eventualities for frequent change of project plans. Also, employees feel like property refurbishing; their PMS also need to be refurbished. PMS, at present, can only share negative feedback and cannot capture holistic performance data for more objective feedback, which could have helped employees in assessing themselves in right earnest. Also, employees could provide more important suggestions, like adequate due diligence in property selection and purchase.

Based on the employees' feedback, the company decided to go for strengthening their MIS, proper identification of the project property, introduction of a system of resolving differences through discussions, provision of role clarity and strengthening the communication with focus on transparency.

In line with the aforementioned action plans, the company first redefined its KPIs, helping employees to assess themselves more objectively and to understand how they are performing. From organization point of view also, employees could be given more fact-based performance feedback. Different metrics were chosen at this stage to guide employees' activities objectively. These metrics could help in measuring performance, plotting data in a general format, across all the project sites. Such objective measurement helped in effective discussion on deterrent issues in project sites and helped the team in focusing attention to ease out the situation.

To motivate employees further, in review meetings, the company shared the data with the employees to objectively make them understand cost implication, wastage and so on, and its corresponding effect on the profitability of the organization, for any eventual project delay. With data, employees could recognize the issue, understand its gravity and, as a team, could take concerted actions for driving the success of this real estate company.

Question: Based on this case study develop some metrics, which you think are appropriate to drive change through teamwork.

FURTHER READINGS

Bassi, L. (2011). Raging debate in HR analytics. *People & Strategy, 34*(2), 14–18.

Bassi, L, Carpenter, R., & McMurrer, D. (2010). *HR analytics handbook: Report of the state of knowledge.* Amsterdam: Reed Business.

Davenport, T., Harris, J., & Morison, R. (2010). Analytics at work: Smarter decisions, better results. Boston, MA: Harvard Business School Press.

Falletta, S. (2013). In search of HR intelligence: Evidence-based HR analytics practices in high performing companies. *People and Strategy, 36*(4), 28–37.

Fitz-enz, J. (2010). *The new HR analytics: Predicting economic value of your company's human capital investments.* New York, NY: AMACOM.

Levenson, A. (2011). Using targeted analytics to improve talent decisions. *People & Strategy, 34*(2), 34–43.

Saari, L., & Scherbaum, C. (2011). Identified employee surveys: Potential promise, perils, and professional practice guidelines. *Industrial and Organizational Psychology, 4*(4), 435–448.

Sesil, J. C. (2014). *Applying advanced analytics to HR management decisions: Methods for selection, developing incentives, and improving collaboration.* Saddle River, NJ: Pearson.

APPENDIX

Factor Analysis Problem

Factor analysis is often done to analyse the survey research reports. In human resources, we use survey research particularly in those cases for which we do not have any quantitative data or information. One such case where we use survey research is measuring of employee engagement. Employee engagement is considered important for talent retention, increased performance, increased customer satisfaction and collaborative work culture, among others. For measuring employee engagement, let us assume we have a data file (Annexure: Excel Employee Data File) of 50 HR people who are working with our company. All these HR people have been asked specific questions on the aforementioned parameters using a 5-point Likert-type scale. In this case, our purpose is to assess whether the aforementioned questionnaire items could actually measure the construct. In simple terms, can we say from the questionnaire responses that it follows a specific pattern? When we observe responses group together, it indicates that the questionnaire items are measuring the construct. Let us explain this using analogy. It is expected that all the following questions can measure employee engagement and can elicit a similar answer.

1. Do you receive career guidance from your boss?
2. Do you feel your boss is concerned about your career development?
3. Do you feel your boss helps in making you successful?
4. Do you think your work environment is hygienic?
5. Are room fresheners used in your office?
6. Do you feel the urge for bathing after you reach home from office?

Careful study of this questionnaire can explain that as an HR professional our expectation would be to get similar responses from questionnaire items 1–3. These questionnaire responses help us in measuring support from the boss, which is a construct in this case. While for questionnaire responses against items 4–6, the construct is different, as it is intended to measure the hygiene of the workplace. In terms of factor analysis, our expectation here responses against questionnaire items 1–3 from 50 HR people will vary, i.e., will either go up or down, depending on how supportive are their bosses. Likewise, responses against questionnaire items 4–6 will vary depending on the degree of hygiene of the workplace.

Now, let us come to our employee engagement survey. Let us assume we have our own employee engagement scale with nine different parameters and each parameter is measured using a 5-point Likert-type scale, where 1 indicates strongly disagree and 5 strongly agree. Parameters here are hypothetical and not developed based on any standard employee engagement scale. It would be our expectation that respondents (here, it is 50 HR people) will answer all questions in a similar pattern (selecting similar point on 1–5 scale for all the items). With lower engagement, respondents would tend to select answer 1 or 2, while with higher engagement such answer selection would be 4 or 5. Assumptions here is that variation in the response pattern across all these items should not be too much, rather responses are expected to be consistent. For such results we use factor analysis. Factor analysis results can map the responses from HR people in a consistent manner across all the nine questionnaire items. Results can confirm any of the following four outcomes:

1. Responses are consistent; hence, questions are a good measure of employee engagement.
2. Responses are not consistent; hence, questions are not the good measure of employee engagement.

3. Responses are consistent for some of the items, indicating some questions are a good measure of employee engagement while some others are not.
4. Responses are consistent for two or more sets of items, indicating that in addition to employee engagement, questionnaire responses measure other constructs too.

When questionnaire responses measure more than one construct, it indicates our questionnaire items are poorly designed; hence, it needs reframing of questions. Or it could be a two-factor structure, namely employee engagement and bosses support.

Let us now frame our problem, assuming we have a two-factor structure, i.e., employee engagement and bosses support. Raw hypothetical data are presented in the Annexure. Here, we have 13 variables, first four of which indicate biographical variables, while rest nine employees' responses on their engagement and bosses support. Responses have been measured using a 5-point Likert-type scale, where 1 indicates low and 5 indicates high. Gender data are even though in xls file, being a categorical variable we have not considered it for ultimate analysis.

We have indicated the same as follows:

1. Gender (for female 1 and for male 2)
2. job_level (job level, where 1 indicates lower and 5 indicates higher)
3. age_group (where 1 indicates lower and 5 indicates higher)
4. experience (where 1 indicates lower and 5 indicates higher)
5. eq1 (engagement questionnaire 1)
6. eq2 (engagement questionnaire 2)
7. eq3 (engagement questionnaire 3)
8. eq4 (engagement questionnaire 4)
9. eq5 (engagement questionnaire 5)
10. bs1 (boss support questionnaire 1)
11. bs2 (boss support questionnaire 2)
12. bs3 (boss support questionnaire 3)
13. bs4 (boss support questionnaire 4)

Now, we will perform exploratory factor analysis to identify underlying relationships between measured variables.

We need to open SPSS and go to 'Analyze' menu and select 'Data Reduction', then the 'Factor' option (as presented in Figure A6.1).

Thereafter, we need to select all the 13 variables and move them over to the right-hand side Click on 'Variables' selection box and move using the arrow 	button. Then click on 'Rotation'. This can be seen in Figure A6.2.

Now, we select 'Rotation' to rotate factors. With clicking on the 'Rotation' box, we get a dialogue box and here we have to click the button 'Varimax'. This will analyse factors independently. After this, we go for 'Rotated solution' and the 'Loading plots', and then click 'Continue' and then 'OK'. It is shown in Figure A6.3.

After this, we get an output, which includes 'Total Variance Explained' and the 'Rotated Component Matrix'. Figure A6.4 shows 'Total Variance Explained'.

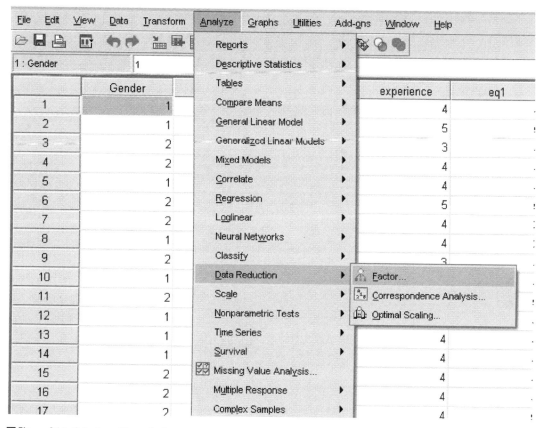

Figure A6.1: Selection of Factor Option

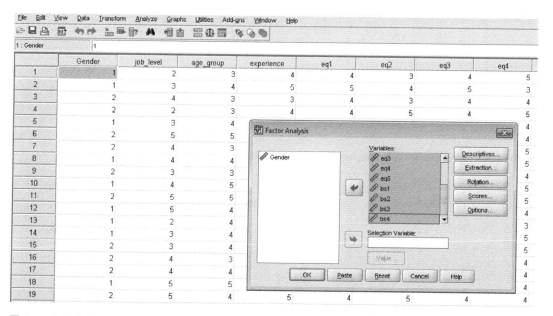

Figure A6.2: Selection of Variables

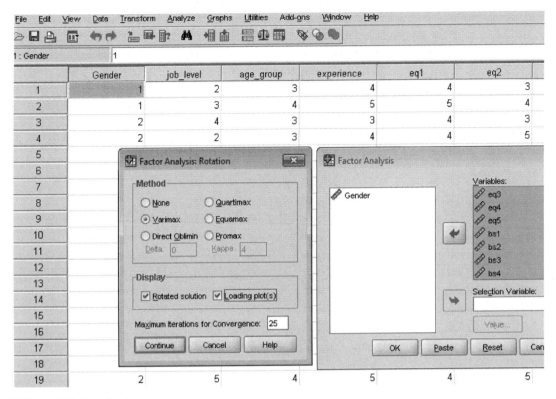

■ Figure A6.3: Factor Rotation

Total Variance Explained

Component	Initial Eigenvalues			Extraction Sums of Squared Loadings			Rotation Sums of Squared Loadings		
	Total	% of Variance	Cumulative %	Total	% of Variance	Cumulative %	Total	% of Variance	Cumulative %
1	2.657	22.139	22.139	2.657	22.139	22.139	2.352	19.598	19.598
2	1.991	16.593	38.732	1.991	16.593	38.732	1.890	15.754	35.352
3	1.583	13.189	51.920	1.583	13.189	51.920	1.762	14.680	50.033
4	1.295	10.793	62.713	1.295	10.793	62.713	1.416	11.799	61.832
5	1.189	9.907	72.620	1.189	9.907	72.620	1.295	10.788	72.620
6	.892	7.437	80.057						
7	.648	5.403	85.459						
8	.600	5.001	90.460						
9	.444	3.699	94.159						
10	.320	2.667	96.826						
11	.204	1.704	98.530						
12	.176	1.470	100.000						

Extraction Method: Principal Component Analysis.

■ Figure A6.4: Factor Analysis Total Variance Explained

Based on the data, SPSS here produces 5 factors or components from 13 initial factors or variables. Excluding gender, however, it is 12 factors or variables. We call these 'Components' and basically this groups the questionnaire items together in different combinations to find if any of them seem to be measuring the same underlying construct. This we understand when two variables behave similarly, i.e., when two variables have high correlation with each other. When SPSS produces a new component (grouping measure—such as engagement), then it will calculate the correlation that each item has with that component.

Rotated Component Matrix^a

	Component				
	1	2	3	4	5
job_level	.845	.115	.004	.031	.077
age_group	.926	−.032	.081	−.022	−.051
experience	.848	.078	.169	−.054	−.038
eq1	.172	.843	−.188	−.048	−.108
eq2	.016	.357	.187	−.605	.553
eq3	−.006	.900	.039	.129	−.076
eq4	.014	−.112	.355	.131	.707
eq5	.002	.377	.171	.805	.065
bs1	.151	−.062	.729	.079	.160
bs2	−.065	−.149	−.513	.585	.110
bs3	.031	.185	.382	.045	−.647
bs4	−.056	.081	−.747	.100	.040

Extraction Method: Principal Component Analysis.
Rotation Method: Varimax with Kaiser Normalization.
a. Rotation converged in 8 iterations.

■ **Figure A6.5:** Rotated Component Matrix

These are called 'factor loadings' or 'component transformation matrix' as shown in Figure A6.5.

In order to determine which components should be included, SPSS calculates the square of the factor loadings and then adds them together to give what is called an eigenvalue. As a rule of thumb, if the eigenvalue is greater than 1, we get a factor that we can use. If it is less than 1, this grouping of items does not correspond to a meaningful construct. In our analysis, we have six components with eigenvalues of more than 1, which indicates these six factors can be used as our constructs.

Looking at Figure A6.4, we can see that SPSS has calculated (after rotation) the eigenvalues for each of the 12 factors. First five factors have eigenvalues greater than 1. Therefore, the other factors are ignored. Looking at component 1 (or factor 1), we see it has a total eigenvalue of 2.352 and accounts for 19.598 percent of variance in the items. Component 2 (or factor 2) has a total eigenvalue of 1.890 and accounts for 15.754 percent of the variance in the items.

Looking at all the five factors together, the cumulative percentage value tells us that they account for 72.620 percent of the variance in all of the items.

The next step is to identify which items (questions) load together into which factors. This is where the subsequent rotated component matrix (Figure A6.5) comes in. Figure A6.5 shows the loadings of each item on each component (factor) after they have been rotated. It is possible to see from the table which questions get loaded to which (values more than 0.5). For example, eq1 and eq3 have gone to Component 2. Similarly, job_level, age_group and experience have gone to Component 1. Likewise, we can find the variables loading to their respective components. Close examination of the table could further reveal that bs2 is loading on both Components 3 and 4, which is not desirable. In such cases, ideally, it is advisable to delete that variable and redo factor analysis.

In a diagrammatic form, six components which have the highest factor loading have been shown in the rotated space in Figure A6.6. The variables that make up each component fall close to each other in three-dimensional sample space.

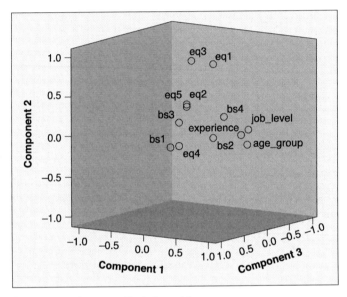

Figure A6.6 Component Plot in Rotated Space

Here, our purpose was to measure two latent variables: employee engagement and bosses support. The results of factor analysis could provide overall picture on these constructs and also could indicate which factor could do well on these measures. We could reduce initial 12 variables to 5 variables for gauging employee engagement and bosses support.

In conclusion, therefore, we can say our responses are consistent for some of the items, indicating some questions are a good measure of employees' engagement and bosses support while some others are not.

ANNEXURE
Excel Employee Data File

EMPLOYEE DATA FILE												
Gender	job_level	age_group	experience	eq1	eq2	eq3	eq4	eq5	bs1	bs2	bs3	bs4
1	2	3	4	4	3	4	5	4	3	4	5	5
1	3	4	5	5	4	5	3	4	4	4	5	4
2	4	3	3	4	3	4	4	5	4	4	4	5
2	2	3	4	4	5	4	5	4	5	4	4	4
1	3	4	4	4	4	5	4	4	4	5	5	4
2	5	5	5	5	5	5	4	4	5	4	4	5
2	4	3	4	3	4	4	5	4	5	4	3	3
1	4	4	4	3	3	3	5	4	4	5	4	5
2	3	3	3	4	4	4	4	5	5	5	5	4
1	4	5	4	4	5	4	5	4	5	4	5	4
2	5	5	5	5	5	5	5	5	5	4	4	4
1	5	4	4	4	4	4	4	4	4	5	5	5
1	2	4	4	4	3	4	3	4	3	5	5	5
1	3	4	4	4	5	4	5	4	5	5	4	4
2	3	4	4	4	4	4	5	4	5	4	5	4
2	4	3	4	4	3	5	4	5	4	5	3	4
2	4	4	4	5	4	5	4	5	4	5	4	5
1	5	5	5	5	4	4	4	4	4	4	4	4
2	5	4	5	4	5	4	4	4	4	4	4	4
1	4	3	4	4	3	4	3	5	5	5	4	5
2	5	4	4	5	5	5	4	4	4	4	5	5
2	3	4	2	4	4	4	5	4	3	5	4	5
2	3	2	2	5	5	5	4	4	3	5	4	5
1	2	2	3	4	4	5	5	5	4	4	5	4
1	1	1	1	4	4	4	5	4	5	5	4	4
1	2	2	3	5	3	5	4	5	4	4	5	5

EMPLOYEE DATA FILE												
Gender	job_level	age_group	experience	eq1	eq2	eq3	eq4	eq5	bs1	bs2	bs3	bs4
2	3	3	2	3	4	4	5	4	5	4	5	5
2	2	2	2	2	5	4	3	4	3	4	3	4
2	3	3	4	5	4	5	4	4	4	5	4	5
1	3	3	5	5	5	5	5	5	4	4	4	5
2	3	2	2	5	4	4	4	4	3	5	4	5
1	4	4	4	4	5	4	5	5	5	4	5	4
2	3	4	4	5	4	5	4	5	5	4	5	4
1	2	2	2	4	5	4	5	4	5	4	3	5
1	3	2	2	5	4	5	3	4	4	4	5	4
2	3	3	3	4	3	4	4	4	5	5	4	5
1	3	2	2	5	4	5	4	5	4	5	4	5
2	5	3	3	4	4	5	5	5	4	4	5	4
2	4	3	3	4	5	4	5	4	4	5	4	5
2	5	4	4	5	4	5	4	4	5	4	5	4
2	4	4	3	4	3	4	3	4	5	4	5	4
1	4	4	2	5	4	5	4	5	4	5	4	5
2	4	4	4	5	4	5	5	5	4	5	4	5
1	3	4	3	4	3	4	4	5	4	5	4	5
1	2	2	2	5	5	4	4	4	5	4	5	5
1	2	2	2	4	4	4	4	4	4	4	4	5
2	3	3	3	4	4	5	5	5	5	5	5	4
1	3	3	3	5	5	5	4	4	4	4	4	5
2	2	2	2	4	4	5	4	5	4	5	5	4
1	3	3	3	5	5	5	4	4	4	4	4	4

7

HR ANALYTICS AND PREDICTIVE MODELLING

LEARNING OBJECTIVES:

After reading this chapter, you will be able to understand:

- Basics of HR analytics and predictive modelling
- Different phases of HR analytics and predictive modelling
- Examples of predictive analytics
- Data and information for HR predictive analysis
- Predictive analytics tools and techniques
- Practical process of using predictive analytics for HR decisions

INTRODUCTORY CASE

Predictive Modelling of Employees' Behaviour and Consequent Success

Talent shortage is a critical area of concern for most of the organizations across the world. The problem is more acute for manufacturing organizations. One such manufacturing organization based in India has a headcount of 20,000 employees and is successfully operating over three decades. This organization has tremendous market reach across the globe and as high as 75 percent of its sales revenue comes from export. The company maintains a large inventory of technology manpower. However, ageing workforce is now one of its major concerns. Added to this problem is a mid-career job shift for many engineers, particularly in technology solutions consulting and information technology organizations. Such problems were never envisaged by the company as employees in general are happy with the way the company manages, so also with the compensation and benefits plan. Increased rate of voluntary employee turnover, particularly of those who are talented, has put the company in great difficulty and prompted for immediate intervention. For this the company made extensive use of HR analytics. To start with, the company started collection of employees' data (focusing more on talent-related data), financial and operational data, and also data from customers' and other stakeholders. With these data sets, the company then could come out with predictive models of employees' behaviour, even cascading it to the individual level. Such predictive models were tested for validity, analysing the behaviour of the employees who had already left the organization. With such validation, the company then initiated corrective measures, such as enhancing high employee engagement, work-life balancing, career growth opportunities and so on. All these were identified as possible weak areas in the data analysis phase. Such predictive modelling of employees' behaviour and corrective HR decisions could help the company to reduce employee attrition drastically and so also to introduce a compelling culture of performance.

INTRODUCTION

HR measurements can be done with metrics, analytics and predictive analytics by using big data. Understanding the process of using these requires specialized skills and knowledge on various statistical tools for developing a suitable algorithm. Right in the beginning, HR managers need to acquaint with the meaning and connotations of all these terms. In the previous chapters, we have discussed these terms. Here again, briefly, we will examine these terms for pacing the discussions of this chapter.

A metric is a fact. It can be in terms of counts, percentages, ratios and so on. HR metrics help us in simple measurement, such as the level of employee engagement, attrition rate, performance score, employees' satisfaction level, training effectiveness score, recruitment efficiency and so on. Therefore, metrics are capable only to track HR activities, particularly those which are quantifiable. Metrics cannot establish cause-effect relationships, namely, what causes employees' attrition and so on.

Analytics refers to measurement and reporting facts or metrics over a time period, explaining how these relate to one another. HR analytics per se can study how each of the aforementioned HR metrics can drive or affect the performance of an organization, can we see any pattern in these HR metrics and so on. For finding proper answers to all these queries, along with the analytics, we also use statistical tests.

Predictive analytics is a step forward, as with this we can even assess the probability of the future occurrence of an event, which may have significant implications on HR decisions. Predictive analytics help in measuring predictive patterns of HR issues combining algorithms, metrics, data and so on with a forward-looking approach. It helps in solving problems that may occur in future, getting answer(s) to specific question(s). For example, with predictive analytics, we can identify talents who are likely to leave the job of the company in the next one year and find out what could be the appropriate HR initiatives to ensure the retention of such talents. All these are now important to ensure HR decisions are effective in future.

Predictive modelling for HR decisions: Focuses on the predictive patterns of HR issues, measuring probability and making use of various statistical tools.

HR analytics and **predictive modelling for HR decisions** being focus on analysing predictive patterns of HR issues in terms of probability; it makes use of various statistical tools. For example, positive correlation indicates that one metric relates to another, while negative or inverse correlation indicates just the opposite.

Another term, i.e., big data denotes large and complex collection of data sets, which cannot be managed manually, and requires some database management or data processing solutions. With HR decisions becoming more and more complex, all-encompassing, and business and strategy aligned, big-data analysis for HR decisions help HR managers to get better insights.

For any organization, HR analytics application follows certain distinct phases of activities. Although we cannot have a model-based approach for successful application of HR analytics, emulating the professional practices, we can have a stepped approach for data collection; data analysis; development of HR metrics, scorecards, dashboards and so on; understanding effectiveness in terms of KPIs by using analytics; understanding how value creation takes place by using predictive analytics and finally overall impact analysis. More or less, this approach can benefit organizations in structuring their journey through HR analytics and predictive modelling of HR decisions.

DIFFERENT PHASES OF HR ANALYTICS OR HR PREDICTIVE MODELLING

Different phases of HR analytics from an organization's perspective can be described using the Bersin by Deloitte's maturity model (O'Leonard, 2013) of talent analytics. The model details the scientific progression from operational reporting to predictive analytics by using four distinct levels. We can also call it a roadmap for the gradual adoption of predictive analytics for human resources. These four distinct phases are as follows:

1. The operational phase. This involves the task of operational reporting; say performance, compliance matters and so on. This is also known as reactive phase.
2. Advanced reporting phase. This phase performs multidimensional analysis by using dashboards and others alike. In this phase, organizations also go for benchmarking. We also call this the proactive operational reporting phase.
3. Advanced analytics phase. This is the phase of proactive identification of problems or decisional issues for reaching to actionable solutions. In this phase, various statistical modelling techniques, root cause analysis and so on are performed for solving business issues. This is the phase from where we actually begin the use of HR analytics solutions to solve our business problems.
4. Predictive analytics phase. In this phase, we develop predictive models, develop scenario plans, perform risk analysis and so on, integrating with strategic plans and alike. This is the phase where ultimately HR functions must focus on to derive the benefits of HR analytics.

For the advanced analytics and predictive analytics phases, HR managers require strong statistical and data analysis skills. In this chapter, we have performed one case analysis by considering a specific HR issue, illustrating the phase-wise activities, for better understanding of the application of HR analytics and predictive analytics for futuristic HR decision-making.

EXAMPLES OF PREDICTIVE ANALYTICS

To develop predictive models for HR decisions, right at the beginning, we critically study the data volume. This can be explained with the real-life corporate example. It is common for organizations to develop a risk model to understand who among the talents are vulnerable to attrition risk. Let us assume that a company has a headcount of 20,000, and the past records indicate that the voluntary annual attrition rate is 5 percent. Based on this information, we can deduce that our sample data size is 1,000 employees for those who may be at voluntary attrition risk. Now this data volume further needs refinement in terms of certain other parameters such as service seniority, performance level and so on. Let us assume we need to develop our predictive models for attrition risk measurement taking into account those talents who left the job of the company voluntarily over last five years. This increases our sample size to 5,000. Here, we may put one data filter, such as from this sample size, we will only consider those who have delivered performance at the 'exceeds expectation' level. Let us assume 50 percent of these employees performed at the 'exceeds expectation' level. This reduces our sample size from 5,000 to 2,500. To further filter the data, we may consider factoring of some demographic variables, such as age group, education level and so on. Further, the data filter can be demonstrated competencies in work that are reflected in their performance records. With all these, let us assume we could ultimately reach a figure of 500 headcounts for those who may be vulnerable to voluntary attrition risk. Now our predictive models will measure the probability of these identified talents (500 in numbers) retention with possible HR interventions such as new career development opportunities, new compensation and benefits plans, employee engagement programmes and so on.

We can elaborate our ideas by using the following graphical presentations.

A typical metric for talent attrition when plotted in a graph (Figure 7.1) can be shown as follows:

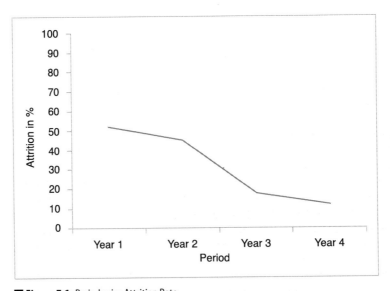

■ **Figure 7.1:** Period-wise Attrition Rate

Source: Author.

Figure 7.1 represents the number of talents who had voluntarily left the organization over the last four years. This is a fixed measurement in terms of absolute headcounts.

When we correlate the aforementioned data sets or metrics by using analytics, we can present the data as shown in Figure 7.2.

Figure 7.2 shows a graph that plots both voluntary (the upper line) and involuntary (the lower line) attritions over a time period, showing how they correlate with each other. Analytics can also help in measuring inverse correlation, time series analysis and so on.

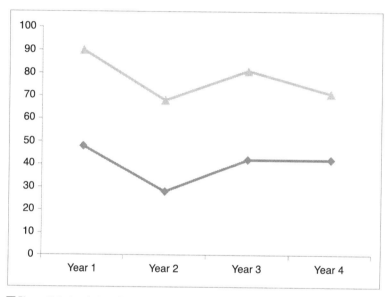

■ Figure 7.2: Correlation of Attrition
Source: Author.

Predictive modelling or predictive analytics by using regression can then simulate probable outcomes of a metric correlated with other metrics; e.g., predicting attrition risk on the basis of number of days availed leave during last one year.

In Figure 7.3, we have divided time period in four different time frames so as to compare how voluntary and involuntary attritions in different time frames correlate with each other. With data availability for longer time period, we can design more accurate regression models for predicting talent attrition. Regression models may further get complicated when we draw other data sets or metrics in addition to the leaves availed, such as engagement level, interpersonal relations, new initiatives, innovation, and so on, for further precision-level measurement of the attrition probability.

Predictive modelling: Predictive analytics using regression can simulate the probable outcomes of a metric correlating with other metrics, e.g., predicting attrition risk based on the number of days of leave availed during last one year. It can also be done using HR analytics solution in alignment with the business and strategies of the organizations.

Predictive analytics can be used as a critical HR decision-making tool duly diagnosing the underlying problems. To develop a predictive model, it is important to select the appropriate predictor variables. This requires HR

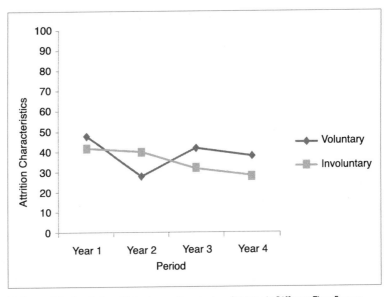

■ Figure 7.3: Correlation of Voluntary and Involuntary Attrition in Different Time Frames
Source: Author.

managers to understand which predictor variables can have a potential effect on specific HR issues. Again limiting predictor variables to only a few is not desirable here, as this may cause inaccuracy in the results. Predictive modelling is done by using software solutions which can handle large number of data sets. Also, developing a predictive model needs to be validated, and the performance of the model needs to be assessed. When results are inaccurate, models require re-examination and calibration. Almost in all critical HR decision-making processes, predictive analytics can help providing value insights into the prevalent trend and future outcome.

One of the most important areas of application of predictive analytics is talent retention. Common metrics like employee turnover, both voluntary and involuntary, can help us in understanding the trend. But when comparison of such a trend over a time period across all divisions, all functions and hierarchical levels is necessary, we have to go beyond metrics and make use of predictive analytics. Similarly, with standalone metrics like pay for performance, we can understand the pay differential of high performers compared to other employees of the organization; but how pay contributes to the business value of the organization can be understood through analytics. Further, how change in pay will alter future business value can be understood by using predictive analytics. Predictive analytics bring change in HR reporting going beyond transactional details and, thus, can add value to human resources.

Despite our discussions emphasizing analytics and predictive analytics, we cannot undermine HR metrics as HR metrics form the basis of our further analysis with analytics and predictive modelling.

In Box 7.1, some strategically important HR metrics which can help in adding value to HR reports through analytics and predictive modelling are presented.

Box 7.1   Strategic HR Metrics

- **Employee Turnover Rate.** This can be calculated for different time periods by using the following formula: (Number of separations during a time period/Average number of employees during the time period) × 100.
- **Revenue per Employee.** This can help in assessing the cost of employee turnover and can be calculated by using the following formula: Total revenue/Total number of employees.
- **Yield Ratio.** This can help in understanding the importance of various recruitment sources and can be calculated based on the percentage of applicants for different recruitment sources.
- **Human Capital Cost.** This can tell us the investments made in employees in terms of compensation and benefits, and can be measured with the following formula: Total compensation and benefits cost/Number of full-time employees.

The aforementioned list is only indicative. Depending on the organizational need, couple of other **strategic HR metrics**, such as human resources to staff ratio, ROI, promotion rate, female employees' representation at the management level, rate of employees' absenteeism, average age group of employees and so on, can also be considered.

Strategic HR metrics: Assess the strategic knowledge and skill sets, competencies, quality of cross-functional teams, ratio of pay at risk and so on.

The success of HR analytics and predictive modelling of HR decisions largely depends on the use of statistical tools combining human resources and business data. Relating human resources with business data can churn out information on customer satisfaction, market share trend and nature of products sold, e.g., premium products, mass products and so on. Some of the universal lessons for HR managers to make HR analytics and predictive modelling successful are combining intuition with analytics, making analytics more business centric, identifying skills that are required to use HR analytics, developing predictive models, ensuring involvement of subject-matter experts in analytics projects, trying to be realistic, taking decisions that are actionable and so on.

We use predictive models to guide different decisions through a series of predictions. Therefore, with predictive models, we cease to focus on the data, but rather focus on the underlying theory of reality. Hence, predictive models need to be accurate, reliable and credible. The assessment of the quality of a predictive model is done by simulating the future eventuality. To illustrate which incentive schemes will have more motivational effect on workers, the workers can be assessed comparing our predictions with the outcome that had actually occurred. In fact, we have built our predictive models based on the data sets of past occurrences. Any predictive models in human resources make use of cross-sectional data. For measuring reliability and validity, we make use of two random partitions: training or learning data set and testing or validation data set. The underlying thought processes for such data division are data sets, based on which we develop predictive models, represent real-life situation, and the real-life situation or processes are stable over a time frame; say previous quarter data may reasonably be stable during the following quarter. Data division between training and testing is done through simple random assignment. Training data sets are larger than the testing data sets. Predictive models developed based on training data sets are tested against testing data sets to assess the performance, and this also helps in model validation. However, we also see a trend in dividing data into a third data set, i.e., validation data sets. In such cases, we use test data to refine our model and validation data to check the accuracy of our predictive models. In some cases, the cross-validation of predictive models may be required. In such cases, we divide the data into multiple sets and run our model against each data set to check the accuracy. For checking and re-checking the accuracy of the models, we require double-checking our work, developing new algorithms when the one available does not yield results, selecting different variables, discussing with business domain experts for clarity on data sets and variables and so on.

Some of the known contributions made in the literature of HR analytics recently are the works of K. Edwards and M. Edwards (2016), Fitz-enz and Mattox (2014), Sesil (2013) and Smith (2013). All these contributors acknowledged the importance of HR analytics, including predictive HR analytics in making HR decisions more strategic and business aligned. When HR analytics are predictive in nature, they make use of predictive modelling based on inferential statistics for assessing the causal factors and deriving a solution visualizing the future. This obviously requires HR managers to acquire statistical knowledge to infer and understand the meaning of the results. In true sense, in the corporate world, we still find the use of HR metrics and partly HR analytics to process HR data sets and generate HR reports. Predictive analysis of these data sets with statistical techniques is found to be less. However, the new generation of HR managers is expected to meet this gap.

Descriptive HR reports with HR data sets, though traditional, benefit HR managers and organizations to monitor HR functions, helping managers understand whatever is going on. However, with descriptive HR reports, HR functions today cannot sustain. HR functions today being more strategic and business aligned, HR reports need to be more predictive. Bersin (2012) highlighted the importance of predictive analytics, as it can help us in interpreting HR data more meaningfully with due identification of trends and patterns, and causal factors including recommended action plans to avoid the recurrence of problem of HR issues. Huselid (2014) also endorsed the importance of HR analytics and predictive analytics as it facilitates strategic decision-making.

Some of the important HR data that are commonly required for HR analytics and predictive modelling of HR decisions are as follows:

- Demographic data of employees
- Data on knowledge, skill and competencies
- Training-related data
- Data on employee engagement
- Performance-related data
- Compensation- and benefits-related data
- Data on customer satisfaction
- Data on employee attrition or turnover.

We run our predictive models making use of such data sets to arrive at decisions that are likely to be less flawed and risky. Along with the concepts of predictive HR analytics that help us in predicting the future and taking our decisions more strategic and business aligned, we need to have clarity on other related terms that often interfere with the operational meaning, e.g., the term prediction which denotes the identification of predictors or potential causal factors for measuring a variation like predictors of employees' attrition. Predictors, thus, drive an outcome; also, these can be potential causes of variation of any HR issue that we are envisaging to predict. Predictive HR analytics denotes predictive modelling which helps in the identification of a series of factors for variations, e.g., in employees' performance level, and then use the model to predict the future outcome, i.e., the employees' performance level, when we take some actions, such as raising of incentives, increase in employee engagement, creating career development opportunities and so on. Also, predictive models are capable of predicting the future employees' performance level and suggest possible remedial actions to make future employees' performance level more satisfactory.

> **PRACTICE ASSIGNMENT**
>
> Based on your study of any organization, cite some examples of predictive analytics, which could help in improving the quality of HR decision-making.

DATA AND INFORMATION FOR HR PREDICTIVE ANALYSIS

We have already said data availability largely depends on the nature of an organization. Many organizations do not recognize the strategic and business roles of human resources. For them, HR functions are managed in silos. This is most common; hence, for illustrating cases of HR predictive analysis, we will restrict our focus only on HR data. By linking data sources and thinking broadly across the whole organization, we are able to model organizational patterns of behaviour and link human resources and people-management practices directly with revenue and efficiency. In order to link and analyse the information available with ease, we need to use a statistical analysis package, of which there are many available on the market.

■ Table 7.1: Possible Sources of Information/Data for Use by Human Resources

Information/Data Source	Description	Example
HR database. Commonly used HR databases are SAP or Oracle.	Information on all HR activities, and also personal details about the employees.	All demographic data, performance ratings, job role, compensation and benefits, attendance, leave information, health status, training and so on.
Employee survey data. Organizations conduct surveys from time to time to measure employees' attitude, motivation level, satisfaction level, response to change and so on.	All information based on survey responses received from employees on various issues. Common employees' survey can be attitude survey, employee engagement survey and others alike.	All survey data or information on employees' attitude, engagement level, motivation and job satisfaction level, employees' perceptions on workplace equity and so on.
Customer survey data.	All information on customers' preferences in alignment with the employees' profile, operation, service delivery, sensitivity to customers' needs and so on. These data and information can benefit organizations in bringing change in customer services and processes, employees' behaviour and skills and so on.	All customer ratings data pertaining to customer services, data on customer satisfaction, customer preferences and so on.

Source: Author.

Table 7.1 illustrates some of the possible information/data sources, nature and examples of such information.

Such data and information widely vary in terms of their scope depending on the degree of alignment of HR functions with the business and strategies of the organization.

SOFTWARE SOLUTIONS

Once data and information are available from multiple sources, as explained, we perform predictive HR analysis by using various software solutions. Some known software solutions available on the market are as follows:

- SPSS
- Minitab
- Stata
- SAS
- R
- JASP

Almost all software solutions have common features and are capable of performing HR analytics jobs along with predictive decision modelling. In this chapter, we have shown the process of doing HR analytics and so also predictive decision modelling by using IBM SPSS predictive analytics software. Hence, our discussion will centre on its process of use. However, similar analysis and predictive decision modelling can also be done with other software solutions, the processes used there are different.

IBM SPSS predictive analytics software can perform statistical analysis and reporting, predictive modelling and data mining, decision management and deployment, and big-data analytics. It can enhance the decision-making process related to business through various analyses, hypothesis testing and predictive analytics, establishing causal relationships among large amounts of time series data. At the end of this chapter we have developed predictive decision models for futuristic HR decision-making, based on real-life HR data, making use of IBM SPSS predictive analytics as a tool.

PREDICTIVE ANALYTICS TOOLS AND TECHNIQUES

Predictive analytics extracts information from raw data and makes use of the same to predict the future pattern of behaviour or trends for getting better insights into HR decision-making. Broadly, predictive analytics tools are divided into regression techniques and machine learning.

Regression analysis helps us in estimating relationships among different variables. For predictive analytics, the following types of regression analysis can be of use:

- Linear regression. This helps in modelling relationships between a dependent variable (Y) and one or more explanatory variable (X). Suppose an HR manager wants to assess the association between performance and pay. Here, performance is the dependent variable and pay is the independent or explanatory variable. In regression analysis, we denote the dependent variable as 'Y' and the independent variable as 'X'.
- Discrete choice models. Using these models, we can describe, explain and predict our choices between two or more discrete alternatives. Here, we limit our choices to those alternatives for analysis which we feel are critical for the problem or decision issue. This we can understand based on our previous knowledge, or through previous survey or qualitative research. Suppose as an HR manager you want to find out what matters more for employees' satisfaction: Should it be better deferred benefits for a secured future, some extra vacation plan or a better insurance coverage? We put before the employees various alternatives, so as to enable them to make their choice based on trade-offs between cash payout and deferred benefits, payment in monetary terms and extra vacation and so on. Responses from all employees are combined and then the best alternative that can increase the level of satisfaction for the employees and at the same time optimize the costs for the organization is identified by using the model.

- Logistic regression. This type of regression helps us to predict the outcome of a categorical or dependent variable (e.g., employees' performance) based on one or more independent or predictor variables (such as pay, career development opportunities, promotion and so on).
- Multinomial logistic regression. This regression model can generalize two outcome (dependent) variables with the linear combination of the predictor (independent) variables. For example, employees' career choice (outcome or dependent variable) can be studied in relation to his/her level of education or mother's influence (predictor or independent variables). Similarly, employees' choices of a training programme, either conceptual or skill specific, may be modelled against the performance score and the education level.
- Probit regression. This regression model helps to study a problem when the outcome or dependent variable can only take two values, i.e., yes or no. Let us assume an employee may or may not get promotion. The predictor or independent variable in this case would be the performance score, age, number of years in same job position, leadership capabilities and so on.
- Neural network. In predictive analytics, **neural networks** denote enhancing computer capabilities, configuring it with required hardware and software so that like human neurons in human brain it can solve complex signalling and pattern-recognition problems. For example, in employee recruitment if we want to predict how a particular applicant can achieve the best job performance, we require data on the application such as personal information, previous jobs, level of education, previous performance, social network data and so on. This requires neural networks or machine learning, rather than regression modelling discussed earlier. More appropriate use of neural networks in profiling a target hire is checking his/her background characteristics. In some critical areas, such as handwriting recognition for cheque clearance, facial recognition, speech analysis, text analysis and so on, neural networks can help. It requires the use of multiple processors simultaneously to receive information (like optic nerves of human beings). The first-level processors receive raw input information. After processing, the data pass on to the next level of processors and then get transferred to the last level of processors to churn the results or the output.
- Decision tree and scenario analysis. A **decision tree** is an important decision-making tool. Before taking decisions, HR managers can understand different choices, risks, gains and so on by using a decision tree. With multiple decision alternatives plotted on a decision tree, HR managers can critically assess each alternative and select the best one. A sample decision tree is illustrated in Figure 7.4.

Neural network: In predictive analytics, neural networks denote enhancing computer capabilities configuring it with required hardware and software, so that like human neurons in human brain it can solve complex signalling and pattern recognition problems.

Decision tree: A decision tree is an important decision-making tool. Before taking decisions, HR managers can understand different choices, risks, gains and so on using a decision tree. With multiple decision alternatives plotted in a decision tree, HR managers can critically assess each alternative and select the best one.

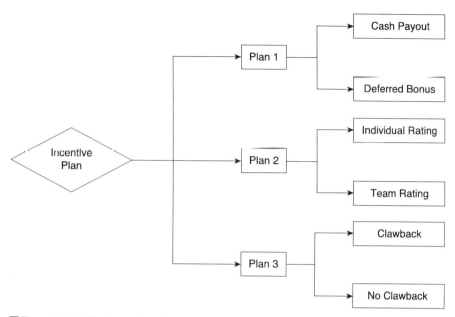

■ Figure 7.4: Decision Tree on Incentive
Source: Author.

Nodes and branches indicate a host of choices available for decisions. The model combines different choices (actions) with detailing of different possible events when a particular choice is selected for the decisions.

Scenario analysis helps us to understand the expected outcome of a decision in different situations. Like simulation, this analysis considers two extremes of a scenario or a base case. Both best and worst possible outcomes of a decision can be ascertained and accordingly decisions are taken. Although its usage is more appropriate in financial decision-making, we can also use it in human resources. HR managers need to perform scenario planning from time to time for assessing uncertain shifts in the environment of an organization and accordingly calibrate the decisions. In human resources, scenario analysis can help us in integrating organization-wide HRM activities with business scorecards, thereby helping in strategic decision-making. The analysis follows the system dynamics approach to model complex systems with computer-aided simulation. Systems dynamics methodology can encapsulate complex HR factors like performance management in understanding which factors contribute to specific performance outcomes, linking HR metrics, competencies and organizational business scorecards. Such causal relationships once understood with scenario analysis can be used as the basis for HR decisions.

Scenario analysis: It helps us to understand the expected outcome of a decision in different situations.

> **PRACTICE ASSIGNMENT**
>
> Like a decision tree on incentive presented in this chapter, develop a decision tree on talent retention strategies.

ANALYTICS HIGHLIGHT

HRP in Google is a strategic HR function. Google does HRP through trend analysis and scenario analysis. While trend analysis is a quantitative tool for forecasting, scenario analysis is a qualitative tool used by Google for HRP. Scenario analysis analyses different mix of variables for predicting the demand for human resources for different resultant scenarios. Using both quantitative and qualitative tools, Google does effective HRP.

In this book, we have restricted our focus only on data analysis and making HR decision-making process more data driven. Therefore, though both decision tree and scenario analysis are important in nature, we will not discuss their application in the HR decision-making process.

Predictive analytics tools today are more user-friendly, and in the market we have a number of vendors who can provide business solutions. Such tools can help us in predicting the outcome of a decision issue by using multiple techniques. In this chapter, we have illustrated a case detailing right from the stage of data collection, analysis, statistical analysis and predictive modelling (see the appendix).

Summary

HR measurements can be done with metrics, analytics and predictive analytics by using big data. Understanding the process of using these requires specialized skills and knowledge on various statistical tools for developing suitable algorithm.

To develop predictive models for HR decisions, right at the beginning, we critically study the data volume.

Predictive analytics can be used as a critical HR decision-making tool duly diagnosing the underlying problems. To develop a predictive model, it is important to select the appropriate predictor variables. This requires HR managers to understand which predictor variables can have potential effect on specific HR issues.

The success of HR analytics and predictive modelling of HR decisions largely depends on the use of statistical tools combining HR and business data. Relating HR with business data can churn out information on customer satisfaction, market share trend and nature of products sold, e.g., premium products, mass products and so on.

Predictive analytics extract information from raw data and make use of the same to predict the future pattern of behaviour or trends for getting better insights into HR decision-making. Broadly, predictive analytics tools are divided into regression techniques and machine learning.

General Review Questions

1. Explain the concepts of HR analytics and predictive HR decision modelling.
2. What are the different phases of HR analytics and HR predictive modelling?
3. Elaborate some of the examples of predictive analytics in the context of human resources.
4. Explain the process of churning data and information for HR predictive analysis.
5. What are the tools and techniques for predictive HR analytics?
6. Write short notes on the following:

   - Decision tree
   - Scenario analysis
   - Neural network
   - Descriptive HR reports
   - Yield ratio
   - Algorithm for HR decisions

Multiple Choice Questions

1. HR measurements can be done with the following, except

   a. Metrics
   b. HR analytics
   c. Predictive analytics
   d. Fish-bone diagram
   e. None of the above

2. HR metrics cannot help us in measuring

   a. Level of employee engagement
   b. Attrition rate
   c. Cause–effect relationships
   d. Performance score
   e. Recruitment efficiency

3. Identify the most appropriate statement for predictive analytics from the following:

   a. It can measure and report facts or metrics over a time period
   b. It can explain how metrics relate to one another
   c. It can see a pattern in HR metrics
   d. It can see how HR metrics can drive or affect the performance of the organization
   e. It can assess the probability of future occurrence of an event and its implications on HR decisions

4. Predictive analytics matches with the following statement, except

   a. It involves predictive patterns of HR issues
   b. It combines algorithms, metrics and data
   c. It is a forward-looking approach
   d. It helps in solving problems that may occur in future
   e. It cannot get answer to a specific question

5. Predictive modelling of HR decisions focuses on the following other than

   a. A forward-looking approach to human resources
   b. Predictive patterns of human resources

    c.   Explain how metrics relate to one another
    d.   Measure probability
    e.   Make use of various statistical tools

6. Successful application of HR analytics follows a stepped approach, covering the following points, except

    a.   Data collection
    b.   Data analysis
    c.   Developing of HR metrics
    d.   Developing scorecards and dashboards
    e.   Modelling of HR decisions

7. The roadmap for gradual adoption of predictive analytics for human resources involves

    a.   Operational phase
    b.   Advanced reporting phase
    c.   Advanced analytics phase
    d.   Predictive analytics phase
    e.   All of the above

8. Indicate which of the following is not a strategic HR metric:

    a.   Ratio of human resources with respect to employees
    b.   Employee turnover ratio
    c.   Revenue per employee ratio
    d.   Yield ratio
    e.   HC ratio

9. Some of the important HR data that are commonly required for predictive modelling of HR decisions are

    a.   Demographic data of employees
    b.   Data on knowledge, skill and competencies
    c.   Training-related data
    d.   Data on employee engagement
    e.   All of the above

10. HR decisions can be made predictive based on which of the following:

    a.   Data on employees' hobby
    b.   Performance-related data
    c.   Compensation- and benefits-related data
    d.   Data on customer satisfaction
    e.   Data on employee attrition or turnover

11. A standard predictive analytics solution is expected to perform the following, except

    a.   Statistical analysis and reporting
    b.   Predictive modelling and data mining
    c.   Decision management and deployment
    d.   Big-data analytics
    e.   None of the above

12. Regression analysis helps us in estimating

    a.   Relationships among variables
    b.   Modelling relationships between a dependent variable (Y) and one or more explanatory variable(s) (X)
    c.   Association between performance and pay
    d.   All of the above
    e.   None of the above

Critical Review Question

1. Like the example cited in this chapter, develop predictive models for the recruitment function of a large technology solutions company spread across 10 countries and employing 8,000 people at present. The company requires global sourcing of talent and their growth is significantly influenced by the availability of right skill sets.

PRACTITIONER SPEAKS

It is believed that the 'line of sight', i.e., the alignment of HR activities with the business of the organization can be ensured by HR analytics. The first stepping stone to create the 'line of sight' is measuring human resources with suitable HR metrics. Realizing this, an HR manager of a large manufacturing organization developed the following metrics. The manager feels that with such metrics he can get better insights and accordingly can calibrate his HR function for getting business results.

HR Functions	Nature of Metrics
Recruitment	Performance score of new hires. Attrition rate of new hires. Difference between the performance of new hires from the external and internal sources. Average cost of manpower replacement.
Employee engagement	Percentage of employees who feel enthusiastic to come to work and also feel satisfied with the way the organization is managed. This can be measured with a survey covering questions on challenge and excitement in work, functional autonomy, identify with the work, learning, recognition and rewards, and so on.
HRD	Percentage of employees with the required level of competency, ROI from training, employee satisfaction about training and learning, and so on.
HR costs	Average cost of compensation and benefits, incremental performance change achieved through new compensation and benefits programme, HR costs and revenue generation ratio and so on.

However, the CEO of the company believes that the earlier described HR metrics cannot give a 'line-of-sight' in aligning HR activities with the business. These are nothing beyond reactive operational data. Do you agree with CEO's observation? What are your arguments?

CASE STUDY

Predictive Analytics for Hiring: Case of Wells Fargo

Wells Fargo, a diversified financial services company founded in 1852, operates from 36 countries with a headcount of 269,000. This company, despite carrying a legacy of more than two centuries, today possesses USD 1.8 trillion in assets and could achieve a market capitalization of USD 245 billion. The company provides banking, insurance, investments, mortgage, and retail and commercial financial services through 8,800 locations and 13,000 ATMs spread across the globe. This San Francisco-based financial services' company with a 70 million customer base today embraces predictive analytics for hiring. For several years, the company has been using predictive-analytics-driven talent assessment solution to ensure they get the right-fit for the job positions and selected employees continue in their employment with the company with a long-term plan. Likewise, Wells Fargo could screen over two million candidates over the years. With predictive analytics Wells Fargo is recruiting those who are more likely to perform better and stay longer. The company believes in the unique culture of 'need-based selling and customer service'. The recruitment process needs to focus on this aspect to ensure candidates who are hired are best-fit with the culture of the organization.

The company needs to use predictive analytics to centralize recruitment functions and for standardizing the selection process, performance review and employee incentive processes. Rather than using psychometric tests in recruitment, the company emphasized the use of biometric data. Analysing such biometric data, the company could know about the number of jobs a candidate had, the duration of stay in each job, the number of promotions the candidate had, the highest level of education and so on. Using these inputs, the predictive analytics solutions of Wells Fargo can predict the best candidates based on the analysis of their background experiences, career motivation, performance, life/work skills and so on. Predictive models developed by the company could demonstrate high reliability for predictive future performance of the recruited employees. Any candidate seeking job positions in Wells Fargo needs to answer a set of questions online. These questions seek biometric data and also test the functional knowledge and skill of the prospective candidates. The predictive solutions are so built that any candidate scoring high (as considered by the company) in his/her interview automatically gets scheduled. The prospective candidate can accordingly meet Wells Fargo's representative on the scheduled date, time and venue. This process also could substantially reduce the cost of recruitment and selection.

Even with this, the company could identify who are the team members for future leadership positions and accordingly groom them right from the beginning with different onboarding processes, assigning special coach and mentors, and so on.

Rather than making these predictive models one-size-fit-all solutions for recruitment, the company also analyses the statistical significance on an ongoing basis and could get the results even at 90 percent confidence levels. With improved performance and retention, the company could make its predictive recruitment solutions its basis for hiring.

Question: Based on Wells Fargo's experience, your company has given you the task of developing predictive analytics solutions for increasing the employee engagement. Indicate your line of action.

REFERENCES

Bersin, J. (2012). *The HR measurement framework* (Bersin and Associates Research Report No. CA 94612). Oakland: Bersin and Associates.

Edwards, K., & Edwards, M. (2016). *Predictive HR analytics*. London: Kogan Page.

Fitz-enz, J., & Mattox, J. R., II. (2014). *Predictive analytics for human resources*. New Delhi: Wiley India.

Huselid, M. (2014). The corporate mirror. D'Amore-McKim School of Business. Available at: http://www.damoremckimleadersatworkblog.com/corporate-mirror-looking-big-data-analytics-work force-management/#sthash.4qx5y7F3.dpuf (accessed on 30 November 2015).

O'Leonard, K. (2013). Getting started with talent analytics. Bersin by Deloitte. New York: Deloitte.

Sesil, J. C. (2013). *Applying advanced analytics to HR management decision: Methods for selection, developing incentives and improving collaboration.* New Jersey, USA: Pearson.

Smith, T. (2013). *HR analytics: The what, why and how….* USA: CreateSpace.

FURTHER READINGS

CIPD. (2013). Talent analytics and big data: The challenge for HR. Available at: http://www.cipd.co.uk/hr-resources/research/talent-analytics-big-data.aspx (accessed on 30 November 2015).

Holley, N. (2013). Big data and HR: Henley Centre for HR Excellence. Henley Business School. Available at: http://www.henley.ac.uk/html/hwss/files/Henley-Centre-for-HR-Excellence-Big-Data-Research-paper.pdf (accessed 30 November 2015).

Huselid, M. A., & Becker, B. E. (2005). Improving human resources' analytical literacy: Lessons from Moneyball. In D. Ulrich, M. Losey and S. Meisinger (Eds.), *Future of Human Resource Management.* New York: John Wiley & Sons.

IBM. (2010). Analytics: The new path to value. IBM and MIT Sloan Review. Available at: http://www-935.ibm.com/services/uk/gbs/pdf/Analytics_The_new_path_to_value.pdf (accessed 30 November 2015).

KPMG. (2013). People are the real number: HR analytics has come of age. Available at: https://www.kpmg.com/GR/en/IssuesAndInsights/ArticlesPublications/Documents/workforce-analytics-download.pdf (accessed 30 November 2015).

Pease, G., Byerly, B., & Fitz-enz, J. (2016). *Human capital analytics: How to harness the potential of your organization's greatest asset.* New Delhi: John Wiley & Sons.

APPENDIX

Predicting Employee Performance

Organizations are more performance driven to sustain in competition. Individual, team and organizational performances are now constantly measured and used as critical inputs for major decisions pertaining not only to employees but also business and strategy framing. Using HR analytics, organizations predict the future performance; identify who are the high-performing employees, who can have critical role in improving team performance; driving organizational performance and so on. Also, such predictive measurement of employees' performances helps in making investment decisions for learning and development on those employees who are chronic underperformers. Using HR analytics, we can predict performance and take decisions that are more accurate and business driven.

For an HR manager, the first challenge here is to decide what sort of performance he/she will be predicting. Although we naturally assume that the annual performance rating data are adequate for us to predict the future performance, but this can only help us in getting a partial view. We have many other performance indicators that are capable of providing useful information. For example, for predicting future team performance, we need to measure team function, competence of a team leader, attitude of individual team members, team engagement, customer feedback, customer loyalty, repeat business from customers, employee turnover rate in a team and so on. Similarly, for predicting the future individual performance, in addition to individual performance rating, we need to study behaviour rating, sales performance figures, individual customer feedback, peer feedback, gender, age group, sickness absence, job satisfaction, person–organization fit, compensation and benefits, perceptions on organizational equity and justice and so on. But operationally, many organizations may not have all these data sets. Obviously, in such cases, we have to restrict our predictive performance analysis based on the available data set in organizations. If we carefully observe, some of the data sets mentioned earlier are not directly attributable to the performance level and rating, even then we have used these data sets in predictive modelling, as this can make our analysis more encompassing and holistic.

As performance measures widely vary across organizations, we cannot have any universal approach to collect performance data. In many organizations, customer satisfaction data may not be considered as the performance measure, so also the sickness absences, attrition data and employee engagement score. But all these have direct bearing on organizational performance. Hence, once we are capable to churn these data, we can encapsulate these in our predictive analysis.

Process of Analysis

For performance analysis, we need to look into the relationships and predictors. Some of the points for our line of enquiry are as follows:

- Characteristics of top individual and team performers
- Investment on the training and development of these top performers
- Key employee characteristics, capabilities and attributes of top performers

To answer all the aforementioned points, we need to do multiple linear regressions. It can help us to analyse the number of independent variables, such as gender, age, team leader, country location and so on, and predict a dependent variable (e.g., performance level) by developing a 'best-fit' model. The multiple linear regressions will tell us the proportion of variance in the dependent variable that is accounted for by all the independent variables collectively and also can indicate which independent variable has a significant impact on the dependent variable, and the relative emphasis of each dependent variable. As the process of doing multiple linear regressions can be understood from a basic statistics book, we are not discussing the process here, rather focusing on data collection and analysis for predicting the future performance level of employees.

Let us now get back to our analysis. Based on our imaginary data sets (see the Annexure: Employee Data Set), we can perform the following multiple linear regressions:

- Predicting the individual performance level combining performance ratings data, employees' record of sickness
- Predicting the individual performance level with performance ratings data, sickness records and customer's loyalty
- Predicting the individual performance level with performance ratings data, sickness records and attitude of employee
- Predicting the individual performance level with performance ratings data, sickness records and employee's profile

This is a tentative description of multiple linear regressions that can be done in a hypothetical situation. Depending on the availability of the data sets and understanding how several factors can influence employees' performance, we can have even more multiple linear regressions to build our predictive model. As our purpose is to explain how predictive modelling for decision-making can be done by using SPSS, we will explain with a specific case of predicting employees' performance level and retention (dependent variables) in relation to some independent variables. Let us frame our problem as follows:

We have to analyse based on the imaginary data sets as appended in the Annexure. Ideally, however, in a real-life situation, for this type of analysis, we collect some inputs from employees' through survey and some inputs from the existing data sets available in the organization. Our purpose here is to understand what factors can be attributed as important for employees' performance and retention. For this example, we have created imaginary data sets of 100 employees working in a hypothetical company. For each employee, we have the following seven survey questions: four of these questions are pertaining to employees' performance level issues and the rest three to understand how loyal they are to their organization.

The first phase of the four questions which are intended to measure the performance level in terms of employees' competence and skills are as follows:

- Understanding job (Sat 1)
- Functional autonomy (Sat 2)
- Frequency of interaction with boss (Sat 3)
- Use of technology in job (Sat 4)

Using a scale of 1–5, employees were asked to indicate their responses against the afore-mentioned questions, where 5 indicates highly satisfied and 1 indicates unsatisfied.

Similarly, the next three questions were asked to measure the likelihood of their retention, again using a scale of 1–5, except in case of gender, as follows:

1. Engagement with the organization (Eng)
2. Competitive compensation and benefits (Ccb)
3. Gender (1 for female and 2 for male)

Data sets, as mentioned earlier, represent imaginary responses from 100 employees of the organization.

Looking at the problem, we can see that we have two dependent or outcome variables and seven independent or predictor variables. Our predictive analysis will help us in understanding whether the organization, by bringing change in predictor variables, can improve employees' performance levels and retention.

Our regression model will look as follows:

The performance level = $a + b_1$ (understanding job) + b_2 (functional autonomy) + b_3 (frequency of interaction with boss) + b_4 (use of technology in job).

Similarly, for employee retention, our model will be as follows:

Employee retention = $a + b_1$ (engagement with the organization) + b_2 (competitive compensation and benefits) + b_3 (gender, i.e., 1 or 2).

Now we need to fit these data sets in SPSS, selecting 'Analyze', 'Regression' and 'Linear'. Then, we set the 'performance level' as a dependent variable and four predictor or independent variables, mentioned earlier. The same is repeated for predicting employee retention. This is explained using the following screenshots of SPSS (see Figures A7.1 and A7.2).

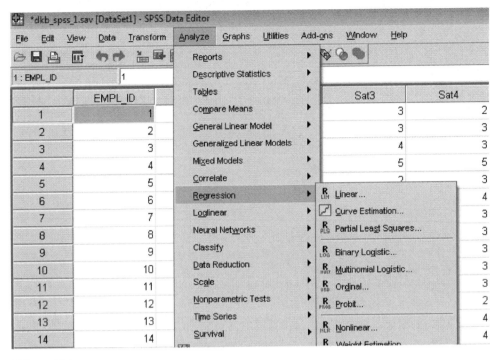

■ Figure A7.1

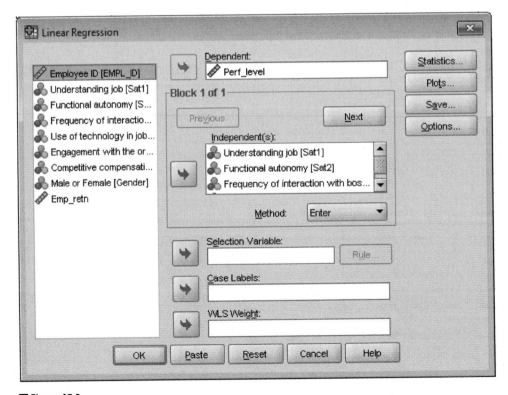

■ Figure A7.2

After arranging data in SPSS (importing from the appended excel sheet), we then click 'OK' to get the output. In our case, our output is as follows:

Variables Entered/Removed[b]

Model	Variables Entered	Variables Removed	Method
1	Use of technology in job, Understanding job, Frequency of interaction with boss, Functional autonomy[a]		Enter

a. All requested variables entered.
b. Dependent Variable: Perf_level

Model Summary

Model	R	R Square	Adjusted R Square	Std. Error of the Estimate
1	.235[a]	.055	.016	1.41788

a. Predictors: (Constant), Use of technology in job, Understanding job, Frequency of interaction with boss, Functional autonomy

ANOVA[b]

Model		Sum of Squares	df	Mean Square	F	Sig.
1	Regression	11.205	4	2.801	1.393	.242[a]
	Residual	190.985	95	2.010		
	Total	202.190	99			

a. Predictors: (Constant), Use of technology in job, Understanding job, Frequency of interaction with boss, Functional autonomy
b. Dependent Variable: Perf_level

Coefficients[a]

Model		Unstandardized Coefficients		Standardized Coefficients	t	Sig.
		B	Std. Error	Beta		
1	(Constant)	5.060	1.057		4.787	.000
	Understanding job	−.408	.286	−.191	−1.428	.157
	Functional autonomy	.074	.295	.037	.251	.802
	Frequency of interaction with boss	.168	.230	.090	.729	.468
	Use of technology in job	−.307	.211	−.171	−1.452	.150

a. Dependent Variable: Perf_level

■ **Figure A7.3**

The summary of the model tells us that the R-square is 0.055. R-square is the square of the multiple regression coefficients between the dependent variable and the predictor variables together. So, the greater the R-square, the more the predictor variables are jointly predictive about the dependent variable. When we multiply it by 100, it tells us the percentage of variance in the dependant variable, i.e., accounted for by the other variables. More technically, it is the percentage of variance accounted for in our dependent variable when taking into account its shared linear relationship with our independent variables (whilst taking into account the interrelationships between the independent variables). So, in this case, the R-square is 0.055, and thus we can say that 5.5 percent of variance in expressions of the performance level is accounted for by the particular combination of predictor variables, as has been used here.

Looking at the ANOVA table, we can understand how well this model predicts variation in the performance level. Here, the regression ANOVA F-value is 1.393 with total degrees of freedom of 99. Although such statistical significance can be interpreted from a statistical table commonly available in any book on statistics, here we could get it from SPSS directly. Here, SPSS has calculated the statistical significance for us to be 0.242 (at 5 percent level of significance). So, we can say that the significance level reached has a p-value of 0.242, which means there is less than about 24 percent chance that we would find this pattern of shared variance (between the performance level and the other survey questions) by chance alone. Therefore, our model is not significant, as the data set used is imaginary.

Had the model being significant from the ANOVA outcome, we could understand which of our independent variables have a significant impact on the performance level, to what extent and also in what direction (i.e., some may potentially improve the performance while others may decrease it). Using our knowledge of the levels of significance and looking at the right-hand column of the table (Figure A7.3, the coefficients table), it appears that four of the predictor variables (excluding the constant) could not significantly predict the performance level. The data sets used for this analysis are imaginary and used only to explain the analytical process. But from this example and with the actual data, it would be reasonable to make the recommendation to invest in helping employees to better understand their jobs, similarly giving more functional autonomy and enhancing the frequency of interaction with boss.

Likewise, we can also predict the employee retention in relation to engagement with the organization, competitive compensation and benefits, and gender.

ANNEXURE

Employee Data Set

Employee Data Set									
EMPL	Sat1	Sat2	Sat3	Sat4	Eng	Ccb	Gender	Perf_level	Emp_retn
1	4	3	3	2	3	3	1	5	1
2	3	4	3	3	3	3	2	3	1
3	4	4	4	3	3	3	1	5	2

(Annexure Continued)

| | | | | Employee Data Set | | | | | |
EMPL	Sat1	Sat2	Sat3	Sat4	Eng	Ccb	Gender	Perf_level	Emp_retn
4	3	4	5	5	3	4	1	5	4
5	3	3	2	3	3	2	2	2	5
6	4	5	3	4	4	3	1	3	3
7	3	2	3	3	3	2	1	2	4
8	4	3	3	3	3	3	2	5	5
9	4	3	3	3	3	3	2	5	2
10	3	3	3	3	3	3	1	3	5
11	4	3	3	3	3	3	2	4	3
12	4	4	4	2	3	3	2	2	4
13	4	4	4	4	3	3	2	4	5
14	4	4	4	4	4	4	1	1	5
15	4	3	4	3	4	3	1	3	3
16	4	4	4	3	3	3	1	5	4
17	4	4	3	5	4	5	2	1	5
18	3	3	3	3	4	4	2	4	3
19	4	4	4	4	4	4	2	4	4
20	3	3	3	3	3	3	2	4	3
21	2	2	2	2	3	3	2	4	5
22	3	3	4	4	4	4	2	4	5
23	4	4	4	4	4	4	2	2	5
24	5	5	5	5	5	5	1	3	1
25	4	3	3	3	3	2	2	1	3
26	4	4	4	4	4	4	2	3	5
27	4	4	5	4	5	4	2	4	4
28	4	4	4	4	4	4	2	5	1
29	5	5	4	4	4	3	1	5	1
30	5	5	4	4	4	3	1	3	5
31	5	5	4	4	4	3	2	4	2

				Employee Data Set					
EMPL	Sat1	Sat2	Sat3	Sat4	Eng	Ccb	Gender	Perf_level	Emp_retn
32	5	5	5	5	4	3	2	2	4
33	4	4	5	4	3	3	2	5	1
34	5	4	4	4	4	3	2	3	3
35	5	4	4	4	4	3	2	2	5
36	5	4	4	4	3	4	2	4	3
37	4	4	5	5	4	3	2	1	3
38	4	4	3	3	3	4	2	2	5
39	5	5	5	3	3	4	2	1	3
40	4	4	4	4	3	3	2	2	2
41	4	4	4	3	4	4	1	4	4
42	4	4	4	4	4	4	1	5	2
43	5	5	5	4	4	4	1	5	5
44	4	5	5	5	5	3	2	2	4
45	4	4	4	5	4	3	2	4	5
46	4	4	5	5	4	4	1	2	4
47	5	5	5	5	4	4	1	3	5
48	5	4	5	4	3	3	1	1	3
49	5	4	4	4	4	4	1	4	4
50	5	4	4	4	4	4	1	1	5
51	4	4	5	3	5	4	1	2	5
52	5	5	4	3	4	3	1	5	4
53	4	4	5	4	4	4	1	4	2
54	5	4	4	4	3	5	1	4	2
55	5	5	4	4	5	3	1	1	4
56	5	4	5	3	4	3	1	4	2
57	5	4	4	4	3	5	2	2	3
58	5	5	4	4	4	4	2	1	5
59	5	4	4	4	4	3	2	4	3

(Annexure Continued)

				Employee Data Set					
EMPL	Sat1	Sat2	Sat3	Sat4	Eng	Ccb	Gender	Perf_ level	Emp_ retn
60	4	4	3	4	3	5	2	2	1
61	5	5	4	3	5	3	2	2	1
62	4	5	5	4	3	5	2	4	3
63	5	5	5	4	4	5	1	3	3
64	4	4	4	3	3	5	2	1	3
65	5	5	4	4	5	5	1	5	1
66	5	5	5	4	5	4	1	5	3
67	5	4	4	3	3	3	2	4	1
68	4	4	3	5	5	4	1	3	3
69	4	5	4	5	4	3	2	2	1
70	5	5	5	5	5	4	1	1	4
71	4	4	3	4	3	2	2	3	1
72	5	4	4	5	4	4	2	1	4
73	5	4	3	3	4	3	2	2	2
74	5	5	5	5	4	3	2	1	3
75	4	4	4	5	4	4	2	5	3
76	5	5	5	4	4	4	2	1	5
77	4	4	3	5	3	5	2	4	2
78	5	4	5	4	3	4	2	1	5
79	5	5	4	4	3	4	2	1	1
80	4	4	4	4	4	4	2	1	4
81	5	4	5	4	3	2	2	5	2
82	4	4	5	3	4	3	2	4	1
83	5	4	4	4	5	4	2	1	1
84	5	5	5	5	4	4	2	5	2
85	4	4	4	4	4	4	2	2	5
86	4	3	5	4	3	5	2	5	5
87	5	5	4	5	4	5	1	1	5

				Employee Data Set					
EMPL	Sat1	Sat2	Sat3	Sat4	Eng	Ccb	Gender	Perf_ level	Emp_ retn
88	4	5	4	5	5	5	2	3	4
89	5	5	5	5	4	5	2	3	2
90	4	5	4	5	4	5	2	5	4
91	5	5	4	5	5	4	2	4	2
92	5	5	5	4	4	4	2	3	5
93	5	4	3	4	4	4	2	4	1
94	4	5	5	3	2	1	2	4	5
95	5	4	4	3	5	4	1	4	2
96	5	5	4	4	4	4	1	3	4
97	5	5	5	5	5	5	2	1	2
98	4	5	3	3	4	4	2	5	4
99	4	4	4	3	2	4	2	4	4
100	4	4	4	3	2	4	2	3	3

HR ANALYTICS FOR FUTURE

INTRODUCTORY CASE

Frito-Lay Case Study

Frito-Lay with 50,000 headcounts globally makes tasty snacks focusing on 'performance with purpose'. With more than 80 years in existence, the famous PepsiCo Company reached several milestones in its journey. Frito-Lay had typical talent management and retention challenge (Levenson & Faber, 2009). The company's key talent pool was the route sales representatives (RSR) who deliver company's products from distribution centres to stores, and manage the in-store inventory (which includes show-casing, i.e., displaying products in shelves) and collection of survey-based ratings of each RSR's ability to execute prescribed job dimensions, which are the time spent to cover RSR routes, estimated lost sales, covering routes previously taken away from the supervisors and so on.

Analysing the mean time spent by the supervisors to cover the routes and the estimated loss of sales could provide the logic for reducing attrition of newly hired RSRs' turnover. Encapsulating external labour market data could further bring new insights into the company, that is, it is difficult to hire these people, as the job itself attracts less number of applicants. Contrarily, the demand for the job of RSRs increased over the years in the company to cater to the increasing number of products and market competition. Multivariate regression analysis of the supervisor ratings with the employees' performance could suggest the need to raise RSRs' compensation to the market level. The company could get deeper insights through multivariate analysis in terms of comparison of the importance of task execution across job dimensions both in relation to each other and in terms of different route types. It was further observed that sales skills were important bottlenecks on smaller volume sales routes and that delivery skills were bottlenecks for higher volume sales routes. Such analysis could help the company to go for a new job design, adding dedicated hourly merchandisers, increasing number of stores, route volume and capital utilization. Further with the regression analysis of the role of different types of work experiences before joining, Frito-Lay could relate sales experience to sales volume and both long and short types of route. This could also bring change in the hiring profile for achieving the right-fit with the organization and the job roles.

INTRODUCTION

Future HR managers will be equally thorough with core business operations, will make use of data and analytics for business-aligned HR decisions and will manage human resources as a more specialized function with analytics. Future HR functions will require in-depth knowledge in data analysis. Technology will be an important enabler for future HR functions. Technology-enabled HR decision-making would be evident in all spheres of HR functions. With technology support, human resources will be more matured to drive business outcomes of organizations. Social media also will influence the way human resources attracts, hires, engages and retains talent in organizations. This would require human resources to focus on employer branding, collaborating with the marketing function, so that in social media organizations become compelling news with all positive manifestation.

Future HR analytics will not limit its utilization within HR department; rather, it would be integrated with strategic-level business analytics. Obviously, in future human resources will also become a business function. This could make HR analytics more technology enabled in future and would require specialized skill sets. It is apprehended unless future generations of HR managers are more equipped with the power of data analysis, spread of data being expanding day by day, encompassing social media and various other external data sources; apart from organization-wide data sets, companies may require to outsource the HR analytics function (Inostix, 2015). Obviously, this will be a great future challenge for human resources. Challenge will be not only to identify proper vendor but also to ensure data security to the organization.

Globally, we have examples of many organizations, such as Google, Wells Fargo, Xerox, 3M, Ericsson and so on, that could benefit from HR analytics. Some of these known benefits are Xerox's lowering of attrition for effective hiring through HR analytics, 3M's productivity improvement through scientific succession management, Wells Fargo's achievement of high employee engagement and enhanced performance and so on.

Boudreau (2015) could identify five forces which may change the future of HR functions. These are exponential technology change, social and organizational reconfiguration, truly connected world, all-inclusive global talent market, and human and machine collaboration. All these forces will bring changes in HR functions, requiring more evidence-based HR decision-making using HR analytics and predictive decision models. For example, exponential technology change would require successful engagement of the workers with automation. Social and organizational reconfiguration will influence talent sourcing and employee engagement processes. So also, a truly connected world and all-inclusive global talent market would have effect on the talent management function. Finally, human and machine collaboration will enhance the use of analytics, algorithms, big data for decision-making and so on.

UNDERSTANDING FUTURE HUMAN RESOURCES

In future, HR analytics can substantially do many HR jobs, thus relieving HR managers from drudgeries of lengthy work processes. For example, in future, HR analytics can facilitate employees' performance evaluations more holistically, encapsulating apparently extraneous and exogenous data. Another example is the power of HR analytics to match manpower scheduling based on demand, so as to ensure the availability of right manpower at times of need. This is particularly important in retail and hospitality industries where revenue models encapsulate optimum deployment of manpower. All these would be substantial time-saver, thus leaving ample time for HR managers to focus on employee development and many other strategic and business functions. With the increased spread of digital work environment, HR managers in future are likely to face the challenge of acute talent attrition, and in the process, talent attraction, development and retention would become more challenging jobs, which itself may substantially pre-occupy them. They need to address talent attrition issues engaging employees, and also with early signals, they plan for suitable intervention.

Technology-enabled human resources will be able to answer our age-old questions such as why top talent will work for the company, what would be the future experience of customers with our employees, what can contribute to employees' motivation, how can an organization better relate to employees' previous experience with their job success and so on. The social behaviour of employees will be the determinant for their workplace behaviour and can exert influence on their ethical values, confidentiality, information sharing and so on. All these can help in the better understanding of organizational dynamics and can also enable human resources to make the work more satisfying to employees. Automation of HR jobs for advanced analytics, on the one hand, will make future jobs more talent driven, and on the other, it will make HR tasks more personal, facilitating collaboration, showing concern for people, championing for changes and so on.

HR analytics will gradually penetrate the entire organizational structure and will provide new insights into competitive advantage making use of data. With data-driven informed decision-making in all critical areas of human resources such as recruitment and selection, performance management and so on, future human resources will have direct impact on business growth and the bottom line. With built-in cognitive capabilities, HR analytics solutions increasingly become more user-friendly and will not require specialized knowledge, training or expertise to make the HR decision-making process data driven. A data-driven approach to HRM will gradually expand to entire HR functions, and it would become a language for human resources and the other top managerial functionaries of the organization.

HR functions today are no longer engaged in doing traditional soft HR functions but in helping organizations to gain sustainable competitive advantages. Obviously, this requires a thorough understanding of the impact of everything they do in the business and strategy context, and legitimize their role as a strategic business partner.

With HR analytics, future HR functions will witness growth opportunities. Some of the future changes predicted by experts indicate that routine HR jobs will decrease and companies will go for more outsourcing of HR functions. With new technology, HR functions will be more inclusive and participative, and will become a business process. With self-service computer systems, employees across all functions will do their part of data entry, thus rendering a large chunk of HR jobs redundant. Such redundancy would be more evident at entry-level HR jobs, and also in routine or transactional HR tasks, as this will be outsourced. Contrarily, some HR tasks like compensation and benefits will demand more expertise from future HR professionals, as this function will become more complex with new employment-related regulations.

We can understand such future trend analysing people operations team of Google, the company known for its extensive use of people analytics in all HR decisions. People operations team of Google require the following types of employees:

- Staffing (with focus on talent attraction and recruitment)
- Analyst (to support growth and management strategies)
- Programme manager
- HR business partner
- Strategy and operations
- Learning and development
- Administrative support

Similarly, future HR tasks would demand more strategic thinking, as human resources will increasingly become a strategic business partner. Here also, HR analytics and technology-enabled HR process could make this possible. Human resources can enhance strategic business value to an organization only when HR managers build their future capabilities to project the future trend based on the understanding of the current business situation. Obviously, this requires strategic planning, which can only rest on in-house HR capabilities (as this cannot be outsourced). Such strategic focus may even create new job opportunities in future for human resources, like HR business partners. Future HR managers' expertise would require not only holistic understanding of human resources but also a thorough understanding of business, operations and strategy, more focus on HR specialist role. Quantum jump in using big data and analytics in human resources will also exert influence on future HR tasks, such as management of remote workforces, talent attraction with organizational brand building, social networking and so on.

Boston Consulting Group (2015) could identify six future roles of human resources, such as managing talent, managing demographics, becoming a learning organization, managing work-life balance, managing change and cultural transformation and getting the fundamentals right. Even though the study is more in the context of Europe, we find that its universal applicability, as organizations, across the globe is focusing on building their capabilities in line with the same.

Ducheyne's (2015) study could see five future roles of human resources such as the architect, the people and digital expert, the coach, the data strategist and the advocate. As an architect, the role of human resources would be more on building leadership, cooperation, innovation and entrepreneurship. These would obviously require a new set of expertise for future human resources such as mastering of digital know-how, which among others also include HR analytics, and acquiring of specialized knowledge in addition to human resources in areas such as marketing, finance, service management and so on. Similarly, coaching in future would be more important because of the changing workforce, which needs to be helped to become successful in complex organizational environment. As a data-strategist, future human resources would be expected to have better insights into organizational issues and decide on appropriate interventions. Finally, as an advocate, human resources will get more recognized in organizations for their knowledge and expertise, and they would find legitimacy in their inclusion in a business decision-making process. All these future HR roles when integrated would make HR functions more evidence based.

Wartzman (2015), based on Deloitte's study, could see that a future HR job is changing, as organizations in the future will focus on the empowerment of individual team leaders for evaluating and guiding their direct reports.

Similarly, pioneers such as Coombes (2014), Ulrich (2015), Boudreau and Rice (2015) and Collins (2013) could also see change in future HR roles, primarily driven by HR analytics and technology-enabled HR processes.

Coombes research, commonly known as research by Accenture, could relate to the changing role of human resources based on the change in future business trends. Most of the findings of the research corroborate with our earlier described roles of future human resources. Rise of extended workforce, need for managing individuals, technology-enabled HR process, global talent, organizational agility, social media and increase in democratization of work and so on are the common areas of concern for future human resources.

Ulrich's HR operating model envisaged relationships-based service-centre-focused technology-enabled human resources in future which will require more expertise with deeper understanding of human resources for delivering business results. Ulrich envisaged that this would require establishing a connection of HR activities to the expectations of an external stakeholder, and also tracking and measuring the impact of human resources. This operating model would emphasize sharing a common purpose, respecting differences, governing, accepting, connecting, caring for the other, sharing experiences together and growing together.

Boudreau and Rice (2015), based on Juniper case analysis, suggested future human resources to be more innovative by getting the bigger picture, seizing on insights, applying them wisely and ensuring their impact. This will ensure future human resources to evolve with business alignment.

Changing nature of workforce, which is diverse, younger in ages, geographically dispersed and culturally different would be the biggest challenge for HR managers in future. The challenge would particularly be in managing talent. With intuition and gut feelings, HR managers would no longer be able to manage future generation of workers. They have to take informed decisions, and informed decisions may only be possible when they make them data driven. This would require HR managers to develop their capabilities for using HR analytics so as to understand the changes in the life-cycle of employees and predict future happenings. Skills for data integration, transforming data into valuable insights and then managing and monitoring employees would be essential requirements for future human resources.

We find that technology and analytics are on the top of future HR transformation. We also call it the era of digital transformation of human resources. With such digital transformation, human resources can provide data-driven insights, enhance corporate agility, ensure better talent management and better performance management and even can streamline their routine functions (Baker, 2016). Ingham and Ulrich (2016) could see future human resources can have two times more impact on business performance. Future HR professionals need to focus on transforming individual talent into stronger organizations through teamwork. They need to create value for all stakeholders. Business people integration and value creation for the stakeholders would be primary areas of responsibilities for human resources. Box 8.1 explains Google's way of driving business through people analytics.

Box 8.1   With People Analytics Google Drive Their Business

Google could make extensive use of people analytics and reinvent human resources. Google's human resources could ensure continuous innovation with accurate decisions on HR issues, based on people analytics. One reason that legitimizes extensive use of people analytics in Google is the analytic management of HR function, which is almost 60 percent of the total variable costs. Among others, people analytics in Google could benefit in terms of HC development, talent retention, diversity improvement, predictive modelling, improved hiring and driving of collaboration in workplace. A glaring example of Google's use of people analytics for effective human resources is evident from 'Project Oxygen' launched in 2009. Analysing internal data Google could quantify what their effective managers do, and in the process could identify eight key behaviours. Subsequently, Google encapsulated these in its management training programme, and in the process, brought change in the quality of its managers. Today, HR functions at Google are more future focused, innovative and business driven.

All these scholarly and professional contributions, therefore, unequivocally proclaimed the change in future HR functions in organizations.

Generic Future HR Skill Sets and Knowledge

Although it is difficult to list generic skills of HR managers in future, especially in the context of increasing the use of HR analytics and predictive decision-making models and algorithms, we can list some common skills that are essentially required for future HR managers. These are depicted in Figure 8.1.

Right in the beginning, HR managers of future need to possess thorough knowledge of human resources and business. HR knowledge, namely reasons for attrition and talent management, need to be analysed in the context of business capturing data on sales, customers' satisfaction, sales margins, key sales objectives (KSOs) and so on. Such knowledge on the one hand can help in identifying a cluster of employees who are likely to leave the company and important reasons for their leaving; on the other hand, with business knowledge, HR managers can also predict KSOs at risk and so also can predict the ROI from business.

Statistical knowledge is important for data interpretation. Statistical knowledge today encompasses various technology-driven techniques like machine learning. Core knowledge, however, centres around the mechanism of data collection, survey design and designing of experiments (particularly for finding cause and effect relationships). Statistical and mathematical knowledge can help in developing decision algorithms based on which behavioural modelling for future decision-making can be done.

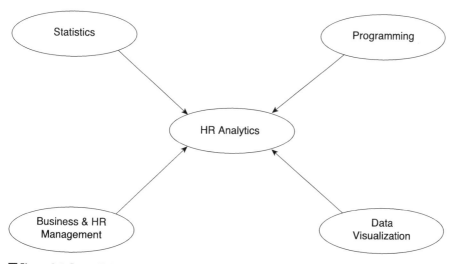

■ **Figure 8.1:** Future Skills of HR Managers
Source: Author.

How HR mines data in retaining talent has been explained in Box 8.2 citing the case of Stantec.

Box 8.2   Mining Data to Retain Talent: Case of Stantec

Stantec, over the years, has acquired expertise in project conceptualization, planning, designing, construction and commissioning. Today, the company operates from 400 locations with headcounts of 22,000, and the gross revenue of the company is C$2.9 billion. The company believes in putting people first, as its core strength lies with its people. HR strategy of the company emphasizes talent segmentation, leadership and succession, learning and development, talent acquisition and employee engagement. Strategically, the company provides to its employees shared expertise and collaboration opportunities, opportunities to broaden experience with new regions and projects, and opportunities for career advancement.

To ensure the best employees continue, the company developed some critical metrics on employee turnover, employee engagement, managerial effectiveness and so on. Such critical metrics could help the company to put a check on talent retention.

With programming skills, HR managers can analyse the data using various available HR analytics solutions. Most of the HR analytics solutions are user-friendly; hence, today these do not require complex programming skills. Like programming skills, data visualization skills are also important. With these skill sets, HR managers can help in understanding the right story from the data and accordingly can persuade people to change their behaviour.

With all these skills sets and knowledge, future HR managers would be able to manage future workplaces which would be more analytics driven.

Ethical Issues in HR Analytics

HR functions by nature require a lot of confidential information, which employees provide to the organization. These are personal to the employees, even though organizations are custodians. In terms of employment contract with the employees, organizations make use of employees' information for managing the business. For HR analytics, employees' data are used for modelling the HR decision-making process extensively and even at times for violating the ethical norms. While the best practice is to take employees' consent for making use of their personal data and information for decision-making, operationally, it may not be always feasible. Technology-enabled HR processes require storing of employees' data about which employees may not be aware. Such data even at times go beyond employees' work spheres, like data from employees' social media interaction. Even data from employees' work spheres also may include some typical behavioural inputs, such as their food choice in staff canteen, their preference for beverages and so on. These require organizations to draw a line between ethical and unethical use of employees' data that are privy to them.

Often analysing employees' data, which may be privy to them, help organizations to get deep insights into future HR decision-making. For example, relating employees' food choice in the canteen to their performance, organizations can come out with ideal meal plan. But again this could be a critical issue of ethics. Unlike survey, where employees' reserve the right to respond to their own fashion and rights, direct and indirect data of employees are collected without their knowledge. This is often construed as managerial prerogative. Good practice, however, calls for communicating the employees' organizational intention to make use of their information for modelling future HR decisions, so as to ensure both people and organizations deliver their best in achieving business goals.

Organizations at times also face security challenges when HR analytics support is outsourced. Here, it is very important to ensure data security with clear ethical guidelines. Issues such as stereotyping, prejudice and discrimination are a critical ethical concern for employees' data. Although organization-wise ethical standards in using employees' data or HR analytics widely varies, CIPD, UK (2012) could come out with some specific guidelines in this respect. These ethical guidelines have been given in general for HR professionals, rather than specifically for HR analysts; but adhering to these guidelines can ensure compliance with the ethical issues pertaining to the use of employees' data also. CIPD emphasizes the need to

- establish, maintain and develop business relationships based on confidence, trust and respect;
- exhibit and defend professional and personal integrity and honesty at all times;
- demonstrate sensitivity for the customs, practices, culture and personal beliefs of others;
- advance employment and business practices that promote equality of opportunity, diversity and inclusion and support human rights and dignity;
- safeguard all confidential, commercially sensitive and personal data acquired as a result of business relationships and not use them for personal advantage or the benefit or detriment of third parties.

A more specific form of human resources 'analyst ethical standards' based on Schwartz (2011) can be listed as follows:

1. Compliance with the legal, cultural and social norms.
2. Safeguard against the interest of all stakeholders.
3. Accountability for the HR analytics process.
4. Safeguard against the security of information.
5. Concern for information sensitivity.

HR managers while making use of HR analytics need to ensure that they are not ignoring the employees' privy without their consent. However, we have conflicting claims on ethical issues in HR analytics, more specifically in predictive HR analytics. This was evident in the debate on

SHRM (2015). For example, it is claimed that the real beneficiaries of predictive HR analytics are employees, as through this, an organization can develop its structures, develop its performance management systems and rewards systems, can retain its talent and work on succession planning more effectively. All these can substantially contribute in creating an enabling environment for employees to give their best. Another claim is that predictive HR analytics while developing decision algorithms and models based on employees' data often violate ethical norms. Many companies often collect data on employees' attitudes, preferences and values, which are in general privy to the employees. This requires certain code of ethics to ensure predictive HR analytics are not prejudicing the privy of the employees and that they are adequately informed about the possible use of their data.

HR Feel More Empowered with HR Analytics

Empowerment of HR function can be possible once HR managers can manage HR activities with HR analytics. HR analytics can help in performing many transactional HR jobs at a much faster pace, thus leaving HR managers to focus more on strategic HR activities to justifiably align human resources with the business. True empowerment of human resources is possible when we are able to bring HR functions closer to business. This can also make human resources responsible for the bottom line and the ROI for the organization.

With HR analytics, HR managers can significantly improve the performance of a company, can build engaged human resources, increase their productivity and in the process can achieve the goals of the company. Many critical HR decisions when taken based on HR analytics, human resources feel more empowered, as HR managers can get insights into the issues and take decisions more accurately. With predictive analytics, HR managers can even go beyond in managing HR functions with a forward-looking approach. Also, predictive analytics can help HR managers in driving HR strategies with future perspectives.

PRACTICE ASSIGNMENTS

1. Critically evaluate any globally dispersed organization and identify what could be the possible generic HR skill sets in future for this organization. Give your answer with a logic.
2. Discuss with specific example how human resources can be empowered with HR analytics with reference to any organization.

Summary

Future HR functions will require in-depth knowledge in data analysis. Technology will be an important enabler for future HR functions. Technology-enabled HR decision-making would be evident in all spheres of HR functions.

Future HR analytics can substantially do many HR jobs, thus relieving HR managers from drudgeries of lengthy work processes and leaving ample time for them to focus on employee development and many other strategic and business functions.

HR analytics will gradually penetrate the entire organizational structure and will provide new insights into competitive advantage, making use of data. With data-driven informed decision-making in all critical areas of human resources such as recruitment and selection, performance management and so on, future human resources will have a direct impact on business growth and the bottom line.

Also, future HR tasks would demand more strategic thinking, as human resources will increasingly become a strategic business partner. Here also, HR analytics and technology-enabled HR processes could make this possible.

Some common skills essentially required for future HR managers are statistics, programming, business and HR management and data visualization.

For HR analytics, employees' data are used for modelling HR decision-making process extensively. This requires strict adherence to ethical norms.

Empowerment of HR function can be possible once HR managers can manage HR activities with HR analytics. HR analytics can help in doing many transactional HR jobs at much faster pace, thus leaving HR managers to focus more on strategic HR activities to justifiably align human resources with the business.

General Review Questions

1. Discuss the potential influence of HR analytics on future of human resources.

2. As an HR professional, what are the possible changes envisaged by you in future utilization of HR analytics?

3. Write a detailed note on generic future HR skill sets and knowledge, especially in the context of HR analytics and predictive decision modelling.

4. What are the ethical issues in HR analytics?

5. Describe how HR analytics can empower HR managers in future.

6. Write short notes on the following:

   - Five forces of future HR functions
   - Technology-enabled human resources
   - Ethical issues in HR analytics
   - Empowerment of HR functions
   - Data visualization

Multiple Choice Questions

1. Identify the incorrect statement on future HR functions out of the following:

   a. HR functions will require in-depth knowledge in data analysis
   b. Technology will be an important enabler
   c. Technology-enabled HR decision-making would be evident in all spheres of HR functions
   d. With technology support, human resources will be more matured to drive business outcomes of organizations
   e. Social media will override technology-enabled HR functions

2. Indicate what out of the following is not relevant for social media in the context of human resources

   a. It will influence the way human resources attracts, hires, engages and retains talent
   b. It will focus on employer branding
   c. It will focus on innovation
   d. It will collaborate with the marketing function
   e. It will become compelling news about the organization with all positive manifestation

3. Future generation of HR managers needs to be more equipped with the power of data analysis because

   a. Spread of data is expanding day by day
   b. HR data even encompass social media
   c. HR analytics even require external data
   d. All of the above
   e. None of the above

4. Indicate which of the following is not an identified force that may change the future of HR functions as per Boudreau (2015)

   a. Exponential technology change
   b. Social and organizational reconfiguration
   c. Connected world
   d. Development of local talent market
   e. Human and machine collaboration

5. Digital work environment can bring the following challenges for future HR managers, except

   a. Talent attrition
   b. Talent attraction
   c. Talent development
   d. Talent retention
   e. Exclusive approach to talent management

6. Technology-enabled human resources cannot answer our age-old questions, for example

   a. Why top talent will work for a company
   b. What would be the future experience of customers with our employees
   c. What can contribute to employees' motivation
   d. What could be the future research in human resources
   e. How an organization can better relate employees' previous experience with their job success

7. Social behaviour of employees is important because

   a. It determines workplace behaviour
   b. It can exert influence on employees' ethical values
   c. It can measure employees' score on confidentiality
   d. It can show employees maturity on information sharing
   e. All of the above

8. Automation of HR jobs for advanced analytics will help in the following, other than

   a. Making future jobs more talent driven
   b. Making HR tasks more personal, facilitating collaboration
   c. Showing concern for people
   d. Enforcing discipline in an organization
   e. Ensuring championing for changes

9. Built-in cognitive capabilities in HR analytics solutions in future can

   a. Make it more user-friendly
   b. Will not require specialized knowledge, training or expertise
   c. Will make HR decision-making process totally data driven
   d. Make data-driven approach become a language for human resources
   e. All of the above

10. Identify which of the following is not an identified future roles of human resources as per Boston Consulting Group

    a. Talent management
    b. Managing demographics
    c. Making human resources more competitive
    d. Managing work-life balance
    e. Managing change and cultural transformation

11. As architects, the role of human resources would focus more on

    a. Building leadership
    b. Cooperation
    c. Innovation
    d. All of the above
    e. None of the above

12. Identify the incorrect statement out of the following:

    a. Future human resources will require entrepreneurship skill
    b. Future HR will require poaching skill
    c. Future HR will require to be data-strategists
    d. Future HR would require to be employee advocates
    e. None of the above

13. Statistical knowledge is important for future human resources because

    a. It is important for data interpretation
    b. It encompasses various technology-driven techniques
    c. It helps in machine learning
    d. Only (a) and (b)
    e. All (a), (b) and (c)

14. Indicate which of the following is not an ethical issue pertaining to the use of employees' data in line with CIPD

    a. Establish, maintain and develop business relationships based on confidence, trust and respect
    b. Exhibit and defend professional and personal integrity and honesty at all times
    c. Demonstrate sensitivity for the customs, practices, culture and personal beliefs of others
    d. Safeguard all confidential, commercially sensitive and personal data acquired as a result of business relationships and not use it for personal advantage or the benefit or detriment of third parties
    e. None of the above

15. All the following points indicate ethical standards for an analyst, except:

    a. Compliance with the legal, cultural and social norms
    b. Safeguard against interest of shareholders
    c. Accountability for the HR analytics process
    d. Safeguard against the security of information.
    e. Concern for information sensitivity

16. Some common skills essentially required for future HR managers are

    a. Statistics
    b. Business
    c. Human resources
    d. Only (a) and (b)
    e. All (a), (b) and (c)

Critical Review Question

1. By making your HR decision-making process 100 percent data driven, your company feels that the quality of HR decisions over the years has significantly improved. You are the CHRO of the company and more than 100 HR professionals are working with you. With HR analytics and predictive decision-making systems, you feel HR professionals are left with time that can be gainfully used. Identify some of the new areas for your HR team where they can work to connect human resources with the business of your organization.

PRACTITIONER SPEAKS

Analysing behavioural data of job applicants based on social media interaction, your company shortlists candidates for a job interview. Your company also assigns higher weightage on such behavioural data. All this your company does without the knowledge of the job applicants. As an HR professional, do you think this can be a potential violation of ethical issues?

CASE STUDY

Making Your HR Analytics Effective: Lessons from SAS

SAS, the 1976 US-based innovative analytics and business intelligence company with a headcount of 14,158 and revenue of USD 3.16 billion in 2015, today operates from 148 countries. The company believes analytics is always an action-driven approach and it can empower the vision of an organization. It is a stair-step process. Predictive analytics also is one such step. The initial step of analytics is visualization and exploration, followed by data mining and then the process of analytics.

Predictive analytics in human resources denotes the process of examining things that did happen and then predict the probability of occurrence of certain outcome in future. Using predictive analytics, human resources can develop algorithms and predictive models, test and validate them, and use them for more accurate HR decision-making.

Globally, we have a number of companies that function based on analytics. These companies felt the need for analytics to bring changes in their HR processes so that they can attract, acquire and retain the best talent. For SAS, HR analytics is more important because it helps in acquiring the best talent and so also in retaining the talent. Using analytics in every phase of employee life cycle, SAS takes critical talent management decisions. With analytics, SAS can get answers to who should be hiring? Who could be successful in a specific job function? Answers to other critical questions such as expected time frame for a new hire to become successful in job performance, investment required to build the capabilities of the new hires and so on also benefit the company to source the right talent. Similarly, for talent retention also the company predicts factors that increase an employee's risk of leaving the company and then develop appropriate business practices that can mitigate such problems and ensure talent retention. In most of the cases, the company could find investment in more training, including changing of the training location could bring positive changes in the mindsets of the employees. Along with this, the company also emphasizes coaching. With initial success in HR analytics, the company today recognizes the business partnership role of human resources, and could support and empower their business through HR processes.

Note: This case study has been developed based on the inputs from: Tucker (2015).

Question: Using SAS experience as the basis, explain HR analytics implementation experience of an Indian organization.

REFERENCES

Baker, G. (2016). HR to focus on technology and analytics in 2016 as digital transformation initiatives take center stage. New York: Business Wire.

Boston Consulting Group. (2015). The future of HR in Europe: Key challenges through 2015. Available at: https://www.bcg.com/documents/file15033.pdf (accessed on 15 June 2016).

Boudreau, J. (2015). Workplace 2025: Five forces, six new roles and a challenge to HR. Available at: http://www.visier.com/hr-leadership/workplace-2025-five-forces-six-new-roles-and-a-challenge-to-hr/ (accessed on 15 June 2016).

Boudreau, J., & Rice, S. (2015). Bright, shiny objects and the future of HR. *Harvard Business Review*, 93(7/8), 72–78.

CIPD. (2012). Code of professional conduct. Available at: http://www.cipd.co.uk/binaries/code-of-professional-conduct_july-2015.pdf (accessed on 15 June 2016).

Collins, M. (2013). Change Your Company with better HR Analytics, Harvard Business Review Blog. Available at: https://hbr.org/2013/12/change-your-company-with-better-hr-analytics (accessed on 16 February 2016).

Coombes, R. (2014). Ten trends that will reshape the future of HR. Available at: http://www.hrmagazine.co.uk/article-details/ten-trends-that-will-reshape-the-future-of-hr (accessed on 15 June 2016).

Ducheyne, D. (2015). The five future roles of HR. Available at: https://www.linkedin.com/pulse/5-future-roles-hr-david-ducheyne (accessed on 21 June 2016).

Ingham, J., & Ulrich, D. (2016). Building better HR departments. *Strategic Human Resource Review*, 15(3), 129–136.

Inostix. (2015). 12 reasons why outsourcing HR analytics is good for HR. Available at: http://www.inostix.com/blog/en/12-reasons-outsourcing-hranalytics-good-hr/#more-1893 (accessed on 15 June 2016).

Levenson, A., & Faber, T. (2009, June). Count on productivity gains. *HR Magazine,* 68–74.

Schwartz, P. M. (2011, May/June). Privacy, ethics and analytics, privacy interests (pp. 66–69). Available at: http://www.paulschwartz.net/pdf/pschwartz_privacy-eth-analytics%20IEEE%20P-%20Sec%20%282011%29.pdf (accessed on 22 June 2016).

SHRM. (2015). Should companies have free rein to use predictive analytics? Available at: https://www.shrm.org/hr-today/news/hr-magazine/pages/0615-predictive-analytics.aspx (accessed on 02 September 2016).

Tucker, E. (2015, April 17). How analytics can empower your HR strategy. Available at: http://www.greatplacetowork.com/events-and-insights/blogs-and-news/2973-how-analytics-can-empower-your-hr-strategy#sthash.Q6H7r1m1.dpbs (accessed on 17 February 2016).

Ulrich, D. (2015). The future of HR is about relationships. Available at: http://www.cipd.co.uk/pm/peoplemanagement/b/weblog/archive/2015/03/24/the-future-of-hr-is-about-relationships.aspx (accessed on 22 June 2016).

Wartzman, R. (2015). The future of work: Say goodbye to HR? Available at: http://fortune.com/2015/04/02/teams-management-human-resources/ (accessed on 22 June 2016).

APPENDIX

Problem on Resource Optimization

Resource optimization problem is more frequently observed in an HR decision-making process, particularly in manpower planning. We can explain this using the following example:

Suppose you are in a continuous process industry. Your company processes industrial molasses to produce rectified spirit, which is used as raw material for country liquor, homeopathic medicine and other pharmaceutical formulation. For erratic supply of industrial molasses, your company now simultaneously runs three more production lines, i.e., a husk based, multi-feed and sweet-beat-based processing for rectified spirit. With such extended production lines, your company's in-built processing capacity is 120,000 litre per day with 30,000 litre per production line. As the operation is highly dependent on raw materials' availability, your operational manpower requirement varies on a day-to-day basis. For this reason, your company has kept a skeleton manpower in planning, maintenance, quality control, electrical and pollution control jobs. For all other operations, your company follows a flexible hiring policy, i.e., hiring on an as-and-when-required basis.

Being a continuous process industry, when full-scale operation is on, you need to run all the units round the clock. From raw material feed to the incoming pit and till the final yield of the finished product, it requires almost 12 hour cycle time, which again varies depending on the quality of raw material and the yeast strains used for fermenting. In the final stage of fermenting, more workers need to be present for continuous monitoring. Operators who are hired on flexible basis are graded as A, B and C, depending on their skill sets and experience, and their hourly rate of wages is also different. The shift arrangement of your company has been so designed that there is some overlapping time between shifts, and at least 70 workers are present at any point of time. Each operator has to work for 8 hours a day. As per the existing practice, shift arrangement is divided into six types as follows:

Shift 1	6 am to 2 pm
Shift 2	9 am to 5 pm
Shift 3	12 pm to 8 pm
Shift 4	3 pm to 1 am
Shift 5	6 pm to 2 am
Shift 6	9 pm to 5 am

The intervening time period, i.e., 5 am to 6 am is the plant's shut-down time to clear the sludge.

Shift-wise assignment of operators and the cost per operator is presented in the following table:

Decision Variable	X_1	X_2	X_3	X_4	X_5	X_6
Details	Shift 1	Shift 2	Shift 3	Shift 4	Shift 5	Shift 6
No. of operators	40	45	43	51	42	44
Daily cost per operator ($)	180	170	178	180	188	176

To solve this problem, we need to understand the nature of job and the optimum requirements of manpower in each shift.

X_j represents the number of operators in shift j, where j = 1, 2, 3, 4, 5 or 6.

Constraints for different shifts are the number of operators shown against each shift.

Our objective is to minimize the total costs of workers who work in the six shifts, i.e.,

$Z = 180X_1 + 170X_2 + 178X_3 + 180X_4 + 188X_5 + 176X_6$

Subject to

$X_1 + X_2 \geq 70 \leq 85$ (considering the overlapping manpower between shifts)

$X_1 + X_2 + X_3 \geq 70 \leq 128$

$X_2 + X_3 \geq 70 \leq 88$

$X_2 + X_3 + X_4 \geq 70 \leq 139$

$X_3 + X_4 \geq 70 \leq 94$

$X_3 + X_4 + X_5 \geq 70 \leq 136$

$X_4 + X_5 \geq 70 \leq 93$

$X_4 + X_5 + X_6 \geq 70 \leq 137$

$X_5 + X_6 \geq 70 \leq 86$

And $X_j \geq 0$ (non-negativity constraints); for j = 1, 2, 3, 4, 5 and 6.

We need not perform the manual calculation as linear programming now can be performed using various standard software, and even Microsoft Excel Solver. What is important for us is to formulate the problem and proper identification of variables. As HR professional, we may not be that conversant with all operations research tools, but using Microsoft Excel Solver we could obtain the shift-wise hiring pattern of an operator as follows:

Min Z 36860

X_1 1

X_2 69

X_3 3

X_4 67

X_5 3

X_6 67

It means the company must go for shift-wise hiring as per the aforementioned results, meeting all their constraints.

The problem formulation and solution arrived using the Excel Solver is shown in Figures A8.1–A8.3:

		Shift 1	Shift 2	Shift 3	Shift 4	Shift 5	Shift 6			
		x1	x2	x3	x4	x5	x6			
		0	0	0	0	0	0			
Cost ($)		180	170	178	180	188	176			
No of Operators		40	45	43	51	42	44			
Total cost ($) =		0								
Subject to:										
		1	1	0	0	0	0	0 >=		70
		1	1	0	0	0	0	0 <=		85
		1	1	1	0	0	0	0 >=		70
		1	1	1	0	0	0	0 <=		128
		0	1	1	0	0	0	0 >=		70
		0	1	1	0	0	0	0 <=		88
		0	1	1	1	0	0	0 >=		70
		0	1	1	1	0	0	0 <=		139
		0	0	1	1	0	0	0 >=		70
		0	0	1	1	0	0	0 <=		94
		0	0	1	1	1	0	0 >=		70
		0	0	1	1	1	0	0 <=		136
		0	0	0	1	1	0	0 >=		70
		0	0	0	1	1	0	0 <=		93
		0	0	0	1	1	1	0 >=		70
		0	0	0	1	1	1	0 <=		137
		0	0	0	0	1	1	0 >=		70
		0	0	0	0	1	1	0 <=		86

■ **Figure A8.1:** Entering Data in Excel Solver

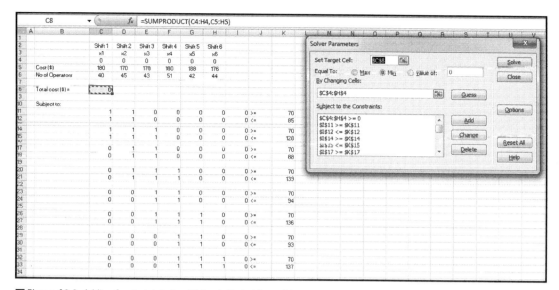

■ Figure A8.2: Adding Constraints in Excel Solver (a Typical Example)

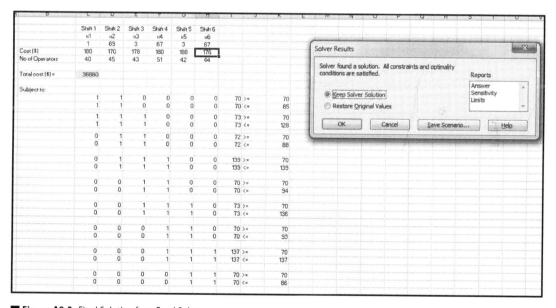

■ Figure A8.3: Final Solution from Excel Solver

*Go to the companion website for the Answer Key.

GLOSSARY

Administrative role of human resources: As per this, human resources contributes to achieve organizational efficiency through the process of reengineering of HR function and HR processes developing shared services.

Advanced analytics phase: This is the phase of proactive identification of problems or decisional issues for reaching to actionable solutions. In this phase, various statistical modelling and root cause analysis and so on are performed for solving business issues. This is the phase from where we actually begin the use of HR analytics solutions to solve our business problems.

Advanced reporting phase: This phase performs multidimensional analysis using dashboards and others alike. In this phase, organizations also go for benchmarking. We also call this proactive operational reporting phase.

Agency theory: This theory suggests strategic approach to HR-aligned agents' (employees) and principals' (employers) interests and thereby ensures streamlining of employment relations and systems within the organization.

Analytics: It is defined as scientific data manipulation, which can measure and report facts or metrics over a period, explaining how it relates to one another.

Architect: As an architect, the role of human resources would be more on building leadership, cooperation, innovation and entrepreneurship. These would obviously require a new set of expertise for future human resources such as mastering of digital know-how, which among others also include HR analytics and acquiring of specialized knowledge in addition to human resources in areas such as marketing, finance, service management and so on.

Balanced scorecard: It measures performance data, and it can also provide valuable insights about employees' potentiality which can substantially influence talent management related decision-making.

Behavioural perspective of HRM: It focuses on embracing those HRM practices which can churn desired employees' behaviour for achieving organizational goals and objectives.

Big data for human resources: It denotes gathering data from several data sources and collates the same using HR analytics tool for decision-making. HR data need to be big data for their obvious alignment with organizational business and strategies.

Business analytics: It is scientific data manipulation for better business decisions. It literally indicates the application of mathematical and statistical techniques.

Casual-comparative research: This research helps in comparing two relationships, e.g., determining the cause of differences between two groups of employees.

Central tendency: It is measured calculating mean, mode and median. Mean is the average, mode is the value that occurs most and median is the mid-value, mid-point or the 50th percentile.

Change agent role of human resources: As per this, human resources is responsible to manage cultural and transformational changes in organizations.

Change champion: As a change champion, HR managers constantly evaluate the effectiveness of the organization, understand the need for change and assess the need for knowledge and skill to execute the change process, and also manage the employees' resistance to change.

Coach: It helps workforce to become successful in complex organizational environment.

Conceptual perspective of HRM: It helps us to relate facts to each other.

Configuration approach of HRM: It focuses on holistic approaches to examine how a pattern of several independent variables can influence organization-level strategies.

Contingency approach of HRM: It aligns organization-level strategic positions with specific choices and practices to achieve the intended results.

Correlational HR decision-making process: It helps in assessing the relationships between two variables. Measuring such relationships, HR managers can understand the possible effect of their decisions and accordingly can calibrate their decision, to minimize the risk of adverse consequences, if any.

Correlational research: This research helps us in determining relationships among variables to establish a cause–effect relationship, e.g., to study how new incentive scheme correlates with employees' performance.

Data-driven HR decisions: It is commonly known as HR analytics.

Data validity: It is measured in terms of describing data assertion, measured in terms of confidence in data using statistical tools.

Data reliability: It denotes trustworthiness of data that become reliable when we get the same result, if we collect it again.

Data strategist: It is the capability to have better insights into organizational issues and to decide on appropriate interventions.

Degree of variation: This can be understood in terms of differentiating characteristics of data. Without such characteristics, decisions may be flawed.

Data usefulness: It is understood in terms of usefulness of data in decision-making. Often HR managers feel burdened with data, which may have little or no relevance.

Data defensibility: It can be understood in terms of all data collection criteria and dimensions. The idea is to ensure data quality and defend the accuracy when data are challenged.

Data visualization: It is data presentation in pictorial and graphical forms. Data visualization or HR report visualization by placing data in a visual context helps us to quickly understand data patterns, trends and data correlations, which otherwise could have been impossible for a layman to understand.

Datafication of human resources: It is the process of turning the existing aspects of a phenomenon into data business, i.e., computerization of data and transforming data into information that has a business value. A good example of this is datafication of our social network data by Google, Facebook or LinkedIn.

Dependency theory: This theory argues that strategic acceptance from stakeholders can unduly enhance the level of influence over organizations from human resources; hence, there exists the need for balancing.

Descriptive HR decision-making process: It makes use of metrics or HRIS to get insights into decisional issues and then take decisions. It can be reinforced by correlational decision-making process also.

Descriptive perspective of HRM: It emphasizes fact-based HRM practices.

Descriptive statistics: This involves describing the existing data, using measures such as average, sum and so on.

Descriptive research: This research engages in data collection and testing of hypotheses, namely measuring the satisfaction level of employees.

Decision tree: A decision tree is an important decision-making tool. Before taking decisions, HR managers can understand different choices, risks, gains and so on using a decision tree. With multiple decision alternatives plotted in a decision tree, HR managers can critically assess each alternative and select the best one.

Discrete choice models: Using these models we can describe, explain and predict our choices between two or more discrete alternatives. Here, we limit our choices to those alternatives for analysis which we feel are critical for the problem or decision issue. This we can understand based on our previous knowledge, or through previous survey or qualitative research.

Dispersion: Also known as variability and is measured using range, quartile deviation and standard deviation. Range measures the difference between the highest and the lowest scores in a data set. Quartile deviation is the difference between the upper quartile and the lower quartile in a data set. Standard deviation is the square root of the variance and it is the distance of each score from the mean.

Employee turnover rate: This can be calculated for different time period using the following formula: (Number of separations during a time period/Average number of employees during the time period) × 100.

Experimental research: This research study helps establish cause–effect relationships by comparison, manipulating one variable while controlling others.

Employee championship role of human resources: It focuses on managing HR operations to elicit employees' contributions to organizational business.

Evidence-based management practices: These facilitate in conscientious decision-making, with effective use of available evidences (data support) so that decisional outcome can benefit the organization and the stakeholders. Analytics-based HR decisions, being evidence based, are more value adding, futuristic and sustainable.

Exponential technology change: This would require successful engagement of the workers with automation.

Financial HR decisions: The common types of decisions under this category are the ROI on training, any financial impact analysis relate to HR decisions and so on. Such decisions are most metrics driven.

Five forces of future HR functions: These forces include exponential technology change, social and organizational reconfiguration, truly connected world, all-inclusive global talent market and human and machine collaboration. All these forces will bring changes in HR functions, requiring more evidenced-based HR decision-making using HR analytics and predictive decision models.

Future HR analytics: It is integrated with strategic-level business analytics. HR analytics in future would become more technology-enabled and would require specialized skill sets.

Glopats: It is also known as global patriates, i.e., employees who will move around the world, wherever organizations have their business presence, both on short-term and long-term assignments.

Hard system approach: This approach to human resources uses well-defined systems to formulate goals, resolve identity problems, ascertain and evaluate options and, finally, select and implement rational plan to achieve the desired outcome.

Human resources as an employee advocate: As an employee advocate, HR managers make use of their expertise in nurturing a work environment that motivates people to spontaneously contribute to organizational needs.

Human resources as a change champion: As a change champion, HR managers constantly evaluate the effectiveness of an organization, understand the need for change, assess the need for knowledge and skill to execute a change process and also manage the employees' resistance to change.

HR analytics: It is defined as the application of analytic logic for HRM function, so that it can benefit organizations in improving the performance of employees, help in rationalizing HR decision-making process and can also improve the ROI from human resources.

HR control: It is the alignment of actions of employees with an organization. In HRM, the concept of control is embedded with the 'agency theory'. In terms of this theory, managers acquiring and allocating resources are empowered to act as a control agent. As a control agent, HR managers focus on controlling the variation in the behaviour of employees and the outcome.

HR control systems: It is primarily the adoption of certain HR practices that can enforce behavioural changes in employees when the results are not meeting the expected standards.

HR dashboards: It primarily helps in monitoring and measurement of HR activities based on various operating metrics. It primarily focuses on short-term or operational goals, helps in visualization of the performance and reports immediately the deviation for interventions. With charts and diagrams, HR managers can track and monitor the performance. Dashboard development requires metrics in KPIs format.

HR decision-making process: It is HR managers' judgemental thoughts, encompassing all stakeholders, on any action. An effective HR decision-making process requires integration of critical thoughts and information.

HR metrics: These assess the impact of human resources on business outcomes of organizations and at the precision level even extend to the assessment of impact of HR functions on customers, processes, people and the finance of the organizations.

HR operating model: This model was pioneered by Ulrich and it envisaged relationship-based service-centre-focused technology-enabled human resources in future which will require more expertise with deeper understanding of human resources for delivering business results.

HR reports: With data collection, we complete the initial requirements of HR analytics, as these data help us to get insights that ease our decision-making processes. Analysing data with HR analytics solutions, we generate various HR reports. Predominantly, HR reports focus on employee data more in the perspective of the cost issues; however, combining these reports with other databases, such as budgets, performance evaluation records, attendance records and others alike, human resources can take better business-focused decisions.

HR scorecard: It provides a framework for measuring human resources. It is designed with the balanced scorecard measurement framework. A balanced scorecard measurement framework, as we know, is developed after four perspectives, i.e., financial, internal process, customer and learning and growth.

HR strategy: It is the pattern of decisions concerning policies and practices associated with the HR system.

HR forecasting: It focuses on measuring the implications of human resources on organizational strategy. HR forecasting is done considering the effects of various economic, technological and organizational forces on the human resources and this requires some structured steps such as framing a business strategy, relating business strategy with various HR scenarios, assessing demand and supply of human resources, assessing the cultural issues, developing the HR forecast and, finally, translating HR forecast into an HR plan.

HR plan: It is the end result of HR forecast, and once the HR plan is developed, human resources has to allocate resources to execute the plan. With an HR plan, HR managers weigh various strategic options, analysing various HR data and information, ranging from data on manpower, HR costs, talent retention and information on culture, training and learning and so on.

HR optimization: It is a process of adding value to the organization.

HR value proposition: It focuses on attraction and retention of talent. Also, it enables employees to assess comparative benefits that they can enjoy over other organizations in terms of compensation and benefits, corporate brand value and so on.

HRD business process: An HRD business process accounts for the budgeting to assess whether training programmes listed in the training calendar can be offered or not. Accordingly, an HRD business process finalizes the training calendar trading off between the needs and the budget constraints. Finally, the HRD business process implements the envisaged strategy, drawn right in the beginning.

Harvard approach to HRM: It emphasizes the need for the alignment of employees with the organization and management. It suggests the need for developing the strategic vision of HRM functions, primarily to assess the extent of integration of HRM practices with organizational policies.

Human resource information system (HRIS): It is a descriptive analytics used by HR managers as a reporting tool for the past and the current happenings. HRIS is not forward looking; hence, it cannot visualize the future outcomes, or future decisional implications.

HRM sustainability: Sustainable HRM sees sustainability in the context of mutual benefits of all stakeholders. It emphasizes the reproducibility of human resources through its nurturing and development.

HRM system: When we consider HRM as a system, different elements or components of HRM, such as procurement (HRP and recruitment and selection function), maintenance (compensation, discipline and industrial relations) and development (performance appraisal and training and development), act as parts.

HRM as a business process: As a business process, human resources provides critical support to value addition to organizational process, leveraging employees' skills and competencies.

Human capital cost: This can tell us the investments made in employees in terms of compensation and benefits and can be measured with the following formula: Total compensation and benefits cost/Number of full-time employees.

Human capital theory: This theory suggests strategic importance of human resources, like other economic assets as knowledge; skills and abilities of the people have also economic values.

Human and machine collaboration: This will enhance the use of analytics, algorithms, big data for decision-making and so on.

Human resource research: This research is carried out to understand how organizations are structured and function, how decisions are made, what factors affect organizational operations and, finally, what strategies are important for gaining sustainable competitive advantages. This research may be descriptive, normative, prescriptive and strategic. Irrespective of research scoping, data collection, analysis, statistical modelling and use of HR analytics for predictive decision-making are required.

Inferential statistics: This helps in finding patterns and relationships in data; it involves statistical testing using various statistical models.

Institutional theory: This theory argues the need for strategic acceptance from stakeholders.

Integrated analytics: It includes those which are holistic and encompassing, such as talent management, workforce planning, succession planning, HR strategy framing and so on.

Interval measurement: It combines the characteristics of both nominal and ordinal measurements. Employees are measured using a measurement tool that can have a scale with arbitrary maximum and arbitrary minimum scores (e.g., zero point).

LAMP framework or model of HR analytics: LAMP represents four critical components of HR measurement which are essential to drive an organization and to achieve organizational effectiveness. LAMP stands for logic, analytics, measures and process.

Linear regression: This helps in modelling relationships between a dependent variable (Y) and one or more explanatory variable (X). Suppose an HR manager wants to assess the association between performance and pay. Here, performance is a dependent variable and pay is an independent or explanatory variable. In regression analysis, we denote dependent variable as 'Y' and independent variable as 'X'.

Logistic regression: This type of regression helps us to predict the outcome of a categorical or dependent variable (say in our example employees' performance) based on one or more independent or predictor variables (say pay, career development opportunities, promotion and so on).

Measurement of relative position: This helps in understanding how well an employee has performed compared to others. Two most frequently used measures of relative positions are percentile ranks and standard scores. A percentile rank indicates the percentage of scores that fall at or below a given score. A standard score is a derived score that expresses how far a given raw score is from some reference point, typically the mean, in terms of standard deviation units. The most commonly reported and used standard scores are z-scores, t-scores and stanines.

Metrics: It tells us about a problem. It is a fact and can be in terms of counts, percentages, ratios and so on.

Michigan approach to HRM: This perspective of HRM emphasized the need for adopting organizational policies that can have effect on the individual performance of the employees. In a sense, this perspective acknowledged the need for strategic orientation of an HRM function.

Multinomial logistic regression: This regression model can generalize two outcome (dependent) variables with the linear combination of the predictor (independent) variables. For example, employees' career choice (outcome or dependent variable) can be studied in relation to his/her level of education, and mother's influence (predictor or independent variables).

Neural network: In predictive analytics, neural networks denote enhancing computer capabilities configuring it with required hardware and software, so that like human neurons in human brain, it can solve complex signalling and pattern recognition problems.

New hire performance ratio: This ratio helps in recruitment validation and can be measured in terms of performance results of new recruitees after onboarding and subsequent to job placement.

Nominal measurement: It is classification of objects in two or more categories; hence, we call it categorical measurement.

Non-parametric tests: Here, data sets are not from normal populations. Hence, we also call it non-normal data analysis or distribution free tests.

Normative perspectives of HRM: HRM is a process of shaping employment relationships to achieve individual, organizational and societal goals. This obviously requires managers to relate their decisions with the prevalent policies and practices.

Operational phase: This phase involves the task of operational reporting, e.g., performance, compliance matters and so on. This is also known as the reactive phase.

Ordinal measurement: It classifies objects in order from the highest to the lowest, from the most to the least. It can indicate one object is better than the other, but cannot say how better it is.

Organizational sustainability: It is achieved through meeting the needs of the present and future stakeholders, balancing through productive internal work relationships and meeting the expectations of employees and the society.

Parametric tests: This test has at least one interval-level measurement, populations from where samples are drawn are normal, variances of the populations are expected to be equal and the sample size is large.

People analytics: It is the other way of naming HR analytics. It integrates HR functions with sales, customer retention, accidents, frauds and quality issues, and then performs management of data to get new insights for better decision-making.

Performance-related pay (PRP): With the help of HR analytics, PRP-related decisions rationalize distribution between fixed and variable pay, decide on important KPIs for performance measurement, allocate weights between individual and group performances, rationalize the total cost of compensation and so on.

Predictive analytics: It can assess the probability of the future occurrence of an event, which may have significant implications on the HR decisions.

Predictive modelling for HR decisions: It focuses on predictive patterns of HR issues, measuring probability and making use of various statistical tools.

Predictive modelling: Predictive analytics using regression can simulate probable outcomes of a metric correlating with other metrics, e.g., predicting attrition risk based on the number of leaves availed during last one year. It can also be done using the HR analytics solution in alignment with the business and strategies of organizations.

Predictive HR analytics: It blends data to develop an algorithm, based on which HR managers can pre-assess future events, as consequences of current HR decisions. It can even help in understanding the behavioural changes of employees.

Predictive metrics: It tells us what should be our action plan for the same.

Predictive decision-making process: It is the process of holistic assessment of decisional outcomes right in the beginning to calibrate decisions for minimizing the adverse effect of decisional impact to benefit both employees and organizations.

Predictive HR decision-making process: It rests on big-data analysis. Two commonly used predictive HR decision-making tools are causation and regression analysis. Through regression analysis, we estimate the trend pattern and accordingly make our decision more robust. It can also be done using HR analytics solution in alignment with the business and strategies of organizations.

Probit regression: This regression model helps to study a problem when the outcome or dependent variable can only take two values, i.e., yes/no.

Process analytics: It is process or HR function specific and is more stand-alone in nature. Recruitment and selection, onboarding, performance management, work-life balancing and others alike are some of the examples of process analytics.

Qualitative data: These data are in the form of words and may even be in form of numeric information. These may be photographs, videos, sound recordings and so on. Qualitative data need to be understood in specific context, namely underlying reasons for specific workplace behaviour, such as mentoring and coaching. Qualitative data collection is done through observations, personal interviews, focus groups and case studies.

Quantitative data: These data are essentially in the form of numbers. Surveys, questionnaire administration, statistical reports and others alike are potential sources of quantitative data. This type of data is more reliable than qualitative data, as these are objective. However, it also suffers from potential weaknesses, such as oversimplification by numbers and rankings, and losing the context of data.

Ratio measurement: Along with the properties of interval measurement, it can analyse differences in scores and the relative magnitude of scores.

Reactive decision-making: It denotes decisions based on historical inputs and actual crisis situation. HR decisions based on dashboards are reactive in nature.

Recruiting cost ratio: This is an important metrics as it has direct relationships with the recruitment efficiency. To calculate this ratio, we require actual costs of manpower hiring and the compensation costs of new employees during the period of their onboarding.

Recruiting efficiency ratio: This ratio is prepared to measure the extent of talented people attracted for a job vacancy. It, simply, is the ratio of talented people recruited over the total people recruited in an organization.

Recruitment success ratio: Measured in terms of the percentage of successful recruitment over the total candidates interviewed. It can measure the efficiency of the screening process or short listing of candidates for interview.

Resource-based perspective to HRM: It differentiates one organization from another in terms of available resource-mix, i.e., physical, organizational and human resources.

Resource-based perspective of human resources: This perspective suggests human resource provides the sustainable competitive advantage for the organization. This is because human resources is characteristically rare, inimitable and non-substitutable source for achieving competitive advantage.

Root cause analysis (RCA): RCA helps us in problem-solving. With the elimination of the root causes; problems get resolved and decisions can be taken. Root causes are defined as the basic reasons attributable to the problems. Thus, RCA is the pursuit for the identification of basic reasons for problems. RCA is done adopting different approaches, tools and techniques.

Scenario analysis: It helps us to understand the expected outcome of a decision in different situations.

Scoring models: It is also known as binary or winners' and losers' model. It is typically used in those types of decision-making which answer in two forms; say the outcome is 0 or 1. For example, we need to measure employees into 'learning' and 'not learning' categories after a specific training programme. Here, this type of predictive model can be fitted.

Smooth forecast model: It helps us in understanding how multiple variables relate to a particular event, measuring which HR managers can predict a specific numerical outcome. For example, if the HR strategy is to ensure the attrition rate should be less than 5 percent in next year, then smooth forecast models can help in arriving at such an outcome after analysing all factors that can have possible impact on employees' attrition in organizations.

Social network analytics: It can provide data on employees behind the scene relationships that can help in tracking their potential and risk. Thus, with organizational HR and business data and data from social media, we can truly transform our HR functions into data driven. With data-driven human resources, we can ensure correct business-aligned and strategic HR decisions.

Social and organizational reconfiguration: This will influence talent sourcing and employee engagement processes.

Soft systems approach: This approach focuses on understanding what the purported HR system should do and how it should behave. More logically, it can be considered as an approach to refer to a problem situation with the intention of developing a conceptual model that defines how the system should operate.

Strategic HR metrics: Assess the strategic knowledge and skill sets, competencies, quality of cross-functional teams, ratio of pay at risk and so on.

Strategic partner: HR managers as strategic partners contribute to the development and also accomplishment of organization-wide business plans and objectives. The HR business objectives are to support the attainment of the overall strategic business plan and objectives.

Strategic partner role of human resource: It requires human resource to help line management to achieve their goals, both in terms of strategy framing and strategy execution.

Statistical analysis: This involves collection, analysis, interpretation and presentation of data for decision-making and also for predicting the future.

Sustainable competitive advantage: It is defined as the unique positioning of an organization that enables to outperform in relation to their competitors. It is the value creating capability of an organization that cannot be replicated by others.

Talent management: It is the function talent attraction, talent recruitment and selection, talent development and talent retention for sustenance and growth of an organization.

Talent analytics suite: It includes all talent management functions, such as recruitment, succession planning, development and retention.

Time to hire ratio: Measured in terms of cycle time required from initial HRP to actual recruitment in terms of job placement.

Total career path ratio: This ratio shows employee promotion as the percentage of employee movement with an organization.

Training investment factor ratio: This ratio represents the average training cost per employee, training transfer ratio, indicated in terms of the rate of utilization of training inputs into actual job and so on.

Transaction cost theory: This theory suggests that strategic HR approach can ensure cost minimization, as this will enhance periodic monitoring and governance.

Universalistic approach of HRM: It is also known as the best practices approach, and it scouts for those policies or practices that contribute to organizational gains in general.

Value proposition: It indicates a clear statement on the specific differentiating value of a service or product. Through a value proposition statement, an organization can communicate to its stakeholders' unique value generating features.

Workforce analytics suite: It usually covers recruitment methods and decisions, organizational structure optimization, job satisfaction measurement, employee motivation and future leadership development actions.

Yield Ratio: This can help in understanding the importance of various recruitment sources and is calculated based on the percentage of applicants for different recruitment sources.

INDEX

Made in the USA
Columbia, SC
19 October 2022

69712616R00139